A VERY SLIPPERY FELLOW

The Life of
Sir Robert Wilson
1777–1849

QA68.12
W75
G58

MICHAEL GLOVER

A VERY SLIPPERY FELLOW

The Life of Sir Robert Wilson

1777–1849

'He is a very slippery fellow ... and he has
not the talent of being able to speak the truth
upon any subject.'

Lord Wellington, 23 April 1810

1478
1978

OXFORD UNIVERSITY PRESS

OXFORD LONDON NEW YORK

JUN 16 1978

202623

Oxford University Press, Walton Street, Oxford OX2 6DP

OXFORD LONDON GLASGOW NEW YORK
TORONTO MELBOURNE WELLINGTON CAPE TOWN
IBADAN NAIROBI DAR ES SALAAM LUSAKA
KUALA LUMPUR SINGAPORE JAKARTA HONG KONG TOKYO
DELHI BOMBAY CALCUTTA MADRAS KARACHI

© *Michael Glover 1977 and 1978*

*All rights reserved. No part of this publication may be
reproduced, stored in a retrieval system, or transmitted, in
any form or by any means, electronic, mechanical, photo-
copying, recording, or otherwise, without the prior permission
of Oxford University Press.*

British Library Cataloguing in Publication Data

Glover, Michael
  A very slippery fellow.
  1. Wilson, *Sir* Robert 2. Soldiers – Great Britain –
  Biography
  I. Title
  355.3′32′0924   DC146.W7   77–30189
  ISBN 0–19–211745–9

*Printed in Great Britain by William Clowes & Sons Limited
London, Beccles and Colchester*

Contents

v

Illustrations

vii

Maps

Introduction

In the north aisle of Westminster Abbey, next to the stone inscribed 'O rare Ben Jonson', is an elaborate monumental brass depicting a knight in full armour and, at his side, his wife also in medieval costume. To those few who take the trouble to decipher the gothicized inscription it comes as a surprise to learn that it marks the tomb of Sir Robert Wilson, who died in 1849, and of his wife, 'Dame' Jemima. Allowing for the fact that the brass was commissioned at the height of the Gothic Revival, it is incongruous that a man who was a radical member of parliament, who travelled by steamship, and whose last commission was signed by Queen Victoria should be portrayed as if he had fought not at Leipzig but at Agincourt.

The incongruity is more apparent than real, for Wilson, who may well have conceived the form of memorial himself, always thought of himself as a knight in shining armour, always ready to do battle for what he believed, at that moment, to be the right. He fought for twenty years against Bonaparte only to become an apostle of the Napoleonic legend. With his sword and his pen he defended the autocracy of Czar Alexander I and sat in parliament as a champion of democracy. He moved from the left wing of the Whigs to the comfortable centre of the Tories. Only his enthusiasm remained constant. His judgement was as changeable as it was unreliable.

Erratic as he was, he never lacked friends. His charm was irresistible and his only constant enemy was George IV who, once they had quarrelled, took care never to meet him. Henry Fox wrote that 'There is something about him that makes it impossible to see and hear him without having an admiration for his high spirit and enterprize, and at the same time great contempt for his understanding and judgment.' Lord and Lady Holland thought him 'a restless busy body' but they continued to ask him to dine at Holland House. The Duke of York, for years Wilson's patron, was at length goaded into agreeing that he must be dismissed from the army but, within ten months, arranged that his son should have an ensigncy without purchase. In 1825 the Duke of Wellington considered that Wilson's conduct 'disgraced his character as a British officer', but approved his reinstatement in the army five years later. 'There is', wrote Lord Howden, 'no understanding your seductive powers.'

One clue to Sir Robert's character can be found on his memorial. On it are inscribed his ranks and titles—General in the British Army, Colonel of the Fifteenth (the King's) Hussars, Knight Grand Cross of the Red Eagle of Prussia, Knight Grand Cross of the Military Order of St. Anne of Russia, Knight Grand Cross of the Imperial Military Order of Maria Theresa of Austria, Baron of the Holy Roman Empire, Knight Commander of the Imperial Russian Order of St. George, Knight Commander of the Royal Portuguese Military Order of the Tower and Sword, Knight Commander of the Order of Merit of Saxony, Knight Commander of the Turkish Order of the Crescent. One title is conspicuously missing—Knight Commander of the Most Honourable Order of the Bath. The knight was without honour in his own country.

If British knighthoods had been given for gallantry, Wilson must have received one. Unfortunately, when the Order of the Bath was reconstructed in 1815, 'the great object', according to the Secretary for War, 'has been to avoid the principle of selection, as being invidious and, for a government such as ours in England, impracticable'. The Bath was given to men who held commands at several of a number of specified victories. Sir Robert had been present at Eylau, Friedland, Smolensk, Maloyaroslavets, Vyazma, Beresina, Lützen, Bautzen, Dresden, Külm, Leipzig, and Vallegio, but none of these counted towards making him a KCB. He blamed, quite unreasonably, the Prince Regent and Castlereagh for depriving him of this honour which he considered to be his due. He never forgave either of them and did everything he could to annoy each of them until they died.

His military services were undoubtedly, in his own words,

'not unprofitable', but he was not averse to embroidering them. In 1818 he was heard at the dinner table telling 'some incredible stories of his battles with serpents in the east', stories which are not substantiated from his extensive journals of his travels overseas. He always put the best possible construction on his own actions. As a Peninsular colleague wrote, 'He will never want a trumpeter while he lives, and no man better knows the *art de se faire valoir.*' The story that it was he who, disguised as a *moujik*, sat on the raft at Tilsit while Napoleon and the Czar conferred, and later reported their words to London, was published by Thomas Hardy in 1906. It is certainly untrue but it is quite probable that its origins derived from one of Wilson's flights of fancy late in his life.

Throughout his life Robert Wilson wrote copiously both privately and for publication. There can be little doubt that he intended writing an autobiography. He kept a detailed journal of all the active periods of his life and stored all the letters he received with, wherever possible, copies of the letters he wrote. Some letters, like the long series to Lord Grey, he recovered from their recipients. He did write an autobiographical fragment which was incorporated in the works of his nephew and son-in-law, the Rev. Herbert Randolph. This earnest cleric set out to write Sir Robert's biography on an extensive scale. Having in 1860 published Wilson's *Narrative of Events during the Invasion of Russia in 1812* (written in 1825), he produced in 1861 Sir Robert's *Private Diary of Travels, Personal Services and Public Events* covering the years 1812, 1813, and 1814. This diary, in a shortened form, was republished in 1964, edited by Antony Brett-James. Herbert Randolph next went back to Wilson's birth and published the *Life of Sir Robert Wilson from autobiographical memoirs, journals, narratives, correspondence, &c.* (1862) which carried the story down to 1807. He had intended to follow this with a volume dealing with Wilson's service in the Peninsula, but this never emerged although Randolph did produce in 1872 a booklet dealing with Wilson's part in the formation of Canning's ministry in 1827. On Randolph's death the voluminous Wilson papers were acquired by the British Museum, where they have lain, almost undisturbed, for a century. In particular Wilson's peninsular journal was unknown to any of the historians of the Peninsular War, including Sir Charles Oman and Sir John Fortescue.

The only substantial use of the Wilson papers was made by Professor Giovanni Costigan who published in the United States a biography in 1932 under the title *Sir Robert Wilson: A Soldier of Fortune in the Napoleonic Wars*. I disagree with Professor Costigan on a wide variety of points but I owe to him and to the Rev. Herbert Randolph an immense debt of gratitude for saving me many weary hours in deciphering Wilson's handwriting. Sir Robert did try to make his writing legible in important letters, and the consequence of the recipient can be accurately gauged from the legibility of any letter. In his journal, written by candlelight, on bad paper with worse ink and a poorly sharpened quill, it is a strain to read any single line. His spelling of place names was at least as personal as that used by every other British officer at the time. I have endeavoured to standardize the spelling of such proper names into acceptable modern forms and, as is frequently necessary for the eastern campaigns, given the new names that have been in use since 1917 or 1945. It is worth adding that the version I have used of the name Lavallette is that used by the count himself. His wife used the variant La Vallette. Most historians seem to have preferred Lavalette.

Acknowledgements

Many people have helped with the research involved in writing this book and I would particularly like to thank Mr. David Chandler, Professor and Mrs. David Curnow, Professor Richard Glover, and Sir Robert Ricketts. I am also grateful to Miss Jean Coburn of the Greater London Record Office, to Major B. O. Simmonds of Home Headquarters, 15th/19th The King's Hussars, and to the staffs of the London Library and the Manuscript Room of the British Museum. I have had abundant help from the Old War Office Library, pre-eminently from my daughter Stephanie, who has been a cornucopia of books, documents, and ideas.

Most of all I must thank my wife for her help, her comfort, and her inspiration.

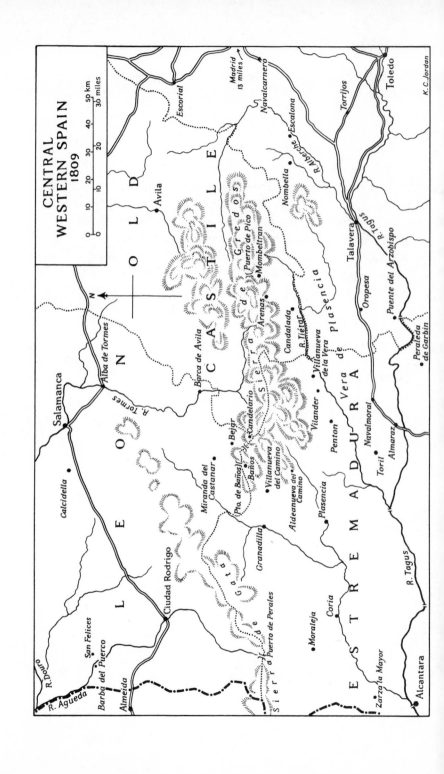

CENTRAL
WESTERN SPAIN
1809

0   10   20   30   40   50 km
0   10   20   30 miles

K. C. Jordan

NORWAY

Christiania

Stockholm

Abo

St. Petersburg

DENMARK &

Copenhagen

S W E D E N

R U S S I A N

R. Dvina

Mittau

Vitebsk

Borodino Moscow
Maloyaroslavets
Vyazma
Kaluga
Tula

Memel
Tilsit
Smolensk

Hamburg
R. Elbe

Danzig
Konigsberg •Friedland

Vilna
Minsk

E M P I R E

R. Beresina
Borisov

PRUSSIA

R. Niemen

Berlin

GRAND

DUCHY

Warsaw

Pripet

Brest-Litovsk

Leipzig

Dresden   Breslau

OF

Marshes

CONFEDERATION

Erz-

WARSAW

OF

gebirge

R. Vistula

Kiev

THE

Prague

R. Dnieper

R. Rhine

RHINE

Jitomar

Carpathians

AUSTRIAN

Kamienetz

R. Pruth

R. Dniester

Vienna

MOLDAVIA

E M P I R E

Jassy

Verona Vicenza Trieste

Fokchani

ITALY

Venice

R. Danube

WALLACHIA

BOSNIA

Bucharest

Giurgeva

Rutschuk

SERBIA

Schumla

Rome

T U R K I S H

Constantinople

NAPLES

E M P I R E

Messina

Sicily

Marmorice

•Malta

EASTERN EUROPE
1806-14

0 ——————— 800 km
0 ——————— 500 miles

K.C.Jordan

Alexandria

CHAPTER 1

A Reputation in the Cannon's Mouth

General Sir Robert Wilson was the son of a painter. There was nothing unusual in a man of such parentage achieving high rank in the British army during the long wars against revolutionary and Napoleonic France. The peacetime sources for the supply of officers, who were for the most part the sons of officers, were quite unable to provide enough men to command a force expanded threefold and with a wastage rate, from death, resignation, and dismissal, of about seven hundred and fifty officers a year. Commissions could still be purchased but, by 1810, four out of five were given free and one officer in twenty had risen from the ranks. At Waterloo the Scots Greys were commanded by the son of a sergeant-major and the chief staff officer for the cavalry was the son of an eating-house keeper from Furnival's Inn, Holborn. All the literate classes of the population contributed their share of officers. The Adjutant General was colonel of a regiment popularly known as 'Calvert's Entire' since he came from a well-known brewing family. The arts contributed their quota. Tom Sheridan, son of the playwright, was a captain in the Inniskillings; W. C. Macready's brother was an ensign in the Thirtieth Foot; the father of Captain C. W. Dance, Twenty-Third Light Dragoons, was one of the original members of the Royal Academy and the architect who designed the façade of Guildhall.

Benjamin Wilson, Robert's father, was one of the most successful painters of his day. He was also a Fellow of the Royal Society. His own father had been a wealthy Russia merchant from Leeds, but bad luck and bad weather ruined the business and Benjamin had to be taken away from school. He had already shown some aptitude for painting and had received lessons from a French artist who was employed at a nearby stately home. After his father's crash he set out for London, walking where he could not persuade a carter to carry him. A relative in the capital gave him a suit of new clothes and two guineas. Thus supplied he found himself a clerkship in the court of Doctors' Commons at 7*s*. 6*d*. a week. Two-thirds of this he saved and lived on the remaining half-crown, in his own words, 'as well as a emperor, being . . . content to stay at home in self-improvement'. Before long he had saved £50 and moved to a better job as clerk to the Registrar of the Charterhouse, earning 15*s*. a week, including fees.

Having achieved this comparative affluence, and continuing to live frugally, he returned to painting in his spare time and was so successful that he was soon able to abandon the Charterhouse. He established a lucrative practice as a portraitist, many of his subjects coming from his native Yorkshire and including such pillars of the Whig establishment as Lord Rockingham, Lord Camden, and Sir George Saville. By 1756, when he was thirty-five, he was earning £1,500 a year and felt able to move into the house in Lincoln's Inn Fields that had been occupied by Sir Godfrey Kneller. Hogarth proposed a partnership, with Wilson contributing the faces to their joint work. When Zoffany first came to England in 1758 he worked for Wilson as a drapery painter, and when Garrick decided to present a portrait of Shakespeare to the town of Stratford upon Avon for the Jubilee of 1769 it was to Benjamin Wilson that he gave the commission for the work.[1]

At an early age he developed an interest in electricity and in 1746, when he was only twenty-five, he read to the Royal Society a paper entitled *An Essay towards the Explication of the Phenomena of Electricity deduced from the Æther of Sir Isaac Newton*. In the following year Benjamin Franklin published his famous work linking electricity with lightning, a discovery which inspired Wilson to make his own experiments. 'On the occurrence of the first succeeding thunderstorm, he happened to be at the house of a friend near Chelmsford, and at the moment was acting with others in one of Shakespeare's plays. He was playing the role of Henry IV when the storm came on, and running out in his royal robes he extemporized an apparatus to test the discovery—a curtain rod inserted in a clean quart bottle, with a pin (or needle) fastened to it at the other end. The bottle he held in his hand as he stood on the bowling green, and the fluid was collected in the rod so that the sparks were drawn from it by himself and all the rest.'[2] In 1756 the Royal Society elected him a Fellow and awarded him a gold medal for his experiments with the electrical properties of tourmaline. His scientific work was also acknowledged by membership of the academies of Bologna, Paris, St. Petersburg, and Uppsala.

Through his friends among the Whig grandees, he made the acquaintance of Edward, Duke of York, brother to George III, who became greatly attached to him. Not only did Wilson dine three or four times a week at York House, but he was appointed director of the Duke's private theatre in St. James's Street. It was through the same patronage that Wilson was appointed Master Painter to the Board of Ordnance.

It is far from clear why the Board of Ordnance, which was principally concerned with the production of cannon, should require a Master Painter since they also employed a number of skilled draughtsmen, or why they should pay this dignitary the generous salary of £4,000 a year in peace and £7,000 in time of war. Although for some time Wilson had to share the salary with the natural son of the previous incumbent, he felt that he could now afford to marry and, at the age of fifty, selected for this purpose a Miss Hetherington, 'a lady of good birth but no dowry except her rare beauty and her many virtues'.

In 1772, the year after his marriage, Benjamin Wilson quarrelled with both the Royal Society and the Board of Ordnance. The Board had asked the Society for advice about lightning conductors for their powder magazines at Woolwich. The Society consulted Benjamin Franklin with whom Wilson had been engaged in a long-drawn-out dispute about the shape of conductors. Franklin maintained that they should have pointed ends. Wilson contended that this would 'invite or solicit' the lightning and that the ends should be rounded. To his fury it was decided that the lightning conductors at Woolwich should have pointed ends. It must have given him some satisfaction when, five years later, by which time Franklin was a notorious rebel, one of the Woolwich buildings was struck by lightning. Fortunately it was only the Board House.

Wilson did little to make himself popular with his brother-artists. He was a formidable craftsman and produced a print in the manner of Rembrandt which convinced Thomas Hudson, whose apprentice Reynolds had been, that it was 'the best piece of perspective and the finest light and shade that he had ever seen by Rembrandt'. Fortified by this authentication, Wilson gave a dinner for twenty-three prominent artists and decorated the sirloin with copies of the bogus print. The joke was not appreciated, least of all by Hudson who was present. At least, however, the company got a sirloin. Wilson's reputation for miserliness was such that he was said to call on a different acquaintance each morning to save himself the expense of providing breakfast.[3]

Through the Duke of York, Wilson had been introduced to the King who consulted him on matters of art and took a lively and practical interest in his electrical work. When Hogarth died in 1764, George III appointed Wilson to succeed him as Sergeant Painter. He exploited this royal connection to the full. In 1788 he asked Benjamin West, who was to succeed Reynolds as president of the Royal Academy, to present to the King a paper in which he 'represented himself as being in very distressed circumstances, thereby hoping to obtain something from his Majesty's bounty'. Three weeks later Wilson died, and at his funeral West, much concerned by his belief in Wilson's poverty, expressed his feelings to the trustees, who told him that, on the contrary, Wilson left £35,000 in the Funds and other property, amounting together to £40,000.[4]

The painter left six children of whom the third, the second surviving son, was Robert Thomas Wilson, born 17 August 1777. Robert was the favourite son. Shortly before he died Benjamin told him that 'I might, if I would, cultivate natural talents and rise to an eminence honourable to myself and beneficial to my family [and] that he had left me £1,000 more than he had left to any of my brothers and sisters; to be applied to the payment of the expenses of my education. . . . My father, on the same occasion, earnestly advised me not to go into the army, and not to marry before I was thirty-five; to make the law my profession and parliament the object of a patriotic ambition.'[5]

Robert showed few signs of talent at school. He was taken away from Westminster after an unprofitable year. A further year at Winchester, during which his mother died, produced little more than an ability to memorize quantities of Greek and Latin verse. Even in those days this was insufficient to satisfy his schoolmasters, but classical tags were to garnish his conversation, his speeches, and his writings for the rest of his life. He completed his education at the hands of a clergyman in Tottenham Court Road and 'I frequently officiated as his clerk at the desk and at funeral services in the burial ground'. He had been made a ward of Chancery and his guardian (whom Wilson was careful not to name in his writings) was unsympathetic and had a dislike of letting young men have any money. Instead of being reasonably affluent, for in those days the interest on a sixth share of £40,000 would have brought in a comfortable income, Wilson was constantly in debt.

If he had little education and less ready money, young Robert was blessed with abundant charm. He also had influential contacts. Benjamin had taken care that the King should meet his family and had presented them to him at Windsor when Robert was three. 'The King took hold of Bob's hand and introduced him to those who were in attendance as an *exceedingly fine boy*. He was admitted to familiar intercourse with the King and several of the Princes who all treated him with marked attention.' George III took a keen and friendly interest in Robert's career as long as his public life lasted, but Wilson's most valuable friendship was the one he formed with Frederick, Duke of York, the King's second son, who supported him for as long as it was possible for him to do so.

Although Robert's dependence on his guardian and the Court of Chancery should have lasted until 1798 when he reached the age of twenty-one, his sister Frances offered him an avenue of escape. In January 1793 she married Lieutenant-Colonel Bosville of the Guards. The marriage was tragically short. War broke out with revolutionary France and the Guards embarked for Flanders in February of the same year. Bosville was killed at Lincelles in August, leaving his widow pregnant. The marriage brought Robert Wilson into the circle of Frances's brother-in-law, William Bosville. He was a wealthy eccentric who always wore the fashionable dress of the previous reign and an old-fashioned powdered wig and queue. He had served in the Guards in the American war and continued to refer to himself as Colonel Bosville, though he had never attained a higher rank than Lieutenant and Captain.* Despite this military pretension, his house in Wigmore Street was a centre of the anti-war party, being frequented by Charles James Fox, Horne Tooke, and Sir Francis Burdett. Robert, though only sixteen, was a welcome visitor at Wigmore Street and among the friends he made was Lieutenant-Colonel John Hely-Hutchinson (later General Lord Donoughmore) who was to give him his somewhat amused patronage for the rest of his life. Hutchinson and the rest of Bosville's circle held a low opinion of the army but this was not enough to deter Robert Wilson, despite his father's last wishes, from deciding to secure a commission.

In 1793 the army was being expanded at a ridiculous and unpractical rate. Regiments of horse and foot, most of which never raised enough men to muster a company, were being authorized almost daily. Nothing would have been easier than to obtain some sort of ensigncy or cornetcy. Purchased commissions were being offered at much below their regulated price and free commissions were available to anyone literate who would accept them. Wilson's problem was to be gazetted into a 'good' regiment, preferably one serving against the French in the Netherlands. Patience was never one of his virtues and he would not wait until Chancery decided whether or not to release £900 for an ensigncy in the Foot Guards or £735 for a cornetcy in the

* Officers of the Foot Guards held rank in the army above their regimental rank. Thus a captain in the Guards was a lieutenant-colonel in the army and a Guards lieutenant was an army captain.

cavalry. Instead he sought an interview with the Commander in Chief. This was Lord Amherst, a veteran of the Seven Years War, who had been restored to the head of the army but who was no more than a figurehead. The pathetic old man had to explain that he had no influence in the giving of commissions. Most were awarded by the Secretary at War, a very dubious politician called Sir George Yonge; the remainder were in the gift of the Duke of York, commanding in the Netherlands. All Amherst could do was to advise the young man to present a memorial to the King asking for an ensigncy in the Foot Guards, where the Secretary at War's writ did not run. 'I immediately drew up myself a memorial recalling to the King's recollection my father's enjoyment of his most gracious favour, my sister's marriage and loss: and I concluded with the expression of hope that I might obtain the opportunity of proving my attachment to his Majesty.'

Going to Windsor to present it he met an old friend, Major-General Gwynn, Lieutenant-Colonel of the Fifteenth Light Dragoons and ADC to the King. Gwynn approved the memorial and 'gave me the opportunity of presenting it in person. The King took it as he was going into chapel: and on coming out, seeing me again, made several encouraging remarks, asked me many questions to no one of which he gave me time to answer. Next day General Gwynn sent for me, and told me, by the King's command, that he would recommend my going to Flanders to the Duke of York who would provide for me. "Tell him", were the words, "Frederick will take care of him." '6

Borrowing £180 from Frances Bosville, Wilson 'bought a beautiful English mare, a very serviceable horse, on credit from a liveryman', engaged a groom, and, accompanied by two Scotch terriers, 'ugly to an exquisite degree of beauty', set off for Ostend, 'with a red coat on my back, something like a surgeon'.

He was well received at headquarters. 'The Duke in the kindliest manner addressed me, and after some general conversation, asked me whether I preferred a cornetcy of cavalry or an ensigncy in the Foot Guards; and if I liked cavalry, whether I had any choice of regiment?' He chose the Fifteenth Light Dragoons, the senior light cavalry regiment of the army, and was gazetted cornet without purchase on 8 April 1794, four months short of his seventeenth birthday and a little older than the average junior subaltern of his day. Two days after he was appointed, the regiment discharged at its depot in Reading one of its most distinguished members. This was Silas Tomkyn Comberback, otherwise the poet Samuel Taylor Coleridge, who had enlisted in a moment of patriotic enthusiasm. Although a complete misfit in the ranks of the dragoons, Coleridge always maintained that the Fifteenth had treated him kindly, a clear indication that Wilson's first regiment was a good and humane one.

The British army acquired little glory from its campaign in the Netherlands in 1793–5. It could hardly be expected to do so. Peacetime economies had reduced its strength to such an extent that even after a year of war and recruiting the expeditionary force consisted of only fourteen regiments of cavalry (each of two squadrons), six battalions of infantry, and six companies (batteries) of artillery. There should have been a siege train but the requisition for it had been lost in the Ordnance Office.[7] It would be flattery to describe the supply services as rudimentary. Reinforcements and men to replace casualties were all but unobtainable, since such men as could be raised were being formed into the skeletal new regiments which Sir George Yonge, not without profit to himself, was authorizing in such profusion. When drafts did reach the Netherlands they consisted, in Wilson's words, of 'recruits from the gaols, sent out in such a state of equipment as to excite shame and derision. Even the recruits sent to the light dragoons came out in many instances with undress jackets and without boots, those who sent them presumed that they might be fitted out from the dead men's kits, as if the effects of the slain were regularly collected and stored.'

The Duke of York had been given the command. He was young and untried but he showed himself a competent, if not a brilliant, general. It would have availed him nothing if he had possessed the combined talents of Marlborough and Wellington. His army was ill-equipped and unbalanced and he was made subject to the Austrian command, the British government extracting promises from their allies that the Duke was to be allowed no freedom of action. His youth might have justified this precaution, but it was unfortunate that the Austrians were infected with a theory of war which would have paralysed the finest army in the world. Under the 'cordon system' they attempted to be equally strong at all points on their extended front. If they had determined on a defensive strategy such a theory would have been no more than extremely dangerous but, although the French outnumbered them by 243,000 men to 160,000, they were set on invading France. Thus they divided their force into a large number of un-connected columns each of which faced superior numbers and had the support of fortresses. Only the gross incompetence of the French, whose military arrangements had been disrupted by the revolution, saved the allies from humiliating disaster in the open-ing campaign.

Sixteen days after being gazetted, Cornet Wilson saw action of the most spectacular kind. Prince Coburg-Saalfeld, the Austrian commander, had his headquarters at Le Cateau while he undertook the siege of Landrecies. On the west side of the besieged town was a covering force commanded by the Duke of York which faced a strong French corps based on Cambrai. The Duke's advance guard consisted of two Austrian squadrons, 112 rank and file of the Ferdinand Hussars, and two squadrons of the Fifteenth Light Dragoons, 160 rank and file. These cavalry-men were commanded by the Austrian General Otto, who learned on 23 April that a strong French column had crossed the Scheldt north of Cambrai, apparently intending to advance against the road leading from Le Cateau to Brussels. He asked the Duke for reinforcements and was sent four regiments of heavy cavalry.

Next morning Otto led his force against the French who had established themselves in the village of Villers-en-Cauchies, eight miles north-east of Cambrai. An impetuous commander, he rode with his four light squadrons and failed to realize that the heavy cavalry, who had received no orders, were not following. When he got within 'half cannon shot' of the enemy, he halted and looked round for his supports. There was no sign of them.

A Very Slippery Fellow

Wilson takes up the narrative:

At this period General Otto received advice that the Emperor [of Austria], who was on his road from Brussels to Cateau was [likely to be] intercepted by the enemy on our front and must infallibly be taken unless they were obliged to throw back their left. He immediately called together the commanders, told them the perilous position of his Sovereign, the desperate condition in which the corps they commanded were placed, and the necessity of perishing sword in hand as assailants. He then added, 'Gentlemen! remember, your numbers do not permit prisoners.'

The French cavalry appeared to be in one line, supported by a wood on the left and the village of Villers-en-Cauchies on the right. No infantry or cannon were visible. On the word *March* being given, although we could ill spare the detachment, a small body of hussars was ordered to move on the wood, as Otto suspected that there was a corps of the enemy concealed in it; his suspicion was quickly justified by two squadrons of cavalry withdrawing from it so soon as the hussars had fired with their skirmishers a few *feeling* shots.

The enemy immediately sent forward from their apparent front line a swarm of *chasseurs à cheval*, who fired at a few paces from us. One fired at me as I was riding on the left flank of the whole, and the ball grazed along my helmet just above the ear, striking off the silver edging.

When we began to trot the French cavalry made a movement to right and left from the centre. They dashed in a gallop towards wood and village and we saw in lieu of them, as if created by magic, an equal line of infantry with a considerable artillery in advance, which opened a furious cannonade with grape while musketry poured its volleys. The surprise was great and the moment most critical; but happily the heads kept their direction and the heels were duly applied to the *Charge*, which order was hailed with repeated huzzas.

The guns were quickly taken; but we found that the *chaussée*, which ran through a hollow with steep banks, lay between them and the enemy. There was, however, no hesitation: every horse was true to his master, and the *chaussée* was passed in uninterrupted career. It was then, as we passed the crest, that the enemy poured in its volley—but in vain. In vain also the first ranks *kneeled and presented a steady line of bayonets*. The impulse was too rapid and the body attacking too solid for any infantry formed in line to oppose though the ranks were formed three-deep. Even horses struck mortally at the bank had sufficient impulse to plunge upon the enemy in their fall and assist the destruction of their defence.

The French cavalry, having gained the flanks of their infantry, endeavoured to take up a position in their rear. Our squadrons, still on the gallop, closed to fill the apertures which the French fire and bayonets had occasioned, and proceeded to the attack of the French cavalry, which, though it had suffered from the fire of part of its own infantry, seemed resolved to await the onset; but their discipline or their courage failed, and our horses' heads drove on them just as they were on the half turn to retire.

A dreadful massacre followed in the chase of four miles. One farrier of the Fifteenth alone killed twenty-two men. The French were so panic-struck that they scarcely made any resistance, notwithstanding that our numbers were so few in comparison with the party engaged that each individual pursuer found himself in the midst of a flock of foes.

We did not stop our foaming horses until we received a salute from the guns of Bouchain, eight miles from our starting point. We then sounded the trumpet of recall, and the dispersed victors collected to retire, but in very reduced numbers; particularly the Austrians as their horses had been unable to keep up with us: indeed, at the original charge, notwithstanding the equal zest of the riders, we certainly gained three yards in ten.

The retreat was not less formidable than the attack; for we had only perforated not dislodged the enemy who had positively *twelve thousand men* with fifty pieces of cannon in his position when we attacked, and through the survivors we had to make our way by force or stealth. We did, however, retrace our steps at a good trot without interruption though squadrons and battalions were formed on both flanks on the plain over which we returned. Some may have been astonished but I believe most of the enemy thought we were a fresh succour coming out from Bouchain.[8]

Few feats of cavalry, heavy or light, have equalled the charge at Villers-en-Cauchies. Less than three hundred sabres had crashed through a three-deep line of infantry, strengthened and supported by artillery. Then they had driven a superior force of cavalry before them like a flock of sheep. The allied losses had been comparatively light. The Fifteenth lost seventeen men and nineteen horses killed and an officer, seventeen men and eighteen horses wounded. The Ferdinand Hussars suffered thirty-one casualties. The French, by their own admission, lost three guns and twelve hundred men. So ferocious had the pursuit been that their dead outnumbered their wounded by two to one.

Whether the action was necessary is quite another matter. There was not a Frenchman within eight miles of the Emperor's road to Le Cateau and their reactions to the attack of Otto's puny force suggest that they had no immediate intention of advancing. It is most unlikely that they knew that the Emperor was riding in that direction. Nevertheless, it was a dashing exploit and the Emperor was easily persuaded that the four gallant squadrons had saved his life. He announced that he would dub the eight officers of the Fifteenth who had been present Knights of the Order of Maria Theresa, an honour that carried with it the rank of Baron of the Holy Roman Empire. Unfortunately, some officious chamberlain questioned whether foreigners were eligible for the Order. The Emperor therefore promised each of the officers a special gold medal. It was four years later that this medal was struck and forwarded to the recipients, and two years after that the question of eligibility was satisfactorily settled and, with the sanction of George III (2 June 1801), the eight, including Wilson, became knights.

During the remainder of 1794 Robert Wilson was involved in most of the British cavalry actions in Flanders. His most alarming experience was at Willems on 10 May. The Fifteenth stumbled across an unbroken square of French infantry which inflicted terrible casualties. 'I was on my English mare who extricated herself by extraordinary activity; but she carried me to the enemy, and I should infallibly have been taken if a soldier had not made a blow at her head with the butt-end of his musket: this frightened her so much that she turned like a hare and ran obliquely along the line until I could find a clear piece of ground, when I succeeded in giving her a new direction. I suppose upwards of a hundred shots were fired at us, of which only one struck her in the neck.'[9]

In September he and another officer led a small patrol deep into the French lines and reached the headquarters of General Vandamme. They failed to seize the general but took prisoner one of his aides-de-camp and two gendarmes. From the ADC they learned the exact disposition and strength of the French forces opposed to them. They also discovered that the enemy intended making a feint at the allied position at Boxtel. In the ensuing skirmish a young lieutenant-colonel, the Hon. Arthur Wesley, came under fire for the first time and displayed the cool courage and skill that were, in the next twenty years, to earn him the title of Duke of Wellington.

As the campaign dragged on, harmony between the allies became increasingly strained. The Austrians lost interest in the Low Countries; the Prussians accepted a large British subsidy but withdrew their troops; the Dutch decided that they would do better to support the French. In the final act the British and Hanoverians had to make a long winter retreat to Emden, a retreat on which the supply services finally collapsed.

Wellington said of this campaign that at least it taught him what one ought not to do. Robert Wilson was horrified by the amount of flogging that was thought necessary to keep order among the gaol-birds who had been sent out to the infantry. He also complained of the drunkenness prevalent in all ranks. This he ascribed to the fact that 'the drink was strong port instead of the pure vintages of France'. Luckily the Fifteenth was a comparatively sober regiment and he remarked primly, 'I was never once inebriated during the whole campaign'.

He had become a lieutenant by purchase in October 1794 and by February of the next year he was with his regiment in barracks in Croydon. There followed a spell of regimental soldiering until, in 1796, he purchased a captaincy. By that time the Fifteenth were stationed in Weymouth and it was there that he met Jemima Belford. She was not only beautiful, she was rich and well connected. Her grandfather was General William Belford, one of the original officers of the Royal Artillery, and two of her uncles were colonels in the Foot Guards. Her mother was an heiress of the Pelham family and Jemima and her sister were the co-heiresses to a third uncle, Lieutenant-General Sir Adam Williamson of Dover Street and Avebury and, at that time, Governor of San

Domingo. Wilson decided to ignore another of his father's injunctions. Benjamin Wilson had urged him not to join the army and not to marry until he was thirty-five. Now, a captain of twenty, he decided to marry Jemima.

They must have made a good-looking couple. Miss Belford was described as the admiration of society and Wilson, although no physical description of him seems to have survived, can be seen from his portrait to have been tall, dashing, and handsome, the kind of man to be perfectly set off by the light dragoon uniform, topped by the elegant fur-combed Tarleton helmet. The immediate problem was that they were both wards of Chancery and, although the guardians were in favour of the match, the Court would not agree to their marriage until both attained the age of twenty-one in the following year. However, the jurisdiction of the Chancery Court ceased at the Scottish border and the betrothed pair accordingly set out for Gretna Green. Unlike most couples travelling to the same destination, they travelled in separate carriages, each accompanied by their guardians. They were married, under Scots law, on 7 July 1797 and the ceremony was repeated, according to the Anglican rite, at St. George's, Hanover Square, in the following March. Their first child, a daughter, was born at their house in Windsor in August 1798 and her godparents were the Queen, the Princess Mary, and, most importantly for the father's career, the Duke of York, now Commander-in-Chief of the Army.

Robert Wilson was not at the christening. He had crossed St. George's Channel in May 1798 to take up the post of brigade major to Major-General the Hon. Frederick St. John, grandson of Bolingbroke, who was commanding a district in the south of Ireland. Wilson says little of his time in Ireland beyond admitting a dislike for the island and claiming that he had done his best to soften the reprisals taken by the protestant landlords after the rebellion in 1798. The reason for his reticence may be that he was not a success as a staff officer. He had many military virtues but an interest in administration was not among them.

He was back with his regiment in time to take part in the abortive expedition to Holland in 1799. The aim was to seize the naval base at Den Helder and the Fifteenth, who were in the second wave of troops to be landed, went ashore on 25 September. Since Britain was still unable to muster sufficient troops for this operation, it had been arranged for a contingent of Russians to land with them. Co-operation between the allies was never good and the expedition almost succeeded in defeating itself with little interference from its French and Dutch enemies. Wilson took what opportunity there was of distinguishing himself. On 2 October the Duke of York had planned an advance out of the beach-head which the force had established, but his plans were frustrated by the lethargy of Sir Ralph Abercromby and the obstinate independence of the Russians. At the end of the day the British light cavalry had their flank on the sea-shore near Egmont-op-Zee. Near them was a troop of guns which were supposed to be under their protection. According to an officer who was present, 'our light dragoons were dismounted to rest their horses, when suddenly came down two squadrons of *chasseurs-à-cheval*, at full speed, and were upon and among the Horse Artillery before they were discovered. They hoped by this feat of dashing gallantry to have carried off some of the guns; but luckily there was a troop of ten or twelve officers chatting together close by (among them were Lord Paget [later Marquess of Anglesey], Colonel Erskine and Captain Robert Wilson) and these, followed by half a dozen sergeants and others, who happened to be still on horseback, plunged at once into the midst of the French, and fought so furiously that the dragoons gained time to run together and mount, and then the thing was over. Most of the *chasseurs* were killed or taken.'[11]

Soon the expedition was abandoned and the Fifteenth were in barracks at Canterbury by November. Sir Adam Williamson had died in October 1798 and half of his somewhat reduced fortune had passed to Jemima Wilson. This made it possible for Robert to think of purchasing further promotion as soon as his six years commissioned service, the minimum insisted upon by the Duke of York, was complete in April 1800. There was no hope of buying a majority in the Fifteenth and there was a seller's market in all the regular cavalry regiments. The best chance was to purchase into one of the new foreign cavalry regiments in the British service, and he found a possible seller in an elderly German officer in Hompesch's Mounted Rifles. This regiment, consisting only of four troops, had started life in 1796 as a mounted offshoot of the Light Infantry regiment raised by Baron Ferdinand Hompesch, the battalion that, in December 1797, became the basis of the 5th (Rifle) battalion of the Sixtieth (Royal American) Foot. The cavalry section survived as an independent unit with a strength, on paper, of 452 other ranks. Most of the officers and all the troopers were Germans, although the army tended to describe any man who came from the east bank of the Rhine and who was not markedly Asiatic as a German. The uniform was a green jacket, faced with red, red breeches, and a black, infantry-style shako surrounded by a red turban and surmounted by a red and white plume. The unit was often referred to as Hompesch's Hussars although there had been another regiment of that name, raised by Ferdinand Hompesch's elder brother, Karl.[12]

Wilson purchased the majority of Wilhelm Bylandt on 28 June 1800. The regulated price was £4,250 and it is unlikely that he would have had to pay more for a rank in a foreign regiment. Most of the price would have come from the sale of his light dragoon captaincy, for which the regulated price was £3,150 but which, since it was in an old-established regular regiment with a good reputation, might well have commanded a higher sum.

In his *History of the British Expedition in Egypt*, written in 1802, Wilson said that 'Being desirous of joining the British army in the Mediterranean under Sir Ralph Abercromby [I] bought the majority of Hompesch's Hussars.' This cannot be true. His new regiment was still in Ireland when he was gazetted and it was not until the following month that it embarked, with 7 officers and 157 rank and file, at Cork to take part in the abortive attack on Ferrol (25–27 August). Wilson stayed in London, while his wife was expecting their second child, until September when he was ordered to take despatches to the British ambassador in Vienna.

Sailing from Yarmouth on 21 September, he reached Cuxhaven two days later and the following day arrived at Hamburg. By the

1. Major General Sir Robert Wilson in 1818.
Engraving by W. Ward after the painting by H. W. Pickersgill

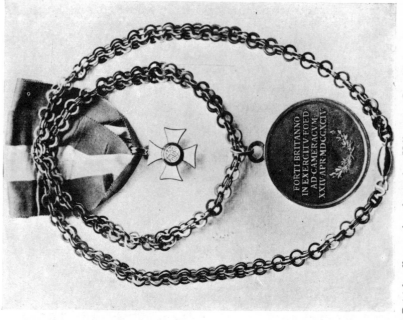

2. The gold medal presented by the Emperor of Austria to the British officers who charged at Villers-en-Cauchies, *left* obverse, *right* reverse

29th he had reached Berlin, 'a handsome city, fine buildings: but thinly inhabited and very gloomy'. Pausing only to collect more despatches, he set out for a non-stop journey by way of Dresden and Prague, reaching Vienna on 5 October. 'At Wolfe's hotel we got excellent roast beef, introduced by Lord Nelson, who had resided there. I slept very soundly the first night; having been eleven days in my barouche during which, from the badness of the roads, repose was impossible.' [13]

The military situation in the Mediterranean was obscure. As far as any policy can be divined from the stream of orders and counter-orders which poured from London, the government intended General Abercromby to land his troops in Italy and co-operate with the Austrians. Unfortunately the Austrian general in Italy, General Melas, had been decisively beaten at Marengo and a local armistice was arranged as a prelude to peace between France and Austria. The news that greeted Wilson in Vienna was that Abercromby had retired to Gibraltar. There was nothing to do but wait until further news arrived. Vienna was agreeable. 'There were many houses open in the evening. An Englishman found universal admittance and respect.' Wilson was introduced to the Emperor, who 'behaved most graciously', and Baron Thugut, the chief minister, who told him that the long-awaited knighthood had been approved.

After a month, letters arrived saying that Abercromby was making for Malta. Wilson immediately set off to join him and reached Trieste on 11 November. He sailed to Venice in a heavy sea in a small boat 'with forty-two oxen below and thirty passengers—Jews, Turks and Christians. It was a miserable voyage.' At Venice, 'as I was a courier and an officer, I was not searched at the custom house. I had the pleasure of conveying for a poor Turk two pounds of tobacco which he told me would be his food during the Ramazan.'

He was in Rome by 9 December and formed a poor opinion of the city. 'The houses are wretched, the streets unlighted, the people miserable and there is a universal want of cleanliness and comfort. I was much disappointed with St. Peter's, the building does not look so vast or so lofty as St. Paul's. Its front I think paltry. The colonnade, however, is very fine. In seven hours I saw everything worth seeing.'

Dawn on 20 December found him at Messina where he lost no time in hiring an open boat to take him to Valletta for £15. They set off but a storm drove them back to Messina. He sailed again on the 23rd in the transport *Anne* but that night the wind blew up again and 'the captain called me and told me he had little hope of saving the ship. . . . When destruction seemed inevitable from the impossibility of clearing a cape, Providence interposed and saved us. In a moment the wind changed from south-east to west. The ship was instantly taken aback. The confusion on board was dreadful—scarcely a single person could stand above or below decks. Trunks, furniture, ladders, a horse, birds, dogs, men and women lay tumbling together.' The *Anne* had to put back into Syracuse for repairs and did not reach Valletta until New Year's Eve. It was all Wilson could do to catch a convoy sailing that day to join Abercromby in the eastern Mediterranean. Again there was a storm and the danger was increased by a fire caused by the troopers of the Twelfth Light Dragoons smoking their pipes in the hay store. It was 12 January 1801 before Wilson reported himself to General Abercromby in the Bay of Marmorice, on the south coast of Turkey, north of Rhodes.[14]

Six weeks passed before the army, 16,000 strong, sailed from Marmorice to recapture Egypt from the French. They landed at Aboukir Bay on 8 March and thirteen days later the main French army was defeated outside Alexandria, a battle in which Abercromby was mortally wounded. The command passed to the senior major-general, Wilson's friend John Hely-Hutchinson. Wilson's diary is missing between 23 February and 27 April and there is no way of telling what he did during the landing and at the battle. A picture exists which purports to show him as being present when Abercromby was wounded. If the picture is correct, Wilson was wearing the Tarleton helmet of the light dragoons rather than the turbanned shako of Hompesch's.

Hutchinson used Wilson as a liaison officer with the Turkish allies during the weary business of forcing the French in Cairo to capitulate. It was an energetic occupation for him, entailing long solitary rides across the desert with every chance of getting lost and dying of thirst. Only once did he see a chance of action. Early on the morning of 14 May, when he had just returned from a long, tiring mission, he saw 'a dark mass on the horizon'. With another officer he rode out after it, ordering a squadron of Twelfth Light Dragoons to follow. Having galloped for seven miles they recognized that their quarry was a large French convoy whose '*tirailleurs* gave me the benefit of their shots; one of which was nearer than I wish another to be in Egypt'. The squadron of the Twelfth came up but they were not strong enough to interfere with the escort of the convoy which was moving steadily northward towards Cairo. The only chance was to bluff them into surrendering.

For some time I could get no white pocket handkerchief. At last a major of the Twelfth lent me one. I stuck the handkerchief on my sword but when I got near the French it blew off. However, I galloped on and asked for the commandant, observing everything at the same time most carefully. Cavalier, the commandant and *chef de brigade* of the dromedary corps, advanced. I said, 'I am come, sir, to propose you should surrender to the English. Our columns are advancing against you, and it is humanity to offer you permission to go to France after laying down your arms.' Cavalier replied: 'You must retire from our columns. It is our duty to fight.' I answered: 'Then, sir, the responsibility rests upon your head; and remember that it is a dreadful one. You sacrifice your people.' I turned my horse to go away. I heard the soldiers ask whether I had not said the words, 'return to France'. I was presently called back, but pretended not to hear. An aide-de-camp galloped after me, and said the commandant wished to hear my proposals again. I repeated them. He said he must consult his officers. At length it was settled that they should lay down their arms and we found ourselves masters of above seven hundred camels, five hundred and ninety seven Frenchmen and above three hundred Arab camel drivers: also one piece of cannon. Our cavalry could not have followed a league further having neither water nor provisions.[15]

The Egyptian campaign ended on 27 June when the French army surrendered. Wilson received the Turkish Order of the Crescent, 'a beautiful Mameluke sabre of great value', a present from the Grand Vizier, and a further reputation for daring. He spent some time arranging for the repatriation of the French troops, but on 11 September he parted with Hompesch's Mounted Rifles and started for England. 'I leave Egypt, and pray I may never set foot on its shore again.'

He sailed in the frigate *Pique* and, as was becoming usual every time he travelled by sea, they ran into a storm, accompanied on this occasion by a waterspout. When the weather became calmer and they were fifty leagues from Malta, 'I beat the second lieutenant, who boasted that he could go up to the top-mast-head and come down again before I could get into the main-tops. I reached it before he had even got to the top-mast-head. I had never gone aloft before.'

On 21 October they learned from a French corvette that the preliminaries of peace between France and England had been signed on the first day of the month. Wilson, therefore, decided to land at Marseilles and continue his journey overland. The French insisted that he undergo twenty days of quarantine, a confinement made less irksome by being shared with Pierre-Joseph Redouté, the famous painter of flowers. He had been among the *savants* taken to Egypt by Napoleon and his drawings 'excell everything of the kind I ever saw—particularly the fishes of the Nile'.

On 26 November Wilson was free and set out for Paris over 'infamous roads'. The journey took three days and once again he formed a poor opinion of a foreign capital. 'Anyone who has been in Dublin can form the best idea of Paris: magnificence and meanness are only more frequently contrasted. All the public buildings are calculated to inspire admiration. But Paris has not a street as good as our Cheapside; all are narrow, dirty, unpaved; the houses old and mean in general, the shops without brilliance. Here are no open squares, no streets denoting wealth and comfort.'

Inevitably there was another storm as he crossed the Channel, but on 21 December 1801 he landed safely at Dover.

CHAPTER 2

The Pen and the Sword

As soon as he reached England, Wilson set about negotiating the purchase of the lieutenant-colonelcy of his regiment and his promotion was gazetted on 27 February 1802. He never saw his regiment again, for Hompesch's Mounted Rifles were disbanded in October of that year and he found himself on half-pay (8s. a day). Although in June 1801 his Austrian knighthood had finally been approved, he was short of money and turned to writing to supplement his income. He published a history of the recent campaign with a fulsome, but not undeserved, dedication to the Duke of York, paying tribute to his work in reforming the army.

The History of the British Expedition to Egypt was not a very memorable piece of military history but it immediately became a best-seller. Two short passages, neither of them directly connected with the subject of the book, caught the taste of the public. Both concerned Bonaparte's actions after the storm of Jaffa in 1799. In the first Sir Robert accused him of the murder of his Turkish prisoners. 'Three days [after the storm] Buonaparte, who had expressed much resentment at the compassion manifested by his troops, and determined to relieve himself of the maintenance and care of three thousand eight hundred prisoners, ordered them to be marched to a rising ground near Jaffa; where a division of infantry formed against them. A signal gun was fired. Vollies of musquetry and grape instantly played against them; and Buonaparte, who had been regarding the scene through a telescope, could not restrain his joy, but broke into exclamations of approval.'

This story was largely true. Bonaparte had ordered the massacre of 2,500, not 3,800 prisoners, although the report of his glee at the massacre was invention. The other story was more dubious and Napoleon was still denying it at St. Helena. The Corsican was accused of murdering his own soldiers who were suffering from plague. 'Opium at night was administered in gratifying food; the wretched unsuspecting victims banquetted and in a few hours 580 soldiers, who had suffered so much for their country, perished thus miserably by the orders of its idol.'[1]

True or not, this was the kind of story the British public wanted to read, especially after the Peace of Amiens broke down and the war was resumed on 16 May 1803. Britain was threatened with invasion, and an enterprising publisher printed as a broadsheet these two extracts with a letter from Wilson giving the sources for his allegations. Entitled *The Tender Mercies of Buonaparte in Egypt: Britons Beware!*, the sheet enjoyed a thriving sale at 2*d*. a copy or 1*s*. 6*d*. a dozen. The book itself was translated into French and Wilson sent copies to the Emperors of Austria and Russia, both of whom sent notes of appreciation to the author. Lord Nelson also wrote to Wilson thanking him for a copy. Sir Robert acquired the nickname of *Jaffa* which, in some circles, stuck to him for the rest of his life, and the French, not unnaturally, were very angry.

The renewal of the war did nothing to help Wilson with his military career. Purchase could take him no higher than lieutenant-colonel and, as there was no large increase in the army, he remained on half-pay. Many other lieutenant-colonels were in the same position and the chances of exchanging into a regular regiment were remote. The best that could be found for him was the post of Inspecting Field Officer of Yeomanry in Devon, Cornwall, and Somerset. It was not a job to appeal to a young officer anxious for action and distinction. 'My duty is most unpleasant, harassing, expensive and unsatisfactory. I have no military authority, a district of 400 miles in circumference to ride thro', no travelling expenses allowed, only allowance for three horses, and 13*s*. 10*d*. per day pay. I dare not resign but I would be very glad to receive my dismissal. Perhaps pride operates to disgust me, for I presume I should have a better employment than what the situation of Adjutant to Yeomanry affords here.'[2]

His relations with the Royal Family continued to improve. On several occasions he was invited to stay with the Duke of York at Oatlands and General Hely-Hutchinson, now Lord Hutchinson, introduced him to the small band of politicians who were personally attached to the Prince of Wales. Before the war resumed he considered going into parliament for Liskeard, a Cornish borough in which the Prince had some influence. He also drafted for the Prince a letter to the King begging that, as heir to the throne, he should be allowed some higher military appointment than that of Colonel of the Tenth Light Dragoons. In September 1804 Wilson renewed his acquaintance with George III at Weymouth. 'Uncertain from various reasons of the reception I should find, I nevertheless posted myself with my wife at the pier head. When the King arrived I attracted his observation and after some slight remarks he desired me to come aboard the [Royal] Yacht that he might question me more about Egypt and turning to Ld. Hawkesbury he observed that they were atrocious crimes of which I had accused Buonaparte. "I believe them all; do you not, my Lord?" Ld. Hawkesbury declined an answer. We went on board but Egypt was totally forgotten, and I thought the King did not appear capable of great recollection.'[3]

Throughout the fourteen months he spent as an Inspecting Field Officer, Wilson was trying to secure some other employment. He volunteered to serve in India or to return to Ireland. He sought the Prince of Wales's help in securing the second lieutenant-colonelcy of the Tenth Light Dragoons. He asked the Russian ambassador if his services would be acceptable in the Russian army, but was told that he would first have to learn Russian. It was not until August 1804 that the Duke of York was able to help by appointing him as second lieutenant-colonel of the Nineteenth Light Dragoons.[4]

Meanwhile Wilson had written another book. This time he eschewed history and launched an attack on the government's military policy. The *Enquiry into the Present State of the Military Force of the British Empire with a View to Its Reconstruction* was an open letter addressed to William Pitt, the Prime Minister. The theme of the book was that the government was devoting too many of the available resources to building up the Militia, the Volunteers, and the Yeomanry at the expense of the regular army. His text was 'Warriors alone can oppose warriors'. 'When a government has formed a sufficient regular army to oppose the force which menaces to attack her, then the addition of an armed populace will ensure a decided superiority and materially contribute to shorten the contest, but until the regular army is completed, all parochial military establishments counteract the proposed object.' He urged that a 'Disposable Force' of regulars should be formed and kept ready to intervene on the Continent at short notice.

The most interesting part of the book was taken up with suggestions for increasing the strength of the regulars. He advocated short-service enlistment and the removal of all British troops from the West Indies—'that charnel house must be closed for ever against British troops'. Their place should be taken by men specially recruited from the countries round the Mediterranean, especially 'Æthiopians, a brave, faithful and warlike people, and great numbers of them come annually to Cairo and are dispersed throughout Asia'. Recruiting would also be encouraged if the amount of flogging was sharply reduced. 'Corporal punishment ought to be so rare in the British service that, whenever inflicted, such an event would be considered as remarkable, and then the impression would be advantageous.' He drew attention to the system instituted by Sir John Moore in the Fifty-Second Foot, where flogging was almost unknown and the incidence of crime very low. The fact that, in some regiments, flogging was deplorably common he attributed to the influence of officers promoted from the ranks who 'are generally more severe than other members of courts-martial or as commanding officers'.

While hoping to save money by reducing the size of the Brigade of Guards, he insisted that the pay of officers should be increased. The existing rate 'is so small that it scarcely affords subsistence: the half pay is absolute beggary'. Curiously enough he asserted that 'The non-commissioned officers and men are paid fully enough and perhaps more than is equal to their wants.' Since the net pay of a private soldier was sixpence a day, less a large number of deductions, and every other authority, from Wellington downwards, was convinced that the soldier was underpaid, it is fascinating to speculate on Wilson's reasons for believing that he might already be paid too much.

In his autobiographical fragment Wilson affected to believe that the publication of the *Enquiry* earned him the hostility of the Prime Minister. 'Mr Pitt complained to the Duke of York of this as an attack on his system, and . . . I was ordered by the Duke of York to India, and only the King's *positive command* obtained the revocation of this edict.'[5] It is unlikely that Pitt, who was daily assailed in similar terms by more substantial critics, such as William Wyndham and Colonel Robert Craufurd, would have paid much attention to Wilson's little volume. There may well have been a suggestion from the Horse Guards that Sir Robert should go to India, but this was not unreasonable since the Nineteenth Light Dragoons was serving there. Certainly the Duke of York put no pressure on him to go abroad and on 7 March 1805 sanctioned his exchange with Lieutenant-Colonel Robert Rollo Gillespie of the Twentieth Light Dragoons. This put an end to all talk of India since two squadrons of the Twentieth were in England and the other two in Sicily.

Wilson saw his last regimental service with the Twentieth. With 230 dragoons he embarked at Southampton for Cork. Meeting, for once, 'a miserable calm', he spent twenty-three days on the voyage. 'I employed myself in finishing a memoir, long since begun, on outpost service. It is a collection of instructions acquired by my own experience, without reference to any other writer . . . I have taken much pains to elucidate the subject in order that the young officers of the 20th may be prepared for this essential service. The ignorance or misconduct of a single individual now hazards my own reputation.'

Cork was the rendezvous for a force destined for 'a particular service', under the command of Lieutenant-General Sir David Baird, a difficult man, soured by forty-four months with a musket ball in his thigh in one of Tipoo Sultan's dungeons.

Wellington called him 'a gallant, hard-headed, lion-hearted officer; but he had no talent, no *tact*'.[6] He always treated Wilson with great personal kindness while constantly finding fault with his military work. At their first meeting, at Cork, he 'was very civil, but made no communication as to our destination'.

Before sailing in the last week of August, Sir Robert had an opportunity of demonstrating, in practical terms, his views on military punishment. The officers 'discovered that our Madeira and porter had been pillaged by the ship's cook, a sergeant and a regimental cook. The ship's cook I shall, at all events, send on board a man-of-war, the sergeant will be broke; and the regimental cook, as he is an old man, I shall punish by a very strong emetic.'[7]

The convoy touched at Madeira and went on to Bahia (S. Salvador) where Wilson was sent ashore to buy fifty horses and incurred Baird's displeasure while doing so. Then they sailed again and, on 4 January 1806, the fleet anchored in Table Bay.

Baird's instructions had been to capture the Dutch colony at the Cape of Good Hope which was thought to be garrisoned 'by not more than 1,500 Batavian regular troops, not of the best description, ... [although] it is not impossible that two French ships of the line, with troops on board, and which are yet unaccounted for, may have thrown themselves into the Cape, with a reinforcement of 1,000 to 1,200 troops'.[8] The government had considered 4,700 men sufficient for this enterprise but Sir David had insisted on having his force increased to 6,500. Even this was not a large corps with which to attempt to conquer a sizeable colony defended by a militia and up to 2,700 regulars. In fact the reinforcements from France had not arrived and, after a skirmish at Riet Viel on 8 January, the governor surrendered.

Wilson missed the fighting. He and his dragoons were landed at Saldanha Bay, fifty miles north of Cape Town, as part of an advance guard under Brigadier-General Beresford. Once they were ashore Baird, to the fury of Beresford and Wilson, decided to land the main body elsewhere, and sailed south. They set off on a long dreary march southward. Wilson led with his dragoons and two companies of infantry, the largest force of British troops he ever commanded. He lost his way and 'the heat was more oppressive than I have ever experienced. The infantry spirits began to droop. One man became sick. I put him on my horse and, taking his musket, marched six miles in great pain for my boots galled me terribly.' At least he was better off than fifty of his dragoons who, having no horses, had to march 'with heavy overalls and [thigh-]boots, carrying their saddles'. When they reached Cape Town they found that the campaign was over.

When the force settled down to occupy the colony, Baird showed himself to be the worst kind of martinet. One of Wilson's troopers wrote that 'Sir David Baird, being a mighty disciplinarian, had all the infantry officers at the balance-step and, watch in hand, appeared himself on the drill-ground, regulating their movements as if he had been the adjutant of a regiment. Meanwhile, in barracks, pipe-claying, heel-balling and other amusements peculiar to soldiers in those days, went forward, which were diversified by guard-mountings, field days, roll calls and a system of drill to which there seemed to be no end. It was otherwise with us in the Twentieth Light Dragoons. Our colonel, Sir Robert Wilson, gave us as little trouble as possible. We took our piquets to be sure, and paraded once a day, besides attending faithfully to our stable duties, and preserving good order; but he never harassed us with work that was not called for; and as to punishments, there were none, because they were not needed. Nay, more—he used to march us two or three times a week, in our stable dresses, to an elevated plain about a mile from the town and there encourage us to play at all kinds of athletic games, himself and his brother officers taking part in them. This latter proceeding, however, accorded not at all with the rigid notions of the general. Having come upon us one day while engaged in our sports, he took no notice of the circumstance, but the very next morning a general order appeared which left us with no leisure for a repetition of the scene.'[9]

Wilson wrote to Lord Hutchinson, 'Baird's manners are cold, and he has rendered himself very unpopular in the army by the peculiar deportment he has assumed towards the officers.' On 11 February he issued an order that the officers of the Twentieth were to wear black leather stocks. Wilson replied by quoting the Dress Regulations which prescribed stocks of black velvet, adding that the Duke of York had permitted the officers to wear 'a black silk handkerchief without any bow in front'. When he quoted an order from the King, Baird replied, 'I am his Majesty here.' Bowing low, Wilson replied, 'Very well, King David, your Majesty's orders shall be obeyed.' The general, who was no more proof against Wilson's charm than other men, had the grace to laugh, but the leather stock had to be worn.

Two months later, Sir David made a formal inspection of the Twentieth and found them in so unsatisfactory a state that he censured the regiment in General Orders. Wilson rushed to their defence, appealing directly to the Horse Guards. He pointed out that Baird had insisted on the regiment recruiting thirty captured Waldeckers from the Dutch garrison and had recently drafted to them a hundred local horses 'completely unbroken to any regular gait'. Baird would not withdraw his criticism.[10]

Relief was at hand. On 12 May the *Porpoise*, sloop of war, reached Cape Town with newspapers announcing the death of William Pitt on 23 January. Wilson was no Tory but he wrote in his diary that this was 'The worst of all calamities. We are all sad and desponding.' The news, however, had a bright side, for a Whig government was being formed. 'Lord Hutchinson, the papers say, has an appointment. I am satisfied he will have some good employment; and I calculate upon his friendly offices, at all events, to remove me from hence.' He applied for leave to go home and 'Sir David sent for me and said he knew I had family reasons, and that my friends were come into office, so that he would not detain me.'[11] Wilson sailed on 6 June in HMS *Adamant*, the first port of call being St. Helena, which he described as one of the most unhealthy and dank climates in the world. Sir Arthur Wellesley, who had visited the island in the same month of the previous year, wrote that 'the climate is apparently the most healthy I ever lived in'.[12]

Wilson reached England after a stormy voyage of thirteen weeks to find his friends in office but in an incomparable muddle.

The 'Ministry of all the Talents', led by Lord Grenville, possessed only one notable 'talent', Charles James Fox, and he died on 13 September. His surviving colleagues' policy for conducting the war (which they had ignominiously failed to end by negotiation) was to repeat all Pitt's strategic mistakes on a wider scale. When they came to office they found available a Disposable Force, such as Wilson had recommended, of 40,000 men ready to intervene at short notice on the Continent. Troop transports for 10,000 men were standing by. This force the 'Talents' immediately dispersed. The transports were paid off as an economy measure. The soldiers were sent to Egypt and South America on expeditions which were as inept in conception as they were disastrous in execution. In February 1807 when Sweden, Britain's ally, asked urgently for troops to assist in the defence of Stralsund, all the 'Talents' could offer was a brigade of dragoons.[13] The strength of the regular army was 199,000 rank and file.

Contrary to Wilson's expectation Lord Hutchinson had received no office. He was not an easy man to fit into the political scene. Although Creevey considered him by far the most interesting and agreeable man he knew, he was an uncouth figure. One of his staff officers wrote: 'Shunning society, abstracted, reserved, slovenly and indolent, with ungracious manners and a violent temper, the general was little calculated to gain the confidence or win the affections of those under his command.' He was a committed Whig but his political ideas were wholly negative. The aristocracy he believed to be 'by nature unprincipled, prodigal, corrupt, unrelenting and severe'. At the same time, 'My proud heart detests the wild, the sanguinary, the dirty ravings of democracy. I would rather submit to the tyranny of a King.'[14]

The same staff officer wrote that 'He was a good scholar, he had read much and profitably; his understanding was strong; his information extensive. Nor had he neglected to study the theory of his profession. On military subjects his views were large; and his personal bravery unquestioned.' It was unfortunate that he regarded military life as 'peculiarly disgusting to men of delicate and reflecting minds'. His most memorable military achievement had been his defeat by a small band of Frenchmen and a mob of Irish rebels at Castlebar in 1798, and he had gained his peerage for clearing up the Egyptian campaign after Abercromby's death. It had been noticed that then he had difficulty in making up his mind and a diplomat remarked that 'a spirit of procrastination rules him on all occasions'. Lord Cornwallis said that he was a sensible man but no general.[15]

In the autumn of 1806 the 'Talents' decided to send him as Military Commissioner to the Prussian court. This was a mission which required all his strong understanding for King Frederick William of Prussia had got his country into a situation of formidable complexity. Having filched the electorate of Hanover, he had been at war with Britain since April 1806. Not content with this, he forced a war on France six months later. To do this he chose a moment when Napoleon, having thrashed the Austro-Russian army at Austerlitz, had a large army ready for operations in Germany. Austria had made peace with France and, although Prussia had made a secret understanding with Russia (of which Napoleon had learned the details from the English newspapers), the Czar had no troops within supporting distance of the Prussians. To complete his catalogue of ineptitude, King Frederick William was conducting a vicious personal quarrel with his northern neighbour, the King of Sweden.

A week after Napoleon received the Prussian ultimatum, he destroyed Frederick William's two main armies at the battles of Jena and Auerstadt. News of these actions reached London on 27 October, the day on which the French armies entered Berlin in triumph. Seven days later Lord Hutchinson embarked at Yarmouth in the frigate *Astrea*. His entourage consisted of his brother Christopher, who had been a lieutenant-colonel but who had abandoned the army in favour of the law and politics, a lieutenant-colonel of the disbanded Irish artillery, another colonel who was Inspecting Field Officer of Foreign Officers, an aide-de-camp, and Robert Wilson.

The *Astrea* was an elderly ship. Twenty-four years earlier she had been present at the capture of the American 40-gun frigate *South Carolina*. By 1806 she had a reputation for leaking even in fair weather. On the night she sailed a gale blew up and Wilson wrote, 'surely there is a peculiar ill-fortune that persecutes me in navigation'. They spent twenty-five days tacking about the North Sea until, on 28 November at 2 a.m., the wind 'rose to tempest violence and blew dead on the Norwegian shore, so that we were obliged to beat out of the *Sleeve*—so called from being a long narrow strait that divides Denmark from Norway—into which we had entered in the hope of getting through into the Cattegat. Our anxiety was great for it was a most terrific storm; and the sea ran so high as to break over the men in the foretops, and there was scarcely an authorized expectation of weathering the Naze of Norway.' Fortunately the wind backed, but *Astrea* was leaking eight inches an hour.

The following day was fine and the wind favourable but, at 7 a.m. on 30 November, the captain 'rushed into the after cabin, and coming to Lord Hutchinson acquainted him that the ship was aground. He had scarcely said so much when we experienced several severe shocks. We rose up; and the day began to dawn: but it brought no other relief that the sight of a lighthouse on a small island called Anholt, distant five miles. Signal guns of distress were fired, but Captain Dunbar judging that we might get off the bank, as he found fifteen foot of water all round her, immediately commenced lightening her by throwing overboard guns, provisions, stores, &c. During this time she occasionally beat heavily; and once the shock was so violent that a ligament of the ham of my leg felt as if broken by the concussion.' Lightening the ship did not refloat her and it was not until the main and mizzen masts were cut away that they got clear. Before a jury mast had been rigged *Astrea* was making thirteen feet of water every hour and 'we all went to the pumps and encouraged the crew by such an example'. On 1 December 'about ten o'clock in the morning was cast anchor in Elsinore roads . . . Lord Hutchinson sent me on shore to wait on the governor, and I sprang on the land with gratitude in my heart to the Almighty Disposer of events who had so miraculously interposed to prolong our lives'.[16]

They were well received in Copenhagen, which they reached

on 3 December. 'It is pretended that the Danes have never for-given the attack on their fleet [by Nelson in 1801]: but we experience only civility, and the Danish government has rendered every assistance to the *Astrea*, which is now lying high and dry in one of the Royal docks ... I wish that my French edition [of the *Expedition to Egypt*] was here; two hundred copies at least would be sold. Even English copies would sell, as most Danes read and speak English.'

A Royal Navy brig took them to Danzig, which they found composed of 'filthy narrow streets crowded with Jews in their national garb and beggars'. Their last stage was overland to Königsberg [Kaliningrad], 'a very large city; irregularly built, but with open streets and much cleaner than Danzig'.

Königsberg was the last major town still in Prussian hands and the King and Queen were both quartered there. Their field army was reduced to a single corps of 6,000 men and their kingdom, apart from Königsberg, was reduced to the beleaguered fortresses of Danzig, Pillau [Baltiysk], and Graudenz [Grudziadz]. How-ever, they had the support of 110,000 Russians, well-trained troops but handicapped by a shortage of staff officers and a chaotic commissariat. The French army facing them was esti-mated at Königsberg at 170,000 strong but was in fact only 140,000 strong.

Since the eastern allies were on the defensive and could base themselves on four fortified towns, the numerical odds were not uneven but the Russian high command was riddled with dissen-sion. The commander-in-chief was General Kamenskoi, whom Wilson described as 'a very distinguished officer and active, notwithstanding that he is seventy-two years of age. He affects to imitate Suvarov, and plays the antics of a semi-savage: but he has the confidence of officers and men.' It was unfortunate that hardly had the British mission reached Königsberg than Kamenskoi suffered a mental breakdown. 'He went, without his shirt, into the streets, and then sent for a surgeon, pointed out all his wounds, groaned as he passed his hand over them, and insisted on a certificate of his incapacity to serve.'[17]

Napoleon had his headquarters at Warsaw and his forward

troops were on a line roughly following the courses of the Vistula and Bug rivers. He started an advance on 23 December, pushing forward in three columns. Next day the members of the British mission were bidden to dine with the King of Prussia. 'Lord Hutchinson was to precede, in order to have his audience and deliver a letter from the King of England; but as he forgot the letter I ran after him. An unfortunate beau-trap covered my boots with mud, and in this condition I arrived at the palace and met Lord Hutchinson coming back for his letter. I went on with him, notwithstanding my misfortune. . . . In the ante-room, the Prince Royal was very curious about my dress and the Turkish medal which I wore and particularly remarked my sword-string, as the Prussians pay particular attention to the tassel of the sword-knot. Hutchinson then came in and as we were talking, a tall lean man with his hands in his pockets rushed bolt up to us, and began to speak before I discovered he was the King. He was very civil, but awkward in his address and general manners; and I observed a wildness of look that I could have imagined denoted an insane state of mind.' Two days later the mission 'went up to sup with Drussini, the British consul, which is the greatest debauch I have committed since leaving England; for nothing is so contrary to my habits as eating meat twice a day, and drinking wine and punch until midnight.'

The first serious fighting took place on the same day, 26 December, at Pultusk, a hundred and forty miles to the south. The first reports reaching Königsberg were of an allied defeat, 'and silent preparations were made for evacuating the city. At ten o'clock news arrived that the Russians had gained a victory. A courier arrived with a note from the aide-de-camp to the king, stating that he had great intelligence to communicate but that he had lost his hat and could not appear before his Majesty in that state. Twenty-four postillions and a hat were sent out to meet the aide-de-camp and about twelve o'clock he dismounted at the palace amidst the acclamations of the populace.'[18]

The first reports had been correct. Pultusk had not been a victory though it had been a most honourable defeat, and after it both sides decided to retreat into winter quarters. The Prussian

court decided to retire to Memel [Klaipeda], on Russian soil.
With the British mission, they set off on 3 January 1807, travelling
'in one of the most tremendous hurricanes, accompanied by a
heavy fall of snow'. Hutchinson's carriage needed sixteen horses
and even then moved very slowly.

It was almost a month before the armies moved again. The
supreme command on the allied side passed to General Bennigsen,
a Hanoverian in the Russian service, and both Prussia and Russia
begged Britain to send an army to fight in Poland. Wilson urged
Hutchinson to promise troops but Hutchinson could only give
limited financial help. His stock did not stand high with the allies
and he made little effort to conciliate them. He disliked foreign
ways and insisted on dining at five. 'The Russian fashion is to
dine at two o'clock, to which Lord Hutchinson will never conform.' Wilson, by contrast, was extremely popular. The Russians
especially admired his skill in driving the mission's four-in-hand
through narrow streets covered in ice. 'I am authorised to boast
of my skill as a charioteer.' He was devoted to the Queen of
Prussia—enraptured by her beauty—and was delighted when she
asked for a copy of his Egyptian book. 'By accident I found a
copy of the quarto edition in Memel and had it bound for her.'

There should have been no more fighting until the spring but
Ney made an unauthorized foraging raid in great strength. He
was driven back and Bennigsen, taking his sally to be the start of a
French offensive, counter-attacked fiercely. The campaign flared
into life, despite appalling winter weather. Wilson and Christopher Hely-Hutchinson rode to join the army in 'an excellent little
barouche. . . . We had not journeyed far before we overtook the
French consul from St. Petersburg, with his wife and family,
stuck fast in the snow. Intense as is my *national* enmity to the
French, I could not humanely do an *inhospitable* act; and therefore
we gave them the assistance of our horses and showed them other
attentions which were very properly received. His name is
Lesseps, a clever fellow.' In the consul's coach was his two-year-
old son who turned out to be another clever fellow. He was to
build the Suez canal.

They reached Bennigsen's headquarters on 1 February 'and

were received by him with all possible and pleasing consideration. We were lodged in his house, were made part of the family and instantly admitted to his confidence.' Each of the British officers had a Cossack attached to him so that 'the strangeness of our uniforms might subject us to no unpleasantness from the Cossacks.' They were lent horses—'the one I sprung upon had been ridden by the Emperor Alexander, and is the most beautiful animal'.

The battle of Eylau was fought on 8 February. It was one of the bloodiest battles in history and was fought in a snowstorm. The French lost 15,000 out of 80,000 present. The allies had 73,000 men in the field and lost 18,000. Sir Robert was everywhere where the fighting was heaviest. 'Having gone to the front, as I was returning from the French side, I was seized as a prisoner by some Hulans, although I had on a fur cap; and was with difficulty liberated after a half-hour's detention. Had I worn my helmet, I must have suffered the penalty of a pot with a lance. One circumstance, remarkable for my short sight, I must mention. I saw a ball coming so true upon me and another man riding beside me, that I spurred my horse and shouted to the unfortunate fellow to do the same; but not understanding me, he only gazed when the next moment both his legs were carried away. After the battle General Bennigsen and all of us were obliged to seek quarters in a house occupied by the dead and dying and mangled, whose shrieks were horrible, while the smell was frightfully offensive. I therefore slept in an outhouse until midnight [when] being within nine miles of Königsberg, and as I had had nothing to eat except a crumb of the sourest black bread given me by my Cossack, I galloped into town to refresh, write my letters and sleep, to return at daybreak.'

Eylau had been a drawn battle. Both sides were exhausted but, despite Wilson's urgings, Bennigsen decided to retreat. The only food for the army was in Königsberg and there were no waggons to bring it forward. Since the French remained on the field of battle they claimed the victory, but soon afterwards they too retreated, although they put in hand the siege of Danzig. Wilson would not concede that Eylau was anything but a Russian victory.

'I was always sure that the French were too much broken to hazard another action; for not only was Buonaparte conquered, but his army was subdued by shame and the consciousness of inferiority in point of courage. I requested Lord Hutchinson to assure the [British] government *on my responsibility* that the battle was decisive of the fate of Europe.' The Russians believed that Bennigsen had been wrong to retreat and the Czar's brother, the Grand Duke Constantine, was overheard to say that if that was how their wars were to be fought, 'the Emperor would do better to order each man to load his musket and shoot himself'. Hutchinson thought all Wilson's talk of victory was nonsense. 'The most that can be conceded is that it was a drawn battle.' 'His lordship', wrote one of his diplomatic staff, 'is deep in the slough of despond and loud in depreciating our resources and magnifying those of Buonaparte. He has strictly forbidden Wilson, whose conduct and language are directly contrary to his, to write to any person.'[19]

On 17 April, while the armies were still in winter quarters, Wilson first met the Czar. He was presented to him before dinner and his first impressions were unfavourable. 'The first conversation was about dress—to officers who had been serving the rudest campaign in the history of the world.' A few days later, when he dined again at the imperial table, Sir Robert was completely won over. 'The Czar talked English during dinner very fluently. . . . Every moment in his society the impression is more favourable; not only from his particular gracious attention to us, but from his particular douceur which proves the benignity of his disposition.' The Czar was equally delighted with Sir Robert 'and expressed publicly the wish that under all circumstances I should remain with the army'.[20]

Napoleon was to say that Czar Alexander was sly, false, cunning, and hypocritical. Wilson thought he had 'all the characteristics of an honest mind'. His formidable grandmother, Catherine the Great, had summed him up when she said, '*Ce garçon-là est la réunion de quantité de contradictions.*' Alexander made a profession of dissimulation. From his youth he had been torn between the education given to him, under Catherine's

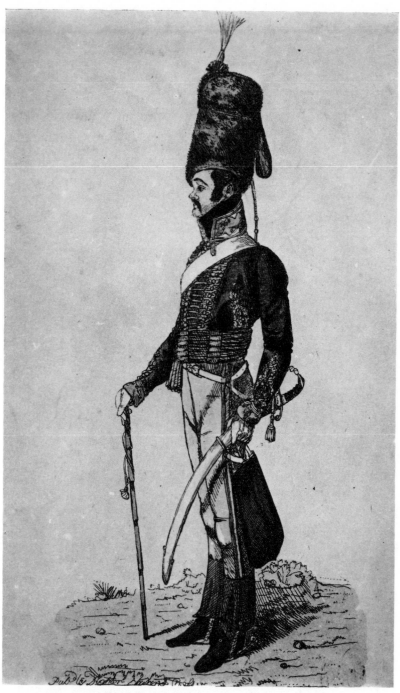

3. Officer of the Fifteenth (The King's) Light Dragoons, 1805.
Robert Deighton Jnr

4. The Battle of Eylau, 8 February 1807. *Sketch drawn on the field by Captain G. P. Bagetti of the French staff*

direction, by a republican Swiss and a Russian priest with an English wife, and the example of his father, Czar Paul, who had a passion for the minutiae of the parade ground. Napoleon remarked that when he first met Alexander, the Czar had counted the buttons on his coat.[21] His instincts were liberal but throughout his life his closest associate was his father's adviser, General Arakcheyev, an honest administrator of great ability but an arch-reactionary with a streak of bestial cruelty.

Alexander could not have ruled Russia if he had not had the facility for being all things to all men. He had to retain the support of the old Russian nobility who were the basis of his power and of the new Russian (and foreign) experts who made it possible to govern the empire. In a single century Russia had expanded from a land-locked grand duchy to a massive empire with outlets on the Black Sea and the Baltic, while her pioneers probed to the Pacific. The old-Russians, who claimed to be the 'real' Russians, were outnumbered, even in European Russia, by the newly acquired subjects, and these new Russians—Baltic Germans, Jews, Poles, Ukrainians—were more than a match for the old-Russians in everything except entrenched power. The administration of the empire and the staff work of the army could not go on without them. At the same time the new men were suspect in the eyes of the twin pillars of Alexander's power—the Orthodox Church and the Russian nobility, brave, conservative, barely educated and intensely xenophobic. The Czar could never forget that only one of his own great-grandparents was Russian. Nor could he forget that, since Peter the Great, every second Czar had been murdered by his immediate, old-Russian, entourage. The last assassination had been that of his own father and the 'first murderer' had been General Bennigsen, the Hanoverian who had got himself accepted as an old-Russian and who was now commanding the army.

To the Czar, lonely on his political tightrope, the appearance of Robert Wilson, a man who might be supposed to stand outside Russian intrigue, was a godsend. George Jackson, Hutchinson's diplomatic adviser, wrote that 'Colonel Hutchinson and Sir Robert Wilson have made themselves much liked here. Both of them behaved so gallantly [at Eylau] that they are to have the

Order of St. George, of the third class; and the emperor has asked for Wilson—who rattles away to him at a great rate, as if laughing and joking with a fellow comrade—to remain with him as military resident. All this suits Wilson exactly and makes him very happy here. I am heartily glad that this is so, though it cannot be denied that he is one of the most harum-scarum fellows that perhaps ever existed, yet there is an immense deal of good in him. Better tempered it is hardly possible to be and I must say he has full need of good temper, for the more he gains ground with the Russians, so much the more do Lord Hutchinson's attacks on him increase in severity. We know that nothing is meant seriously by them and as Wilson parries so well his lordship's thrusts, the spectacle, to bystanders, is amusing enough; but it seems to me that anyone's goodwill would be dearly bought at the price Lord Hutchinson makes Wilson pay for the Russians'.' [22]

Hutchinson was genuinely fond of Wilson but he could not allow him to promise the Russians the help of British troops, since none were available. Equally he had to stop him sending over-optimistic reports to London. He also poured cold water on Wilson's impracticable scheme to raise, in British pay, a huge corps from 'the numerous foreign troops who are dispersed throughout Germany and the disaffected auxiliaries [of the French army]. We may have, in the points of Stralsund and Ostrolenka, fifty thousand auxiliaries and instructed soldiers within a few weeks.' [23]

It was no help to the mission when Wilson went about saying that 'The news of fifty thousand English landing anywhere from Flanders to Danzig would cause more joy here than the gift of three millions of money. I hope that the Duke [of York] will command them. He has had the toil: he should share the glory.' His lordship was already in enough difficulty explaining to the allies that although Britain had no troops to send to the Baltic to fight the common enemy, she had enough to bring on a war with Turkey (29 January 1807) and to invade South America. In the middle of April, Hutchinson's position was fatally weakened. News arrived that the 'Ministry of All the Talents' had resigned on 24 March. Hutchinson, being a political appointment, could look for little support from the new Tory government under the Duke of Portland. Wilson, on the other hand, received a personal letter from the new Foreign Secretary, George Canning, which 'pleased me very much because, without any interested views, it is satisfactory to find friends unchanged by the favours of fortune—with regard to Mr C, I may properly say, by the reward of talent'.[24] Sir Robert was a Whig but Canning was always the politician with whom he felt himself most in sympathy and henceforward, until Canning's death in 1827, a stream of letters, memoranda, proposals, and advice poured to him from Wilson's fluent, if illegible, pen.

Campaigning restarted on 4 June, two weeks after Danzig had fallen to the French. Wilson already had doubts about Bennigsen's capacity as a commander. After Eylau he had written, 'He is not a great officer', and, by mid-May, 'Bennigsen will, I believe, lose the command, much to his own contentment and the utility of the service.' The general himself showed at his worst in June 1807. He tried to isolate Ney's corps but was himself trapped at Friedland [Pravdinsk] on the 14th. He had a river at his back and his position was cut in two by an impassable millstream.

Wilson displayed his usual disregard for danger, and at one time his Cossack orderly tried to tear the light dragoon helmet from his head as it attracted so much fire. When asked for an explanation, the Cossack 'excused his violence by this observation: "The hetman has many Cossacks but only one stranger: it was my duty therefore to do that which might avert him from mischief, and from the sorrow of losing in such a manner a guest whom we esteem."' Sir Robert agreed to wear a fur cap at future actions.

Matvei Ivanovich Platov, hetman or chief of the Cossacks, certainly esteemed his one stranger. He treated him 'as a son and said that he had no other name for me but *Boatt* Wilson, which in the Russian language signifies brother'. On the night of 8 June, Platov had forded a deep river in heavy rain. He slept that night propped against Wilson, 'which gave the cramp to my arms and hands. I could not find it in my heart to wake him by withdrawing, but bore it as best I could, and at last we were quite slushed in mire.'

Friedland cost the allies 10,000 men and 80 guns, and Wilson blamed their commander. 'Had Bennigsen but acted as he ought to have done he would have saved the day, but he seemed physically as well as morally imbecile on this occasion.' The Russian army was extracted from the jaws of the trap, partly because Wilson succeeded in clearing a blocked bridge at Wehlau, but Bennigsen insisted that an armistice was unavoidable. On 25 June Napoleon and the Czar met on a raft moored in the river Niemen at Tilsit.

Next day Wilson wrote in his journal, 'We have this instant received intelligence that Buonaparte succeeded in his project, and that the emperor [of Russia] and the king [of Prussia] met him on a flying bridge on which a hut was erected. . . . The conversation continued an hour, when the sovereigns *embraced* and amicably parted. It is also noted that on gaining the opposite banks the sovereigns again took off their hats and waved a salute. How lamentably ridiculous! Not a month ago I heard the emperor at table speak of Buonaparte as a madman and a tyrant. No communication has yet been made to the English ambassador, so I presume England at present has no voice.' Later he learned that the King of Prussia had been left on the bank for four hours in drenching rain while the two emperors conferred. He also heard of 'a hostile speech of Alexander's relative to England. I hope it is not true.' Report had it that the Czar's first words to Napoleon were, 'I hate the English as much as you do and I am ready to assist you in any undertaking against them.'[25]

There was some fraternization between the French and Russian armies and Wilson, dressed in a pair of grey trousers, a short grey waistcoat, a foreign-cut coat and a cap, crossed the river to see what he could of the French. Despite his disguise he was almost discovered when, surrounded by French soldiers and officers, he was careless enough to refer to the French emperor as Buonaparte. He was also able to see Napoleon as he drove past. He looked 'grossly corpulent, and his countenance presented no commanding talent: his face was very pale and unhealthily full. He was plainly dressed with a cocked hat worn as the old Frederick [the Great] wore it.' He also saw Murat, who 'was dressed exactly like our May-day chimney sweeps, though the cloth of his coat was blue. So thorough a coxcomb I never beheld. His aides-de-camp were dressed *en fantasie* and more ridiculous than anything seen on our stage.'[26]

The Franco-Russian peace made the position of the British mission very difficult, and it was made no easier at the end of June by the news that British troops in Egypt had been heavily defeated by the Turks at Rosetta (31 March). Wilson blamed the 'Talents'. 'If the government will not prefer experience where they have the choice, they should be responsible.' Naturally the officers who had the experience he had in mind were Hutchinson and himself.

It seemed probable that the Czar had agreed to declare war on Britain. There were known to be secret clauses to the Treaty of Tilsit but the mission could discover no more than a rumour that 'France was to have some of the Greek islands and Egypt'. It was fortunate that the government in London had other sources of information. They may have had a spy named Mackenzie who was actually present at the interview between the two emperors; it may have been Talleyrand or Bennigsen who leaked the news to London. What is certain is that on 17 July 1807 the government knew that Napoleon intended to seize Denmark and secure the Danish fleet for use against Britain. The new ministry unhesitatingly gave orders for an expedition—sixteen ships of the line and 20,000 men—to forestall the French at Copenhagen.

Meanwhile life in Memel was tedious. 'We pay our court every morning, and pass our evenings at the house of one or other of the [Prussian] royal family, where the whole assembles. But, although they are very agreeable personages, there are not in this society sufficient *agrémens* to fill out our time without an opening for *ennui*: and the gloomy aspect of affairs prevents imaginary pleasures in prospect.' Sir Robert advised Queen Louise to read Richardson's *Clarissa*.

In mid-July Hutchinson heard that he was to be Military Commissioner to the Russian Army and, with his staff, set out for St. Petersburg. They reached Mittau [Jelgava] on 23 July. There they were presented to the exiled Louis XVIII of France, 'who is very large and unwieldy but with a quick eye and a countenance of benignity. He received us most affably and talked freely and well on general subjects. Our dinner was not good and the wines very bad.'

From Mittau Wilson travelled ahead of his colleagues in a britska, 'a little low carriage just capable of carrying one person and without any springs whatever'. He reached St. Petersburg on 8 August—'What a city! magnificent beyond description or imagination. The whole appears an assemblage of palaces.' Ten days later he dined with the Czar. 'As soon as I entered he took my hand, shook it with affectionate kindness, and led me to the empress. . . . I would have gone to the bottom of the table but the emperor desired me to sit on his right hand and during the whole of dinner we talked in a lively and unceremonious manner.'[27]

At the end of August news reached the city that the British expedition had disembarked near Copenhagen and demanded the surrender of the Danish fleet. This news came to Wilson from the Danish ambassador, 'at which he was much vexed. He said we had been precipitate, for had we waited a few days France would have violated Danish neutrality and then Denmark would have joined us.'

The Czar was also vexed, the more so as succeeding bulletins announced that the British had enforced their demand by bombarding Copenhagen until the Danish fleet was handed over. For months Britain had been denying her ability to help her eastern allies with troops. Now, when her own interests seemed threatened, she had produced 20,000 men at short notice. The British ambassador, Lord Granville Leveson-Gower, was summoned to the palace and an explanation was demanded but he was in a difficult position as he had had no warning that the expedition was to be undertaken and privately disapproved of it. His reply, however, was that Britain had acted for self-preservation. Under no circumstances could she allow the Danish fleet, seventeen ships of the line, to fall into French hands. The Czar was dissatisfied though he appeared to be impressed by this unusual demonstration of British determination. Lord Granville urgently needed to report the Russian reaction and to receive instructions. He chose Wilson as his messenger, largely because Sir Robert had just heard that his wife was seriously ill. Before he could leave, the Czar sent for him. He 'received me alone and for near an hour talked on important political subjects: a conversation very interesting to England'.

Leaving St. Petersburg on 3 September and passing through Stockholm—'the meanest capital in Europe'—he reached London on the 19th. That evening he went to Esher to see Canning at Claremont. He reported his last interview with the Czar, asserting that 'Alexander has repented and was coming round to us again ... that the Treaty of Tilsit could not last; that it was made under the pressure of the moment, with a view to gaining breathing-time; that things must come round again and Russia, England and Austria be united.'[28]

The Foreign Secretary received this information 'with a few scruples of disbelief. He considered Sir Robert as too flighty and as a partizan rather than an able officer and though he applauded his eagerness he made due allowance for it.' He decided that Wilson should return to St. Petersburg with a message for the Czar that 'We were fully disposed to renew our friendly habits with Russia, and to effect this by all practical means.' The Foreign Office view was that 'it is a good policy to send Sir Robert back; he is a military man, has served with the Russians, has been spoken to confidentially by the Emperor, and may do better than a better man. Nothing important, however, is to be left to his sole discretion.'[29]

Finding that Jemima Wilson was 'much better than I had ventured to hope', Sir Robert sailed from Harwich in an 80-ton despatch boat on 3 October. As was almost routine when he travelled by sea, a gale blew up and the ship was driven into Göteborg, but Wilson had taken the precaution of having had a light phaeton lashed to the deck and this he immediately disembarked. Before setting out overland he paused long enough to dine with Louis XVIII, who happened to be in the town. The exiled king 'had the good nature to order a bottle of coffee, some tea, sugar, wine and meat to be packed up for my use on the journey'. He reached St. Petersburg on 17 October.

The Czar refused to see him. Wilson wrote a letter but it went unanswered. Individual Russians, including Alexander's Polish mistress, Madame Narishkin, entertained him, and his popularity was a sore trial to General Savary, the French ambassador. After twelve days he was summoned to the Ministry of Foreign Affairs for an interview with Count Roumiantzev. He delivered Canning's emollient message but the minister firmly denied that his master had intended to make the friendly advances which Wilson attributed to him after their last meeting. Roumiantzev, however, said 'that he would charge himself with my presentation to the emperor and that I might confide in his Majesty's un-alterable friendship to myself . . . I would flatter myself that every hope of a private understanding is not unwarrantable.'[30]

The summons to the palace never came. Instead, Madame Narishkin's son called at the embassy a few days later 'to ask Lord Granville whether, as he was going away, he would not sell his horses'. The ambassador found this inexplicable until, five days later, he was given his passports and told that Russia was at war with Britain. On 8 November Wilson was despatched to take the news to London. He was shipwrecked off Göteborg but still managed to beat the official Russian courier who had six days' start. He announced the declaration of war to Canning at 4 a.m. on 2 December. 'All my conduct was approved and my diligence commended.'

CHAPTER 3

Loyal Lusitanian Legion

The Twentieth Light Dragoons were the first British cavalry to see action in the Peninsula. At Vimeiro, on 21 August 1808, Sergeant Landsheit, who charged with them, wrote, 'we kept laying about us till our white breeches, our hands, arms and swords were all besmeared with blood. . . . We were in the heart of the French, cutting and hacking, and upsetting men and horses in the most extraordinary manner possible. . . . It was here that our colonel met his fate. He rode that day a horse that was so hot that not all his exertions would suffice to control it, and he was carried headlong upon the bayonets of the French infantry, a corporal of whom shot him through the heart.'[1]

It was not Robert Wilson who fell on the French bayonets, although the headstrong charge of the Twentieth was the kind of fighting that appealed to him most. In the eight months that had elapsed since his return from St. Petersburg he had not considered that the superintendence of half a regiment of cavalry —two squadrons of the Twentieth were still in Sicily—was a task worthy of his talents. Instead he had spent his time in London trying to persuade his friend Canning, and anyone else who would listen, that he ought to be employed in an independent situation, preferably in Russia.

The French occupation of Portugal and much of Spain raised a variety of feelings in Britain. After fourteen years of desultory and ineffective intervention on the Continent, few believed that the British army would be able to effect much, but the government was unwilling to miss an opportunity of striking at Napoleon, and their Tory supporters did not dissent although they were haunted by the belief that the country would not be able to afford any sustained operations. The Whig opposition was divided. The right wing, led by Lords Grenville and Holland and, when he was reasonably sober, by Richard Brinsley Sheridan, developed a romantic love for the Spanish patriots and counted on their passion for freedom to free their country from French oppression. The left, for which Samuel Whitbread was the chief spokesman, foresaw nothing but humiliation from the attempt to intervene.

Robert Wilson's political sympathies lay largely with the left but he saw for himself a chance to attain an independent situation. From the government downwards, it was expected that any British help would be directed towards aiding the Spaniards; only the Royal Navy, with their eyes on the all-weather harbour of Lisbon, favoured making Portugal the British base. Wilson believed that he could make a niche for himself in Portugal and, from there, intervene as a free agent in the Spanish war.

His ally in this plan was the Portuguese ambassador in London, the Chevalier de Souza, an ugly, shrivelled little man much sought after by London hostesses, especially those without unmarried daughters. De Souza had a problem. When the French invaded his country in November 1807 and the Portuguese court had sailed for the Brazils, a few hundred Portuguese soldiers of all ranks had made their way to England. Their maintenance was a charge to the embassy. The British government took little interest in them and the men themselves were encamped and dispirited near Plymouth. The ambassador was anxious to disembarrass himself of them. Moreover, the outbreak of fighting between the French and the Spaniards, hitherto allies in the rape of Portugal, left northern Portugal unoccupied by the French. A provisional government had been set up in Oporto headed by the bishop, Antonio de Castro, who wrote to de Souza, an old friend, asking for the support of 6,000 British troops and 'the succour of 3,000,000 cruzades, the entire armament and accoutrements for 40,000 men and for 8,000 horses, 1,000 barrels of powder, and cloth for uniforms; besides this some vessels with salt fish and other necessaries; all upon credit [and] an able general to direct our affairs'.[2]

De Souza bombarded Canning with demands that he send help to Oporto, but there was little that the British could do. Their entire disposable force, 7,000 men, was under orders to sail for Spain with Lieutenant-General Sir Arthur Wellesley in command. It was at this stage that Wilson suggested to de Souza that, at a single stroke, both his problems could be solved. The men at Plymouth should be formed into a Portuguese Legion and shipped off to Oporto with Wilson at their head. The proposal was embodied in a memorandum, drafted by Wilson himself, and sent to the Foreign Office. Canning, delighted to see a way of ending de Souza's importunities and of gratifying his friend Wilson, supported the idea and persuaded the Secretary for War, Lord Castlereagh, to issue the necessary orders.

On 4 August 1808 Wilson was ordered to take the Portuguese refugees to Oporto 'with a view to adding to them a number of recruits as will compose three battalions of chasseurs and a company of artillery'. Arms and clothing were to be supplied from England 'upon the account of the Prince Regent of Portugal, and a sufficient advance of pay should be made until the officers and men now here can arrive in Portugal. . . . An imprest of £300 has been ordered to be placed in your hands to answer contingent expenses.' The complete unit, to be known as the Loyal Lusitanian Legion, would have a strength of 3,216 all ranks, of whom Britain was to provide 36 non-commissioned officers and 10 farriers. None of these British soldiers was actually supplied but two foreign officers, Lieutenant-Colonel Baron Perponcher, a Dutchman, and Lieutenant-Colonel Baron Eben, a German, did report for duty.[3]

Everyone was pleased with this arrangement. De Souza had sent help to the Bishop of Oporto; Canning was relieved of de Souza's constant demands; Castlereagh had made a gesture towards Portugal without incurring any charge to the Army Estimates; and Wilson had got his dearest wish—an independent command. It was, in fact, a very independent command, being responsible to no one except the Prince Regent of Portugal who was in Rio de Janeiro and could not be expected to bother with details even if they were reported to him. The only Portuguese government in Portugal was the Junta of Oporto, which was not recognized by London, and, although Wilson was told that 'on arrival you will report yourself to the General Officer commanding his [Britannic] Majesty's troops in Portugal', no such appointment had been made nor was it envisaged. Even if a general was appointed, Wilson was only instructed to act with that officer's approval and was not put under his command. Although he was instructed to make reports to the Secretary for War in London, he was also told to 'act in concert with the Chevalier de Souza, who corresponds on this subject with Mr. Secretary Canning'. This meant that he had two masters in London and, since the Foreign Secretary and the Secretary for War were known to be on hostile terms, there was every chance of being able to play one department off against the other.

It may have been an additional source of satisfaction to Sir Robert that while his instructions authorized him to raise three battalions and a battery, the schedule of the establishment of the Legion (which he had drawn up himself) included four troops of cavalry, an addition which the War Department had apparently failed to notice.

After a nine-day voyage Wilson reached Oporto on 18 August and received a rapturous welcome from the people of the city. The bishop installed him in a fine house—'quite the pallace of a dictator'—and promoted him to be a brigadier in the Portuguese service, although he refused to accept pay. Bishop Castro 'overwhelmed me with kindness and good intentions and never did a stranger possess his affections to so great a degree', wrote Wilson, who added, privately, that the bishop was an amiable old woman.

There was every reason for this display of episcopal goodwill. 'The fate of the Bishop of Evora, who the Bishop of Oporto states to have had his eyes torn out and to have been stabbed to death, has made a great impression here.'[4] It was a measure of Castro's personality that he had been able to maintain a semblance of order in the city. The only force available to him had been 1,500 regulars, all dispirited and mostly unarmed, who were little less unruly than the mob. Wilson's arrival meant that he would now have a number of trained troops under disinterested officers with which to assert his authority, and he determined to cement their allegiance to him by persuading the Junta to agree that the Legion should have a higher rate of pay than the regulars. This did nothing to improve the discipline of the regulars and raised for Wilson the danger that the bishop would regard the Legion as his personal bodyguard and would object to its leaving the city.

Sir Robert's cherished freedom of action was also being threatened by events elsewhere. The Spaniards absolutely refused to accept the help of Wellesley's small army and its commander, for want of other employment, decided to capture Lisbon. He started to land the troops and some reinforcements from Gibraltar on 1 August. When all were ashore he marched towards the capital, defeating the French advance guard at Roliça on the day before Wilson reached Oporto. On 21 August he defeated the main French army at Vimeiro.

Wellesley was not allowed to profit by his victory. During the battle he was superseded by Sir Harry Burrard; on the following day the command passed to Sir Hew Dalrymple who concluded with the French the Convention of Cintra by which the French army was to be repatriated in British ships with, as it turned out, all their Portuguese loot. Simultaneously large British reinforcements, released from an abortive expedition to the Baltic, arrived in Portugal, making Dalrymple's army up to 30,000 men.

Dalrymple's conduct in arranging the convention aroused a storm of protest in Britain and no less a storm in Portugal, since he had omitted to consult any Portuguese authorities while committing a future government to making large concessions, including an amnesty for such Portuguese as had collaborated with the French during the occupation. He further alienated local opinion by reinstating, by British proclamation, the Regency which had ruled briefly before the French seized Lisbon. Bishop Castro of Oporto was co-opted as a member of this body.

According to his instructions, Wilson reported himself to Dalrymple at Cintra on 3 September, but the general was busy with other matters and gave Sir Robert no further instructions. He therefore made his way back to the Douro, paying on the way a visit to General Bernardino Freire, the Portuguese Commander-in-Chief, whom he found filled with a justifiable anger at Dalrymple's failure to consult him. When Wilson reached Oporto he found the bishop and his junta in session, having just heard of the convention. He was coldly received and, as he wrote to Castlereagh, 'I confess that I was never so pained for the honour of my country as at this moment.'[5]

Wilson's independence was now threatened from three sides. The bishop, although now a member of the Regency, still spent most of his time in Oporto and was reluctant to see the Legion removed from his immediate control. His powers over it were ill-defined but, for the time being, he was in a position to supply the men with rations which could not otherwise be obtained. The second threat came from the Portuguese Regency and their regular army. They claimed that, as a Portuguese unit, Sir Robert and his men should come under their command. Wilson countered both these Portuguese threats by asserting that he owed his allegiance to the British commander in Portugal. This, as he well knew, was sophistry, as he did not hesitate to remind Dalrymple and his successors that they could not give orders to the Legion although they could veto Wilson's proposals.

Wilson was more than capable of keeping these three potential overlords in play against one another in the early months while he was recruiting and training his men. Recruits were raised under British regulations. Each had to be physically fit and not less than five feet three inches tall. Enlistment was for the duration of the war and for six months afterwards, with liability to serve in any part of the world. There was no shortage of recruits and this success of the Legion's recruiting earned Wilson more enmity from the regular Portuguese officers, who saw the best of their conscripts skimmed off to serve under foreign officers. The distinctive uniform was a great lure. Sir Robert had planned to dress his men in the scarlet of British soldiers but de Souza had dissuaded him. Determined to avoid the blue or brown of Portuguese troops, Wilson settled for a green jacket with white breeches. Green was the traditional colour for chasseurs and British experience showed that a green jacket attracted enlistment. It was not only Portuguese who joined. In the first month the ranks were swelled with 26 Swiss, 63 Germans, and 15 Piedmontese, all deserters from the French.[6]

Exploiting the Portuguese custom whereby company officers were appointed by the colonels of regiments without reference to higher authority, Wilson claimed that he had secured the *élite* of Portugal for his officers and he added to them a few unattached British officers. One battalion was entrusted to Baron Eben, another to a lieutenant of the Third Dragoon Guards, and the third to a Mr. William Mayne, who seems to have had no military experience of any kind. A few British ensigns were acquired as company commanders and Wilson secured a Lieutenant James Charles, Royal Artillery, as his aide-de-camp, a post Charles was later to fill in Russia. Baron Perponcher was sent back to England with despatches and Wilson did not complain when he failed to return.[7]

It was hard work to train the Legion for the field. 'Twice a day I am obliged to drill them, for without my presence there is no work done with advantage or cheerfulness.' In addition to the administrative work of the Legion, which fell steadily behind, Sir Robert kept up a constant flow of correspondence with his friends in England. He also wrote, at least once a week and with a wealth of tendentious detail, to the Commander-in-Chief in Lisbon and to the Secretaries of State for War and Foreign Affairs in London. 'Letters, letters, until the mass rises before me in terrifying quantity. The numerous applications have obliged me to give an order that no person shall interrupt me this day, and yet above 40 persons have necessarily been with me and I must go to the bishop for two hours at least, and I must be ready with my voluminous correspondence and I must go to a great party this evening in my honour.'[8]

One of the first acts of the restored Regency was to cancel the augmented pay which the bishop had authorized for the Legion. Wilson at once wrote to Castlereagh begging him for a special subsidy to make up the difference. He took the opportunity to seek permission to march the Legion into Spain, claiming that 'It is in the presence of the enemy, after some incipient organization, that such a corps is formed.' As an afterthought he requested that the Twentieth Light Dragoons might be placed under his command. This letter went unanswered.[9]

On 10 October the Legion underwent its first test. By the Convention of Cintra the French garrison of Almeida was to be repatriated through Oporto. Since their transports could not immediately enter the river mouth, the Frenchmen were lodged in a riverside fort. This caused a riot. Believing that the French baggage was stuffed with plunder, a mob surged round the fort and the Portuguese regulars, siding with the mob, aimed their cannon at British ships in the river. There were only 200 British troops in the city and these Wilson posted round the fort to guard the French. The men of the Legion were stationed to protect the powder magazine. Then the bishop and Wilson rode round the tumultuous city haranguing the mob and urging them to disperse. They were only partially successful but fortunately there was, outside the city, a brigade of Spanish troops, 1,500 of them, and these were marched into Oporto and restored order without bloodshed. This outbreak thoroughly alarmed Wilson and he wrote to Canning, 'I am confident that we must either abandon the country or send a force of 3,000 British troops with some cavalry to this town.' No troops were sent but Wilson enlisted 200 Swiss from among the French garrison.[10]

Meanwhile the position of the British troops in Portugal was changing. Sir Hew Dalrymple had been recalled to face an inquiry and the British government, reverting to their earlier plan, ordered Sir John Moore to march the bulk of the army into Spain to co-operate in the defence of Madrid. The remnant in Portugal was entrusted, as a temporary measure, to Sir Harry Burrard. Sir Harry was worried by the anomalous status of the Lusitanian Legion. It does not, he reported, 'appear to be approved by the Regency, and I shall, therefore, order it to be discontinued unless the objections to it are counterbalanced by much advantage.' To assess the position he asked Major-General Beresford, who was on his way to join Moore's army, to visit Oporto and make recommendations.[11]

Wilson was fortunate that it was Beresford who had been chosen for this examination. They had served together in South Africa and were friends. The general's report made it clear that, although he disliked the way the Legion was constituted, he thought it ought to be retained. 'Without questioning the propriety of forming this corps, his Majesty's orders have been acted upon at very considerable expense, which would be entirely lost if a stop were put to its completion; besides that it would be very disgusting to the bishop, who considers it a measure of his own promoting.' He recommended that the infantry should be completed one battalion at a time and that the cavalry, of whom, according to Wilson, only a few officers had been nominated, should be discontinued.[12]

Sir Robert could hardly have expected a more favourable report, although it was far from meeting his ambitions. He pressed on with raising his cavalry and renewed his plans to escape from Oporto and get to Spain. To gain time he applied formally to be taken under British command but confided to his journal that 'To unite with the British army would be no advantage to my ambitious projects. The order and system of such a force would be fatal to my adventures. I must have freedom of action.'[13]

His chance came early in December, by which time another radical change had come over the war in the Peninsula. Napoleon had entered Madrid unopposed on 3 December. Sir John Moore, with 20,000 men at Salamanca and 10,000 more at Astorga, was deciding to make his gallant attempt to destroy Soult's isolated corps north of Valladolid. Portugal was almost stripped of British troops and a new commander-in-chief was travelling to Lisbon. On his way he called at Oporto.

The new general was Sir John Cradock, whom Wilson had known since they served together in Egypt. Sir John was not impressed by the Portuguese regulars he saw. By contrast, the men of the Legion seemed to have possibilities. 'I really think favourably of them as Portuguese soldiers and Sir Robert Wilson certainly is entitled to much approbation for his exertions.' He was also persuaded that the Legion would improve if it was moved out of Oporto. 'I therefore recommend in the strongest manner (till I have communicated with the Regency in Lisbon I cannot give an order) ... that you should move out of this town the Portuguese Legion under your orders and station yourself at Vila Real.'[14]

Cradock's orders from London were necessarily vague. He was to secure the British base at Lisbon until, as seemed probable, the government decided to abandon it; he was to send supplies and reinforcements to Moore in Spain; to co-operate with the Portuguese in defending their country against invasion. His effective strength was 10,000 men, some of whom Moore had thought unreliable. As long as Moore's main force lay at Salamanca, Portugal was reasonably safe. Cradock could garrison the two frontier fortresses, Almeida and Elvas, and keep a strong reserve at Lisbon. Wilson's Legion seemed the only indigenous help he was likely to get and, at Vila Real, it would block one of the less probable invasion routes open to the enemy.

Wilson marched out of Oporto on 16 December. The second and third battalions, which had not received their uniforms, were left under Baron Eben in Oporto as a sop to the bishop. Sir Robert's column, therefore, consisted only of a single battalion, a squadron of cavalry, and a battery with four six-pounders and two $5\frac{1}{2}$-in. howitzers, 700 men in all. Instead of going to Vila Real, as Cradock had suggested, Wilson turned south-east at Amarante and crossed to the south bank of the Douro. The weather broke and the soldiers were drenched day after day, but 'they marched with one perpetual song and cheer'. Christmas Day was spent halted at Lamego. The soldiers enjoyed themselves but, for the officers, 'Primeval society is never the best for entertainment in any country and here it was villainously rustick.' Wilson wrote to Cradock and let him know that they were making for Almeida.[15]

By a fortunate coincidence this unauthorized move suited Cradock's plans very well. When he reached Lisbon, the general had heard of Moore's intention to attack Soult. Loyally he ordered two battalions at Almeida to move east and reinforce Moore.

The Legion would do as an interim garrison for that fortress. His secretary wrote to Wilson, 'His Excellency cannot but approve and consider it very opportune the arrival of the Legion at that garrison.' In a typically considerate personal letter sent the same day, Cradock advised Sir Robert that he 'should reflect before you shut yourself up in a fortress'. He realized that Wilson's fate, if he fell into French hands, might well be unpleasant. The accusations against Napoleon in the *History of the British Expedition to Egypt* would not have been forgotten or forgiven.[16]

Wilson had no intention of being shut up in a fortress. He left some of his infantry, under William Mayne, in Almeida to guard a depot of stores left there by Cameron's brigade as it marched to join Moore, but, after a few days' rest, Wilson marched across the Spanish border to Ciudad Rodrigo. Rodrigo was a major fortress needing a garrison of 4,000 men and the Spanish troops present consisted of six companies of the Urban Guard, tradesmen in uniform, and a battalion of recruits, 1,400 men in all. Wilson had two companies of infantry, his cavalry, and two guns. Grandiloquently he pledged himself to protect the city.

This was not such an extravagant gesture as it appeared. Wilson was convinced, and continued to be convinced, that the place was in no danger. On 20 January 1809, when he had been there two weeks, he wrote, 'I do not believe the enemy have any intention of advancing in this quarter.'[17] He was also determined to establish himself there for another reason. It contained a large depot of British stores and, on his arrival, he found a commissary making arrangements to transport them back to Portugal. This was an opportunity not to be missed, and the commissary was sent back to Lisbon with a certificate which blandly stated that 'It is impossible and almost unnecessary to send off the commissariat stores in this town.' Wilson recommended that they should be put 'under the care of a gentleman of character in this city, Mr. Taravilla, in order that he may dispose of them to the best advantage for the British or give them to the Spanish or Portuguese troops as circumstances may require.'[18]

This was a master-stroke. It made the Legion independent for several weeks to come. It was the great strength of Wilson's position that he could represent the Legion as a British unit when given orders by the Portuguese, and as a Portuguese unit when dealing with British commanders. It must, however, be fed and the one thing that was clear from the letter of service was that its expenses were a charge to Portugal. Sir Robert's excursion to Rodrigo had infuriated the Portuguese authorities. The Regency and the army disliked the Legion because they could not control it. The Bishop of Oporto had been affronted by the desertion of his 'bodyguard'. For the first time Regency and bishop came to an agreement and refused to send the Legion any supplies. His coup at Rodrigo made Wilson independent of Portuguese food.

In Spain the situation was deteriorating rapidly. Cameron's brigade had found that it could not join Moore and turned back, marching along the north bank of the Douro. Cameron recommended that the Legion should fall back on Oporto. The news from Moore was that he was falling back to north-eastern Spain and his destination was thought to be Vigo.[19]

Back in Lisbon, where there was even less information about Moore, opinion was divided. The admiral commanding in the Tagus was despondent as early as 6 January. 'We must evacuate the Tagus upon intelligence of the French entry into Portugal which we hourly expect.' Cradock was more optimistic. On 11 January, less than a week before Moore embarked at Coruña, he wrote to Wilson that he was sending two more brigades up to Almeida and added, 'The arrival of your corps at Almeida has been most fortunate. ... It does not appear from the general information received that the French will make any approach to Almeida or Ciudad Rodrigo.'[20]

On 14 January two important despatches reached Cradock. He heard from Moore for the first time for a month. He learned that the army was making for Coruña where it was hoped to embark. There was no indication of where the troops would go when they were aboard but Moore was known to favour making Cadiz the British base. A switch to Cadiz also seemed to be implied in the other despatch, fresh orders from London which had been written as long before as Christmas Eve. Cradock was told that, while some British units were to be left in Portugal, most of them would be employed elsewhere in the Peninsula, 'where most advantageous to the common cause'. Until further orders arrived all Cradock's troops were to be held within easy reach of Lisbon and, if the French appeared in great strength, were to be evacuated. As Cradock wrote to Wilson, these orders had been written when 'ministers were not aware of Sir John Moore's retiring upon Galicia. Of course they have not provided us with any instructions to meet actual emergencies.'[21]

Acting on these orders, Cradock recalled the two brigades he had sent to Almeida and made dispositions to make the best possible defence of Lisbon. The Lusitanian Legion set him an insoluble problem. He had no authority to give Sir Robert orders—'I really did not feel myself competent to give him publick orders'—and knew that he would ignore any orders sent to him by the Portuguese command. At the same time he was unwilling to leave the Legion isolated on the frontier where it must be destroyed if a French invasion did come. The best he could do was to write 'a strong recommendation. . . . Composed as the corps is under your orders, and exclusively belonging to the Portuguese nation, it is impossible for his Excellency to prescribe any rule for the government of your conduct. He can only recommend the whole division of the Legion to be collected in the garrison of Almeida; for it is evident that any forward movement (forever to be praised for the spirit it evinces) can, under present circumstances, be attended with no positive advantage to the general cause.' He paid a handsome tribute to the Legion's services and added, 'The present situation of yourself and the English gentlemen attached to the Legion at present appears to be very embarrassing and it would be difficult for his Excellency to hazard, with any chance of being right, a suggestion of the line of conduct they should pursue. The determination is of a nature so exclusively personal that it would seem to rest solely within the breasts of the individuals concerned.'[22]

This letter, which produced no result, crossed with one from Wilson in which he declared his intention 'to *cover* the frontier, or fall upon Seville'.[23] This extravagance prompted Sir John to make another attempt to bring the Legion back. Pointing out that the Regency were demanding Wilson's return to Oporto, he asked him to fall back at least to within the boundaries of Portugal. 'Unless the government of Portugal expressly sanction the departure of your corps for the purpose of aiding the Spanish cause, his Excellency cannot feel himself justified in lending his support, much less give his authority to such a proceeding.' This appeal brought a predictably bland refusal from Ciudad Rodrigo. 'Much as I should wish to consider a suggestion from his Excellency as an order, still I should under present circumstances be wanting in duty to his Excellency if I acted on an opinion given at a remote date and distance, when local knowledge imperiously required another conduct.'[24]

There was nothing further Cradock could do. He did not have the authority to order Sir Robert back to Portugal and he knew that he would not obey orders sent to him by the Portuguese. To hammer home this point Sir Robert sent Cradock a private message saying that even if he had to retreat he would not go to Oporto, as 'it is the government of a mob, of which he had too much experience'.[25]

In parliament in the following year an attempt was made to prove that Wilson's stay around Rodrigo in the early months of 1809 saved Portugal from invasion, and this opinion has been adopted by many subsequent historians. Wilson did not subscribe to this opinion at the time. He did not believe that the French could, or even wished to, advance in that sector and, as late as March, Cradock was reporting that 'Sir Robert's own persuasion is that the French army will retire altogether from Spain'. Wilson's motive in staying in his isolated position was to remain isolated, away from either British or Portuguese control, and to train his soldiers by indulging in desultory raiding operations. He believed that the forces opposed to him were so weak that the Legion could dominate south-western Leon, and in his diary he speculated on the chances of receiving a Doctorate of Laws from the University of Salamanca when he liberated the city.[26]

His estimate of the intentions of the French was right. Napoleon's master plan for the subjugation of Portugal and southern Spain called for two large forces. One, under Soult, was to conquer Portugal from north to south. The other, commanded by Victor, was stationed on the Tagus and was to co-operate in the later stages. In the 300-mile gap between these two corps there was a force under Lapisse consisting of 7,692 infantry and about 800 cavalry. Lapisse had orders to 'form a corps of observation, to establish a supply depot and to subdue and disarm the whole of western Leon'. He was forbidden to invade Portugal until he was ordered to do so by the central command in Madrid, and he was told that this order would not be given until Soult was deep into Portugal.[27]

Lapisse, in fact, had so many duties and so few men that the most he could do was to keep a tenuous screen of outposts in the direction of Ciudad Rodrigo, and these isolated detachments were an ideal target for the small-scale operations which were invaluable for giving confidence to the Legion. Wilson's force was growing greater in strength. The Spaniards put two battalions under his command, he borrowed detachments of Portuguese dragoons from the garrison of Almeida, and he detained many stragglers from Moore's army and formed them into a company of mounted infantry, pressing into service any horses and mules that could be requisitioned from the countryside. With this miscellaneous force, Sir Robert harassed Lapisse's men unmercifully. Vedettes were ambushed, ration convoys seized, and, by means of multilingual leaflets, many of the non-French soldiers were induced to desert.

One of Wilson's forays was described by Benjamin D'Urban, a staff officer attached to the force by Cradock. Hearing that the French had a small post at Calcidella, about five miles from Salamanca, garrisoned by an officer and 30 cavalrymen, Sir Robert set out with thirteen Portuguese dragoons under an officer and three British officers. He sent for two further detachments of dragoons, 110 in all. On the night of 20/21 January the party lay up in an isolated house with a wood between them and the French. D'Urban's journal continues:

January 21st. Neither of the detachments have joined, but it is necessary to do something immediately; the confidence of the people, as well as other ends, are to be gained by it, and we cannot remain long undiscovered which, with our small force is everything. Early in the morning therefore, resolved to move by the wood towards the enemy outposts and be guided by events.

Evening. We have done this day as follows:— On proceeding about half way to the enemy's post at Calcidella, we were joined by a peasant who told us that the enemy occupied two posts—at Calcidella and Torre—that the former was an officer's post, and that what was doing at one could not be seen by the other; Sir Robert determined instantly to attack it; and this he did in the most gallant manner, and it was carried in an instant, but with the loss of Captain Piralugi, who was shot. We saved the prisoners with some difficulty from the rage of the Portuguese dragoons and now found that it was only a small post with a sergeant commanding it.[28]

This kind of buccaneering was much to Wilson's taste and was excellent battle training, but its effect on the course of the war was minimal. Not that much was known in Portugal of events in the other parts of the Peninsula. Wilson did not learn of Moore's death and the embarkation of the army at Coruña until two weeks after the event. At Lisbon Cradock was little better informed. On 26 February he wrote to Sir Robert that 'we are in a deplorable state from want of intelligence. It would appear that ministers meant to leave us to our discretion. ... *I am sure* that England will not send another army into Spain. ... It is impossible to describe the intricacy of our situation here. We shall remain here until we receive orders—or an irresistible force approaches. [With] one that we can cope we shall do our best.'[29]

It was not until 3 March that Cradock heard that the British government had decided on a line of policy. Lisbon was to be held, reinforcements were to be sent, and the organization of the Portuguese army was to be undertaken by British officers. Before this news reached Wilson he had decided to seek glory in another part of the Peninsula. He rode south, with a single companion, to concert an operation against the French with the Spanish general Cuesta, who was rallying a defeated army on the south bank of the Tagus and who had suggested that the Lusitanian Legion should co-operate with him. Sir Robert confided to his journal, 'I have chosen my theatre and the world shall be spectators of my purpose.'[30]

This sudden change of course may have been dictated by boredom. There was little glory in an endless series of pin-pricking raids and Ciudad Rodrigo was in no danger. A contributory factor was that the junta of Rodrigo had seized the remains of the British stores in the town as a security for the debts left behind by Moore's army. Cradock had given Wilson full powers to settle the matter in the best way possible but the loss of the stores spelled the end of the Legion's independence. Possession of them had enabled Sir Robert to avoid acknowledging the authority of either British or Portuguese generals. Without them he would have to go begging for rations and he would get none unless he obeyed orders. He hoped that Cuesta would prove more amenable.[31]

Cuesta was far from amenable. He was touchy, perverse, and indecisive, but he went out of his way to please Sir Robert, appointing him a brigadier in the Spanish service and offering to add 5,000 Spaniards to his command in a joint campaign astride the Tagus which aimed to liberate Madrid. Although Wilson described the Spanish general as a grumpy old gentleman, he wrote in his diary, 'It is a summons that either makes or mars my future fortunes. I have always aspired to command. . . . There is no man that can achieve greatness without responsibility.'[32]

It was Wilson's good fortune that the joint attack was never launched. It could only have ended in disaster. As it turned out, the French moved first. While Wilson was riding back to Rodrigo to collect his men, Victor marched against Cuesta, drove him back and, on 28 March, routed him at Medellin. Wilson had his own piece of bad news. When he returned to the Legion he found waiting for him a letter from Beresford, now Marshal and Commander-in-Chief of the Portuguese army. Sir Robert was to hand over the command of the Legion to the senior officer and was himself to report to the Portuguese headquarters at Lisbon.

CHAPTER 4

A Separation by Detachments

Cradock had written on 3 March to tell Wilson of Beresford's mission. 'This day Genl. Beresford arrives with full powers to command the Portuguese army, & the rank of [British] lieutenant general. He has brought some officers with him who all get one step [in British rank]—so ought you.' Sir John added the unpalatable news that the Duke of York, Wilson's patron, was to undergo a parliamentary inquiry into irregularities in the disposal of commissions.[1]

The Regency had asked the British government to provide a commander-in-chief to organize their army and Beresford had been appointed because, apart from being an excellent trainer of troops and a capable field commander, he spoke some Portuguese. In October 1808 Wilson had written of him, 'We have long been friendly and he is one of the best men I know to do business with.'[2] However friendly Beresford was, Sir Robert could not have imagined that he would tolerate the idea that the Legion stood apart from the Portuguese army. Beresford was authoritarian by nature and the last man to tolerate Wilson's attempts to evade control.

Wilson was in no hurry to obey the summons to Lisbon. A week after it had reached him he was still supervising his thin screen of outposts which stretched eighty miles from the Douro in the north to the Sierra de Gata in the south. He was still at Ciudad Rodrigo when, in the last days of March, Lapisse pushed his own forward posts up to the Agueda river at Barba del Puerco, twenty miles north of the fortress. Wilson, who could never resist the chance of a fight, decided to have a final fling. He called in his scattered detachments and crossed the Agueda with his whole force on 1 April. He captured the French piquets in Barba del Puerco and pressed on to the village of San Felices, where he found himself faced with a solid body of 3,000 Frenchmen. What followed is obscure. It is certain that Wilson's men fell back to the river: what is less sure is how much fighting took place. In a letter to the British minister to Spain Wilson suggests a gallant withdrawal with every inch hotly contested. Writing to Lord Holland he seems to claim a victory. 'I carried the village, and in a sharp action killed and wounded above a thousand men, without any loss to mention on our side.' The French loss was, in fact, trifling, and it seems that the truth of the matter was that Sir Robert saw that the odds were too great for him and fell back to the Agueda with no more than sporadic skirmishing. Nevertheless, he wrote that 'I do not think that [Lapisse] will endeavour to force his way when he finds every step of the way is contested.'[3]

Lapisse had no intention of forcing his way into Portugal. He had marched this column to the gates of Rodrigo knowing that this would lead Wilson to concentrate his men. The French division was under orders to march south to join Marshal Victor on the Tagus. Wilson's sortie at Barba del Puerco played into their hands, for Wilson had called in his detachment which had been blocking Lapisse's way south over the Pass of Perales. Already the French advance guard was racing for the pass and, as Wilson's men stood ready to contest every step of the way to the west, Lapisse's main body made forced marches to the south.

Wilson followed them as soon as he realized what was happening. 'Unfortunately I could not overtake the enemy with my infantry or, weak and unsupported as I was, we should have shattered him considerably. With my cavalry I made prisoners but no serious impression.' When the Legion reached Alcantara they found that the French had sacked the town but were a day's march ahead and already on the south bank of the Tagus. Ordering Mayne to garrison the wrecked town with his battalion of the Legion, Wilson rode off alone to meet Beresford.[4]

They met at Thomar, midway between Lisbon and Coimbra, on 20 April. The marshal, Wilson wrote, was 'employed in a Herculean labour, but he will partially succeed. Altogether he cannot, to any solid degree, unless there is a general reform of the state, and even then much time is required for the extinction of old habits and the exercise of a new education.'[5] Not for the last time, Wilson underrated the capabilities of other commanders.

The interview was a difficult one. Beresford knew his friend well enough to realize that he would not be happy to lose his independence, and did his best to sugar the pill. He had arranged that Wilson should be appointed a brigadier in the British service from 1 April. This gave him 28s. 6d. a day and 15s. bât and forage money in addition to his pay as a lieutenant-colonel of cavalry (23s.). He also appointed him to the command of a brigade which was potentially the best in the Portuguese army—three battalions of light infantry (*caçadores*) with two companies of German riflemen of the Sixtieth Foot.

Wilson's first thought was to resign. He wrote in his journal, 'With a British army I have too many commanders, or powerful rivals, to prevent opportunities for distinction.'[6] He was dissuaded by the prospect of action. On 22 April Sir Arthur Wellesley had returned to Lisbon as Commander of the Forces. This time he bore the additional title of Marshal General of Portugal and had the right, lacked by his predecessors, to direct both the British and the Portuguese armies. He lost no time in mounting an operation against Soult, who had been in possession of Oporto since 29 March. In the plan Beresford, with a column of Portuguese troops, was to operate independently against Soult's escape routes.

On 12 May Wellesley's force crossed the Douro in broad daylight and surprised the French in Oporto. Soult's corps fled north but the full manœuvre did not quite succeed. Through no fault of his own, Beresford failed to block every one of the roads to Spain and Soult managed to escape over the mountains having lost all the army's baggage, its artillery, its military chest, and 4,500 men. Everybody was pleased except Robert Wilson. His brigade had formed Beresford's rearguard and throughout the fighting he had been at Lamego without seeing an enemy. He was depressed and angry, describing himself as 'an invalid garrison governor, when the game's afoot'. On 21 May he wrote in his diary that 'If I cannot pursue my career on Spanish ground, I am not disposed to vegetate in Lusitanian swineries.'[7]

Two day later he sent a letter to Beresford. 'I can only connect myself with the Portuguese service by the Legion which the Ministry directed me to raise, discipline and command, and if that command should be averse to your Excellency's plans so that it cannot be combined with some general service, I must request your Excellency to present to HRH the Regent [of Portugal], my resignation as Chief of the Legion and Brigadier General in the Portuguese Service.'[8]

One of Beresford's close associates wrote that 'his faults were ungovernable temper and obstinacy'. He knew that he could not reform the Portuguese army unless he could extract unhesitating obedience from his subordinates, and it might be expected that Wilson's resignation would provoke him to anger. Another general who, at the same time, requested leave to return to England 'if it is intended to employ his services again in co-operation with the Portuguese troops', had been sent packing. Beresford took trouble to dissuade Wilson from resigning. 'The request you make, or rather the principle on which you desire to serve is so totally incompatible with all military system that I cannot for a moment hesitate to reject holding out an example that would be so prejudicial to HRH's service.' Nevertheless, he urged Sir Robert to think again.[9]

Wilson was not convinced. He wrote in his diary, 'There is no place for me in the *dramatis personae* beyond that of a candle-snuffer. I prefer being a scene-shifter in the hopes of a better character offering finally.' He replied to Beresford that 'the Legion was raised, recruited, armed and brought to the field and to notice under very peculiar circumstances and that the very appointment of Chief [of the Legion] was established previous to the new military arrangement.' He therefore claimed 'my right, according to the Laws and Usages of Portugal, to its direction and command'.[10]

'In respect of your right according to the Laws and Usages of Portugal, I know of none such', replied the marshal, who was not prepared to let Wilson choose his own wars. He pointed out that he might stay with the Legion if he was prepared to revert to being a colonel, but 'I cannot confine the services of any General Officer to where any particular corps may be, as by that I should frequently be deprived of his services where I might want them and perhaps frequently altogether as the corps may be unfit for a certain time.' This was a shrewd blow for, on 14 May, the Legion had been attacked at Alcantara and had lost almost half its strength. Mayne had reported it unfit for service.

Beresford went on to point out that Wellesley was already planning a new operation, this time against Marshal Victor, and added, 'It appears to me that this is a case where personal feelings, however justly founded, ought to be laid aside, and I will go as far as to hope you will view the case in its general and more liberal view, and will assure you that I shall be extremely happy if you see it as I do and that you will be willing to serve on the principles that other officers of your rank serve.'[11]

Wilson was won over. 'The prospect of immediate service, the state of the Legion and more than all the kind manner of your Excellency on this occasion has influenced me to continue in the command with which I was honoured and I shall proceed with the troops to Castello Branco, there to await further orders.' Not that he gave up his struggle. He wrote direct to Castlereagh suggesting that he was being harshly treated. 'I never proposed that I should not give every assistance in my power to the general army of Portugal and render myself generally useful. I only desired that the Legion should continue to serve under my direction as I was gazetted its chief.'[12]

He did not have to stay long with his brigade at Castello Branco. On 18 June Wellesley gave him a command that delighted him. A joint Anglo-Spanish offensive was being concerted with Cuesta. The British contingent required a flank guard and Wilson was to command it. He was allocated the 1st and 2nd battalions of the Lusitanian Legion and the 5th *Caçadores*, the only Portuguese troops to take part in the campaign. This, he wrote, 'heals all my woes and reconciles me to service in the Peninsula.'

He rejoined the Legion at Zarza la Mayor, just over the Spanish frontier, on 25 June. He had an ecstatic welcome. 'As soon as seen, cheers rent the air and *vivas* echoed from post to post. It was a grateful reception and the more so because I know that to be popular I have not sacrificed any one duty. But I was vexed to see the state of the 1st battalion, filthy to the extremes of misery, many with ulcers, all the cloaths in tatters, bare-footed, arms in horrid order and accoutrements in worse, without pay for a month, no money in the chest and no medicine in the hospital store. Such was the state of this gallant band, and indeed I confess that Col. Mayne had reason to report them unfit, a report at which I was extremely angry. . . . For a moment I was frightened at the state of the infantry but I quickly rallied. I spoke to the officers so energetically and successfully that one general spirit of emulation was excited. The result is that in two more days I shall have 800 prs of trowsers made, 300 prs gaiters, all the jackets mended, the hairs cut, the bodies purified and then decked with 600 new shirts and the feet consoled with as many prs of shoes.'[13]

Even before he had got his men washed and clothed, Wilson was restless to be in action. He looked forward to a triumphant campaign ranging the length of Spain. 'It is supposed that Victor will leave Madrid on his left, and in all cases, I expect a stern chase. It is, however, a most serious object to prevent the enemy from collecting his forces installed on the Ebro.' He was impatient at the delay in starting the fighting. 'We are snails in our operations when vigour is necessary. . . . I would forfeit my head if with the Legion alone I did not do more mischief to the French before they reach the Ebro than the British army now does. The Spaniards are indignant. . . . This is sad, very sad and to me unaccountable for I know Sir Arthur Wellesley is ardent, ambitious, active and brave.'[14]

Sir Arthur was equally anxious to be started but he had his own problems. The army was without medical supplies—'We move without a disposable medical officer or a blanket to cover a sick man'—and there was no money—'The army is two months in arrears; we are head over heels in debt everywhere.' Worst of all the problems was that of reaching agreement with Wilson's friend General Cuesta who was providing the bulk of the allied strength, 33,000 Spaniards to add to Wellesley's 22,000 British. Cuesta was an impossible ally. Wellesley found him 'more and more impractical every day. It is impossible to do business with him and very uncertain that any operation will succeed in which he has any concern owing to the whimsical perversity of his disposition.'[15]

On 4 July Sir Robert was allowed to make a limited advance. This took him to Toril, south-east of Plasencia. He was visited here on 10 July by Wellesley, who was provided with 'a comfortable hut ... a good dinner with the luxury of excellent lemonade and a fine doe, a brace of rabbits and a partridge'. He was able to tell Sir Robert that he and Cuesta had agreed a plan for a joint advance against Victor at Talavera de la Reina. Wilson's part would be to advance parallel to the main armies, using the valley of the Tiétar. From its eastern end he was to cross the hills to the valley of the Alberche, taking up his station at Escalona, 28 miles behind Victor's right flank. Cuesta had agreed to increase his strength by adding two Spanish battalions to his three Portuguese.[16]

Written orders followed telling him to 'alarm the enemy towards the rear of his right flank, [but as] the force of his corps is not sufficient to make a serious impression upon the enemy if he is found to be strong in that direction, Sir Robert must act according to circumstances, endeavouring to give the enemy as much jealousy in regard to his operations as possible. He will continue to report daily to headquarters and to give all assistance he can towards providing supplies to the army from the districts through which he moves.'[17] Nothing could have pleased Wilson better. 'This is a noble allotment for me and God grant that I may bear my honours blushingly and prosperously. I am, however, so flattered that it really does require wisdom to retain humility.'[18]

By 23 July his whole force, about 4,000 men, Spanish and Portuguese, was assembled at Escalona, but there was not a

Frenchman in sight. He decided that acting 'according to cir-cumstances' could be interpreted as covering a single-handed attempt to capture Madrid. He marched to Navalcarnero where he was received with enthusiastic *vivas* and learned that the French had evacuated the town on the previous day. He pressed on and by the evening of 26 July had reached Mostoles, within fifteen miles of the capital.

He omitted to tell Wellesley of his intentions but the general found where he was through a letter Wilson had written to Cuesta's chief of staff. Just as Sir Robert was contemplating a suitable form of words in which to summon Madrid to surrender, a letter reached him from headquarters mildly saying, 'I beg you will return to Escalona without loss of time.' Wellesley went on to remind him of his other duty of sending food into the main army, which was already on half rations as the Spaniards had failed to fulfil their promises to provide food.[19]

Wellesley's forbearance in writing so gentle a letter to his wandering subordinate is remarkable. He had much to irritate him. Cuesta's 'whimsical perversity' was becoming more apparent every day. Sir Arthur had proposed that the combined armies should attack Victor, who had only 22,000 men against the allies' 54,000, on 23 July. The Spaniard refused on the grounds that it was a Sunday. Victor retired next day and Cuesta insisted on pursuing him with the Spanish army alone. Having advanced twenty-five miles he was brought up short by the sight of the French, reinforced by Sebastiani's corps to 44,000 strong, in position at Torrijos. The Spaniards retreated in disorder on their allies. Even then Cuesta, apparently to assert his independence, insisted on their encamping with the river Alberche between them and the British. It was not until 27 July that Sir Arthur was able to persuade him to put his troops in a strong position to the west of the river, with their flank secured on the Tagus and the town of Talavera. On that day and the next a series of French attacks were repulsed, the British bearing the brunt of the fighting and suffer-ing 5,363 casualties, a quarter of their strength. Wilson's brigade was deployed far in advance of Wellesley's left flank and took no part in the battle.

'Talavera', wrote Wilson, 'will pass from posterity to posterity with rapturous delight to every Briton, and terror and reproach to France.' He was convinced that the road to Madrid, to the Ebro, even to the Pyrenees, lay open to the allies. He was astonished and reproachful when he was ordered to move westward to Plasencia to block the pass of Baños. Leaving his men to start their march, he went to dine with Wellesley at Talavera on 30 July. Sir Arthur explained to him that there were reports of a strong French column coming over that pass from Salamanca and threatening the British communications with Portugal.[20]

That evening there was a long and difficult conference with Cuesta. The Spaniard was inclined to minimize the threat from Baños; Wilson agreed with him. It was eventually decided that the British should retreat to Plasencia while the Spaniards remained at Talavera to keep Victor in check. Wilson, at Cuesta's request, was to return to Escalona to cover the Spanish left. 'It was 11 at night before I could leave Talavera and the passage over the field of battle was not very agreeable to the olfactory senses for the dead bodies of men and horses still covered the surface.' By 3 a.m. he had caught up with his brigade and turned them about for Escalona. Reluctantly, but in accordance with his orders, he sent his battery to join the British artillery.[21]

Written orders reached him on 3 August, telling him to act so as to prevent the French probing round the Spanish left and discovering that the British had marched to the west. This he took to mean that he 'should go back to Escalona and as much nearer the capital as circumstances would permit . . . to menace the flank and rear of the enemy so that he might retire from his position'. He failed to tell Cuesta where he was going but, equally, Cuesta failed to tell him, or Wellesley, when he abandoned Talavera and 1,500 British wounded, on 3 August.[22]

Sir Arthur heard of the Spanish retreat on the following day. At the same time he heard that the French column against which he was moving consisted not, as he had believed, of 15,000 men but of 30,000 (in fact it was 50,000 strong). The French advance guard had already crossed the pass of Baños, which Cuesta had undertaken to block, and their leading cavalry had reached

Navalmoral. This meant that they were already across the British communications and Wellesley instantly sent the newly arrived Light Brigade on a forced march across the grain of the country to the bridge at Almaraz, thus securing the flank of his retreat. The rest of the army crossed to the south of the Tagus at Arzobispo. By 6 August the British were safe but Robert Wilson, still on the east bank of the Alberche, was blandly planning the liberation of Madrid. He had with him 4,000 tired, eager, and undertrained Portuguese and Spanish soldiers and he was sixty miles from the nearest allied troops.

He learned of his predicament on 6 August in a letter from Wellesley:

> Peraleda de Garbin [12 miles sw of Arzobispo]
> 5th August 1809.
> My dear Sir Robert,
> It is difficult for me to instruct you when every letter I receive from you informs me that you are further from me and are carrying into execution a plan of your own. The last instructions I gave you were to communicate with, and of course follow the motions of, the Spanish army. The day before yesterday General Cuesta abandoned Talavera and arrived on the morning of the 4th at Oropesa. . . . You will do well to march, directly you receive this, by Calera to Arzobispo, and there cross the river and send word to General Cuesta that you are coming there, that he may not break the bridge before you arrive. I doubt whether you would find your way through the mountains of the Vera [de Plasencia] at present.
> P.S. You should have followed the movements of Cuesta here.[23]

Wilson was under pressure before this letter had reached him. Victor had detached a division to hunt for him round Nombella and Escalona while other French troops had blocked the passes over the Sierra de Gredos at Arenas and Mombeltran. He found French cavalry between his position and the bridge at Arzobispo. He supposed these to be some of Victor's men but they were Soult's, who had come south over Baños. He took the only way that seemed open to him and marched along the north bank of the Tiétar, making for one of the westerly passes over the Sierra. His main advantage, though he could not know it, was that the

French greatly overrated his strength, believing him to have '12,000 or 15,000 Portuguese'.[24]

The brigade reached Candalada, in the foothills of the Sierra due north of Oropesa, on 7 August. From the church tower Sir Robert saw Victor's cavalry riding parallel to him in the plain to the south. To his astonishment he saw *chasseurs à cheval* coming from the west to meet them. These could only be men of Soult's force which had come south from Salamanca. It was clear that Plascencia and the western end of the Vera would be swarming with Frenchmen.[25]

The only way out of the trap seemed to be by the track which led up the Sierra by the Penton stream. The first stage was a march of twenty-two miles to the entrance of this pass. On the way his handful of cavalry surprised a small enemy post at Villanueva de la Vera. There he learned that the next town on the road, Vilander, had a French garrison. He decided to storm it that night.

As William Mayne told the story, they waited until it was dark and 'moved quickly towards the gate, the 5th *Caçadores* forming the advance, but we were perceived by the sentries placed at the gate, and fired upon, which immediately alarmed the garrison: however, we forced our way forward to the town and found the garrison formed in the streets, who poured a heavy volley amongst us, which was returned in an irregular manner by the 5th *Caçadores*, who had halted and appeared unwilling to proceed in consequence of the hot fire kept up by the enemy, the darkness of the night, and the narrowness of the street; Sir Robert Wilson therefore ordered forward one of the battalions of the Loyal Lusitanian Legion from the rear, who eagerly advanced, proud of the circumstance and their selection on this occasion, and gallantly moved forward until they were brought in front, when they immediately poured in a well-directed volley, and coming down to charge, advanced with cheers upon the enemy, whom they drove into the greatest confusion, and drove before them at the point of the bayonet.'[26]

The capture of Vilander scarcely improved Wilson's position. He learned from his prisoners that the French had already blocked the Penton track. The only way out was to use goat paths. The people of Vilander provided guides and some bread for the troops, and the column immediately marched into the mountains for what Wilson described as 'a passage of the Sierra de Gredos, a mountain covered with snow, and which heretofore was used only by peasants on extraordinary occasions in three months of the year'.[27]

The first stage of the march took them over the Sierra to the village of Bohoyo on the upper waters of the Tormes. Some men were lost, 'from the severity of the climate of the mountain summit'. The remainder, after 'a few hours' refreshment', followed the road beside the river which brought them, after a further fourteen miles, to Barca de Avila, on the main road from Plasencia to Avila and Valladolid. From there they struck off uphill and westward, reaching Bejar, below the crest of the pass of Baños, on 10 August. In five days they had marched, according to Sir Robert, 160 miles.

This estimate may be a slight exaggeration but the march was a very remarkable feat, since it was carried out by men who had no experience of forced marches. The greatest credit is due to Wilson who was at his best in this kind of crisis. At times they had passed the 8,000-feet mark which would certainly have increased the fatigue of the soldiers, and, in the higher reaches, they marched through snow which many of the men would never have seen before. Food was very short. There had been no time to forage in the Tiétar valley and, apart from the bread given them in Vilander, no supplies would have been obtainable in the mountains. The march baffled the French, who continued to search for the brigade in the southern valley.

It was typical of Wilson that, having extricated his men from apparently certain capture by his skill and determination, he should immediately hazard them unnecessarily. They spent the night in Bejar and left the Spanish Regiment of *Seville* in the town as a safeguard. The other four battalions crossed the pass and slept the next night in Baños. On the morning of 12 August they marched off again towards the south on the main road leading to Soult's headquarters at Plasencia. After seven miles they came to the crossroads near Aldeanueva del Camino where they took the road leading west to Granadilla and, eventually, to Portugal. Since leaving Bejar they had been moving along the road which carried the main French north–south communications. Now, at last, they were safe.

Their safety did not last long. A peasant pointed out a cloud of dust moving slowly up the high road from Plasencia. Through his spy-glass Sir Robert saw a very large body of French troops preceded by a screen of cavalry. 'I immediately returned and took post in front of Baños with my piquets in front of Aldeanueva, selecting such points of defence as the exigency of the time permitted.'

The force which Wilson was engaging so lightheartedly and so needlessly was the whole of Ney's corps which had been ordered back to Salamanca. There were 12,000 Frenchmen including four regiments of cavalry and thirty guns. They were marching, according to their commander, 'well closed up'. Sir Robert proposed to oppose them with four raw battalions, a handful of cavalry, and no guns. The total number had been reduced by their marches and the detachment of *Seville* to not more than 3,000 men. All were footsore and underfed. The ground might have helped them but, as Wilson himself pointed out, the position at Baños 'on the Estremadura side is not a pass of such strength as on the side of Castille'. To make matters worse there was no time to reconnoitre or to settle in a position. 'I had but just time to face about the columns, send off the baggage and take my advanced post, before they were engaged.'

Sending his dragoons to the south of the crossroads to skirmish and gain time, Wilson concealed 200 Spanish infantry near Aldeanueva. They lay hidden until the leading French horsemen, riding in column, were almost on top of them. Then the *Merida* infantrymen fired a volley which emptied many saddles. There was a moment of confusion while frightened horses reared and trampled on the bodies of the dead and wounded; a few troopers loosed off their carbines; then they wheeled away and reformed out of musket shot. The Spaniards felt a moment of elation as the enemy galloped away. Then the 3me *Hussards* came into line and charged. They were greeted with a spattering of ill-aimed shots before the Spaniards fled, the horsemen at their heels, slashing with their sabres.

Four miles up the road the French could see Wilson's Portuguese getting into position above Baños. The ground in front of them was steep and difficult to climb but Sir Robert had not enough men to guard his flanks. Ney called forward his guns and told them to bombard the heights, while two battalions moved round the right of the Portuguese, a flank held by the remnant of *Merida.* Seeing themselves threatened, the Spaniards fled. Wilson ordered his remaining three battalions to retreat to the pass, to which he had earlier summoned the *Seville* battalion from Bejar. There were two roads across the crest; both led to Bejar but one made a detour by Montemayor. It was on this second road that *Seville* was stationed. They managed to kill an officer and some dragoons who had advanced and called on them to surrender, but as soon as a formed body of French cavalry came forward they broke and followed their comrades of *Merida* into the hills.

By this time the Portuguese, astride the main road, were melting away under French artillery fire. Wilson rallied a body of them and with the Spanish light companies, which had not yet been engaged, urged them to stand their ground. But, 'at six o'clock in the evening, three columns of the enemy mounted the heights on our left and poured such a fire on the troops below that longer defence was impracticable, and the whole was obliged to retire on the mountain road on our left, leaving the main road open along which a considerable column of cavalry immediately passed.'

The last quotation, from Wilson's official report, was putting the end of the action in its most favourable light. It is clear from his journal that his troops fled and left him on his own. 'I waited to the last moment and was pursued two leagues* by the French cavalry. . . . I stopped as night closed in at Candelario and

* At this period four different types of league were in use in Spain. The shortest was 2·63 miles, the longest 4·21. The English league of 3 miles corresponded with none of the Spanish types.

collected some men.' Next day he crossed the main road and established himself at Miranda de Castanar, sending out such men as he had with him to collect stragglers.

It must have occurred to him even at that stage that he had made a serious error of judgement, but he was not prepared to admit such a possibility even to himself. In his journal he wrote, 'It was a well-disputed battle and, altho' the enemy gained his point, he has won a bloody field.' He explained to himself that he could have held the pass if the *Merida* battalion had stood its ground. In his report to Wellesley he wrote, 'I lament that I could not longer arrest his progress; but when the enormous superiority of the enemy's force is considered, that we had no artillery, ... I hope that a resistance for nine hours, which must have cost the enemy a great many men, will not be deemed inadequate to our means.'[28]

A resistance of nine hours sounded impressive, but one fact was omitted. The distance from Aldeanueva to the crest of the pass is twelve miles, little less than an average day's march. The French had already been marching some distance before the fighting started and they ended the day beyond the pass, probably at Bejar. They thus covered more ground in the day than they would otherwise have done and the effect of the battle was to accelerate their progress rather than retard it.

The attempt to present the day's work as at least a moral victory was helped when Ney's report to Soult appeared in *Le Moniteur*. Ney, who was no more truthful in his despatches than his brother-marshals, decided to increase his own prestige by representing Baños as a major action. He claimed that Wilson held the position above Baños town with 4,000 or 5,000 men, who 'had added to the difficulties of the ground by obstructing the accessible paths with *abatis*, ditches and masses of rock', a remarkable effort for men who had only reached their ground a few minutes before they were attacked. Of the final scene at the pass he wrote, 'General Wilson rallied his troops for the third time, and even endeavoured again to act on the offensive, hoping to overthrow us in turn; but this attempt was extremely disastrous to himself. The advance guard had united, and an engagement with the bayonet commenced in which the enemy was overwhelmed.' This last engagement was wholly imaginary but helped Ney to justify his claim that Wilson's corps 'left 1,200 in the field'. The French loss he put at 185, including some lost in earlier skirmishes and several who 'dropped dead in the ranks from heat and fatigue'.[29]

In a handwritten *Narrative of the Services of the Loyal Lusitanian Legion*, compiled after the war, Wilson justified his decision to court battle on the grounds 'of doing [Ney] mischief, giving time to General Beresford's army posted at 2 leagues' distance to attack him on flank and rear, and to give time for the persons who had returned to Salamanca after Soult's evacuation to quit the city'.[30] The first and last of these reasons may have been true. The second was not true and it is probable that Sir Robert knew it. Beresford was not two leagues away but at Moraleja, forty-five miles as the crow flies from Baños.

On 13 August Wilson sent an official report to Wellesley which was forwarded to London with Sir Arthur's commendation. 'Throughout the service he has shown himself to be an active and intelligent partisan, well acquainted with the country and possessing the confidence of the troops which he commanded; and although unsuccessful in the action which he fought, which may be well accounted for by the superior numbers and description of the enemy's troops, the action, in my opinion, does him great credit.'[31]

Sir Robert, however, followed up his report with a private letter in which he gave a more truthful account of the action. He explained the rout by saying that, 'Generally speaking, the dispersion was a *separation by detachments*, and not individual flight.' Wellesley was not impressed by this sophistry and concluded that the action 'was nothing at all excepting a dispertion and a flight'. Wilson, he decided, 'is a very slippery fellow . . . and he has not the talent of being able to speak the truth upon any subject'.[32]

Sir Arthur was little mollified by another incident which happened soon afterwards. He had decided that, if the British army was to be fed, it must retire to Badajoz where supplies could be obtained from Portugal. He ordered Wilson, who had collected most of his stragglers, to take them to the south bank of the Tagus to guard the ferry at Vila Velha, the vital link between the British at Badajoz and Beresford's Portuguese north of the river. He was extremely angry to find that Wilson had put his brigade into quarters at Castello Branco. It seemed that Wilson had reverted to his most independent attitude and was trying to treat Wellesley as he had treated Cradock. A sharp reprimand from the Commander of the Forces was sent to Castello Branco.

A week later Wellesley discovered that Wilson was, on this occasion, innocent. He immediately wrote a very different type of letter:

Badajoz, 3rd September 1809.

My dear Sir Robert,

I am afraid I wrote to you more positively than I intended on the 27th to cross the Tagus. The fact is, that I imagined you would receive that letter long before you would reach Castello Branco. Indeed, I did not know that Beresford had ordered you there. . . .[33]

From Wellesley, who was reputed to find it hard to apologize, this was a very handsome letter. It is also significant that he should start 'My dear Sir Robert', since he did not know Wilson at all well. It was rare, except for such close associates as Beresford and Hill, for Sir Arthur to use any more familiar form of address than 'My dear General'.

On the day that that letter was written, Wilson rode down to Badajoz in the hope of learning that the army was to take the offensive again. He found that the Spaniards had proposed a grand concentric manœuvre to capture Madrid. Wellesley, realizing that the allied armies would be outnumbered and defeated in detail and knowing that it was impossible to find rations in Spain, refused his co-operation. He decided that his first task must be to secure his base in Portugal. Wilson, whose grasp of strategic realities was always tenuous, found this attitude inexplicable. Two weeks earlier he had written in his diary, 'If the war is to be carried on defensively, I shall ask leave to go to England for six weeks. . . . I am resolved not to serve in Portugal while a British force is serving in Spain and indeed I much doubt if I would stay in Portugal if the British army was confined to its defence. I should pine to death in such a situation, and I have too many strong attractions in other quarters.' He considered that Wellesley's decision betrayed the Spanish cause. 'Europe and posterity will ever consider our campaign as one of the most remarkable in the world, for the conquerors have in fact been conquered, and the enemy have gained complete possession of a kingdom by licence of their victors. The effects are scarcely to be traced to any *reasonable* cause.'[34]

His discontent was heightened by the news that Beresford had decided that the Lusitanian Legion should no longer have its own artillery. He asked for eight weeks' leave and it was granted. He rode down to Lisbon where he spent some days trying to disentangle the chaos into which the Legion's finances had fallen. Even there he was not out of danger. On 21 September he was stung on the tongue by a wasp and suffered from convulsions and fainting fits. It was an unlucky day for him, as on that morning in England Canning and Castlereagh, the two unwilling patrons of the Legion, met with pistols on Putney Heath. Canning was shot through the thigh and both men resigned from the government. At a stroke the two men who he might have hoped would help him to resist Beresford's encroachments on the independence of his private army removed themselves from positions of influence.

He parted from the marshal on friendly terms. On 29 September they dined together and Sir Robert met Beresford's Portuguese mistress, Madam Lemos. 'She is certainly the handsomest woman in the country—and what is more pleasing, very clean—but still much inferior to any moderate handsome [English] woman.'[35]

In the first week of October he sailed from the Tagus on his two months' leave. He did not return to Portugal for fourteen years.

CHAPTER 5

Smolensk via Constantinople

Thomas Grenville wrote on 10 November 1809 that 'Sir R. Wilson is arrived at Whitehall with accounts of a great success obtained by the Spaniards over the French. Ney's army is said to have been routed entirely with the loss of 3,000 men and all the French artillery, and the city of Salamanca.'[1] This referred to the battle of Tammanes, fought on 18 October. It had been a small-scale Spanish victory but Wilson was so determined to show that Lord Wellington (as Arthur Wellesley had now become) should have been co-operating with the grand concentric design proposed by his allies that he accepted as truth the inflated Spanish accounts of the action. The truth was that the Spaniards had, for a few days, reoccupied Salamanca, but the French loss had been only 1,500 men and one gun. Ney had not been present. The incident illustrates Wilson's ability to believe what he wanted to believe. He was beginning to consider that the action at Baños had been a victory.

He set about importuning the War Department, demanding that they assert that the Lusitanian Legion was not a part of the Portuguese army. Failing that, he asked for another independent situation for himself. He began to pester the Foreign Office for employment in Russia. The new Foreign Secretary was the Marquess of Wellesley, whom Wilson found more sympathetic than his brother, Lord Wellington. He wrote to the marquess proposing that he should be sent out to engineer a peace between Russia and Turkey, who had been at war since 1806. He claimed that he knew many of the Russian generals and, with less justification, that 'I have been an intimate with the Turkish chiefs, so I have nothing to learn as to their characters, habits and qualities. . . . I have connexions with the Croatians and private relations with the Montenegrins.'[2]

Sir Robert's letter went unanswered. Lord Wellesley was one of the idlest Foreign Secretaries in history and seldom answered letters. Seven months later Wilson wrote again, suggesting that 'to mediate between Russia and Turkey [would be] an interference that would be of considerable advantage to England by establishing a claim to the gratitude of the former power'. This letter received an acknowledgement but no more.[3]

Meanwhile, he went into print again with *Brief Remarks on the Character and Composition of the Russian Army and a Sketch of the Campaigns in Poland in the Years 1806 and 1807*. Again the book was dedicated to the Duke of York, 'under whose administration the British Army has recovered its consideration abroad and has been established on a basis commensurate with the Power and Dignity of the British Empire'. The *Brief Remarks* had a modest success. The *Quarterly Review* praised its matter but added that 'its value would not have been diminished if the construction had been more grammatical, and the style less rhetorical and ornamented. There are, indeed, some passages so involved in their arrangement that it requires more pains than ordinary readers can be expected to bestow to discover their real import.' The *Monthly Review* wrote that Wilson's style 'is not only quaint but obscure. . . . We have seldom met with a writer who is more *alert* in displaying his classical knowledge by the introduction of quotations.'[4]

While Wilson devoted his public time to courting the Tory government in the hope of employment, his private hours were spent with his Whig friends and, to the fury of the Prince of Wales, with the Princess of Wales. Henceforward, although the friendship of the Duke of York remained constant, Sir Robert could look for nothing but opposition from the Duke's elder brother who became Prince Regent in February 1811.

His chances of advancement were not improved by the antics of his parliamentary friends who tried to establish him as an alternative military hero to Wellington. Samuel Whitbread suggested in the House of Commons that Wellington had been less than generous in not giving Wilson more praise for his part in the Talavera campaign. 'It did', he said, 'detract a little from [Wellington's] greatness of mind to characterize Sir Robert Wilson as merely a partizan.' The veteran General Tarleton asserted that Wilson's services 'had been more instrumental in producing the retreat of the enemy than any other services that had been rendered'. Christopher Hely-Hutchinson proposed that the House should vote its thanks to Sir Robert. He recounted how, in the early months of 1809, Wilson had 'foiled the projects ... of a corps which at least amounted to 12,000 men and which, at all times, was more than double the force of Sir R. Wilson, whose corps never exceeded 3,000'. He told how General Lapisse had been driven from the bridge at St. Tipics [? San Felice], which he had occupied 'as opening his march into Portugal'.[5] It saved much embarrassment to friends and opponents alike when the Speaker ruled that such a vote would be irregular since, at the time in question, Wilson, as a Portuguese brigadier, was technically a foreign officer. No vote of thanks had been passed for a foreign officer since 1763 and the officer in question, Count La Lippe, had, unlike Wilson, had British troops under his command.[6]

The attempt to inflate his services exposed Wilson to ridicule at home and in the Peninsular army. William Warre wrote home from Portugal, 'Nobody will deny his courage and talents as a partizan, but to those who know the facts, the attempt at thanks in the house are more adapted to make him appear ridiculous than to do him an honour. He can never want a trumpeter while he lives, and no man knows better the *art de se faire valoir*. He must really be a clever fellow to have, with 700 undisciplined Portuguese, checked 30,000 Frenchmen, terrified them so much, and at the same time covered upper and lower Beira, Almeida, Ciudad Rodrigo and ensured the retreat of the British detachments, which the enemy never attempted to impede. Many others of his deeds, mentioned [in Parliament], we never heard of. He is a good fellow as a companion, and an able light troop officer and, if he would not attempt to be more than he really is, would be more respected.'[7]

Nevertheless, at Brooks's Club and at Whig dinner tables, his views on the war in the Peninsula were held in respect. He became chief military adviser to the Opposition, and his prophecies on the future course of the war were regularly regurgitated in both Houses of Parliament as the basis for attacks on governmental and military incompetence.

Sir Robert's prognostications on the course of the war were wrong with a magnificent consistency. His letters to Lord Grey, who usually led the Whig peers *in absentia* from Northumberland, give a weekly commentary on the Peninsular war which is a classic of misinterpretation. When Wellington declined to fight a battle (which he must inevitably have lost) to save Ciudad Rodrigo in the summer of 1810, Wilson wrote that Wellington 'still thinks he can defend Portugal, but I presume his troops must be much dispirited by such an acknowledgement of the enemy's superiority'. When the French took Rodrigo on 9 July, his opinion was that 'No success can compensate for its loss. [It is] an irreparable mischief and a disgrace to our arms.'[8]

A few days later his 'private accounts' assured him that Wellington intended to fight a battle near Celorico. When nothing of the kind occurred, Sir Robert wrote scathingly that 'Lord Wellington is resolved to persevere in his plan and he confidently expects success by a defensive system (which is generally a fruitful mother of disasters).' When the army did check in its retreat to fight and win the battle of Busaco (27 September 1810), Wilson's reaction was that the action 'proved the courage of the allied troops, but I conceive [it] has given the enemy on the instant all the country between the Mondego and the Douro and probably Oporto, and not only enlarged their share of possession but changed their situation from that of need to abundance.' A week later he assured Grey that he had heard from 'a very able source' that Marshal Berthier was leading a very large reinforcement to join Massena's invading army. At that time Massena's men were settling down to starve in front of the lines of Torres Vedras. Berthier had not stirred from Paris.[9]

When the news arrived that the army was safely within the impregnable lines, Wilson was not reassured, although his recent knowledge of the ground must have shown him that Wellington's position was immensely strong. He would not believe that Lisbon could be secure. 'Massena', he wrote, 'has completely discomfited the calculations of Lord Wellington.' He went on to paint a horrifying picture of the consequences of Massena's inevitable breakthrough. Although it was known that Sir John Moore had asserted that the frontiers of Portugal were indefensible, Sir Robert knew better. Wellington should have fought on the Spanish border. 'There never was a country which more required frontier defence, but I fear this knowledge will be obtained with a most severe chastisement for ignorance.' As for the stories reaching London during the winter telling of starvation in the French army in front of Lisbon, they were 'absurdities'. On 11 March, when Massena was retreating as fast as he could go in the hope of finding food for his troops, Wilson commented that 'it appears that the delusions of Lord Wellington, with respect to the state and intentions of the enemy, continue'.[10]

Grey was in London in the spring of 1811 and Wilson did not have to write to him so there is no way of telling how he explained away Wellington's triumphant liberation of Portugal. Nothing, however, affected Sir Robert's expectation of disaster. When despatches arrived in July announcing that the siege of Badajoz had been raised as Wellington was faced with the combined armies of Soult and Marmont, Wilson foretold the imminent destruction of the British army in the plains of Alentejo and 'an immediate evacuation of Lisbon'.[11]

It may be that Wilson's greatest contribution to Britain's war effort against Napoleon lay in the advice he gave to the Opposition spokesmen. By feeding them a diet of misinformation he made them appear so futile that even the weak governments of Spencer Perceval and Lord Liverpool were able to survive because the alternatives were demonstrably worse. What was the country to make of a party when one of its leaders, Lord Grey (duly briefed by Wilson), at a time when the country was at last beginning to win battles against Napoleon's armies, could accuse the government of having learned nothing from the experience of the Coruña campaign and 'of risking another army at the expence of enormous treasure; and the sacrifice of your best blood, only to purchase misfortune, calamity and disgrace'. This was sufficiently discouraging but Grey continued, 'Is the power of Buonaparte lessened since we engaged in that warfare? Is the power of France reduced below what it was when this country embarked in a military co-operation with the Spanish people? I much fear that the contrary will be felt. I apprehend that the powers of the enemy ... have materially increased.'[12] Other members of the Opposition took the same line, each of them inspired with Wilson's belief that the British army could never maintain its position in the Peninsula, that the French resources were inexhaustible, and that Wellington did not understand the rudiments of the military art.

Not everyone in England received Wilson's opinions with the rapt attention with which they were heard at Alnwick and at Brooks's. In November 1810 Lady Holland recorded that 'his enemies accuse him of having taken great credit to himself in the Puerto de Baños, whereas Lord W[ellington] has recently discovered that he did nothing whatever there. Also there is another charge which, if substantiated, is serious but, from his general reputation is considered highly improbable, viz. peculating in his transactions about raising the Lusitanian Legion.'[13]

The charge of peculation was, as Lady Holland thought, groundless, but Wilson ran the risk of another charge. He was absent without leave. In May 1810 Beresford reported to Wellington that 'It is my duty not longer to delay complaining of Brigadier General Sir Robert Wilson who has now been absent without leave between three and four months. It was in November [October] last that his leave was granted for two months, at the expiration of which he wrote to me from England that to conclude the arrangements of his accounts relative to the L.L. Legion he would be detained a short time longer, but I think it three months since, by that letter, he was to be out here. I find by recent letters that it appears he intends to stay longer in England.'[14]

Wellington forwarded this complaint to the Secretary of State, commenting that, if Wilson was attempting to settle the Legion's accounts, he should, by the Secretary of State's own instructions, be doing so in Lisbon. This letter crossed with one from the War Department 'acquainting your Lordship that it is probable Sir Robert Wilson will not return to the Portuguese staff'. In fact his pay as brigadier in Portugal had been stopped on 24 April.[15]

Having given up hope of obtaining a ruling giving independent station to the Legion, Wilson had lost all interest in it and was concentrating his efforts on finding himself some other interesting employment. He was, however, in danger of incurring serious trouble over the Legion's accounts. There was no question of his having misappropriated funds but he had been culpably careless in administration and the accounts were in the greatest confusion. To make matters worse, Lieutenant-Colonel Mayne, who was Wilson's own nominee, appeared to have absconded. In August 1809, Sir Robert had written to Beresford that 'Colonel Mayne has not only absolutely deserted, but he has left the accounts of the corps absolutely unsettled. . . . There are several hundred pounds he has left unaccounted for.'[16] How this problem was resolved is a mystery submerged, apparently for ever, in one of the darker recesses of the archives of either the British or the Portuguese War Office. No proceedings were taken against either Mayne or Wilson.*

When he knew that Wilson would not be returning to Portugal, Beresford started an investigation into the state of the Legion. He found that 'there are no documents in the corps. . . . It was never conducted upon any fixed or determined principle. . . . The irregularity of the corps had arrived at such a point that I have had infinite trouble to ascertain who are the officers that belong to it, Sir Robert having appointed, promoted and dismissed at his

---

* Mayne had applied to Wellington for leave and, although it had been refused, had taken himself off to Seville. While there he had resigned his Portuguese rank (he had no British rank) on the pretext that the Portuguese had refused to make him a brigadier. He later applied to the War Office to be made an ensign in the Royal Staff Corps but his application was not accepted. He published a *Narrative of the Campaigns of the Loyal Lusitanian Legion* in 1812.

pleasure and it is not a month since I discovered that almost all the officers in the regiment were receiving pay for, and acting in, a rank above what they had a right to and this from simple orders or appointment of Sir Robert, Colonel Mayne or whoever commanded this irregular corps and the appointments of officers have been made without any apparent judgment or discrimination, in some instances sergeants becoming captains in two months and absolute children (at least 14 or 15 years of age) being appointed to lieutenancies in cavalry and infantry.'[17] With Wilson out of the way, Beresford took the opportunity to incorporate the three battalions of the Legion into the Portuguese army as battalions of *caçadores*.

None of these problems seems to have affected Sir Robert's popularity with the Royal Family (excepting, of course, the Prince of Wales). On 25 June 1810 he was appointed an aide-de-camp to the King. This was not only a notable honour, it carried the possibility of accelerated promotion. The purchase system stopped at lieutenant-colonel and promotion beyond that rank depended entirely upon seniority. The only exceptions were the officers appointed ADCs to the King and, after 1811, to the Prince Regent. As it happened, the gain to Wilson was minimal as it only promoted him to colonel over the head of one senior lieutenant-colonel, a Waldecker, but, since the appointments were personal to the Sovereign, it showed that he was under the protection, if not of George III, who was at this time sinking into his final incapacity, at least of the Duke of York, the Commander-in-Chief.

A more equivocal honour was his appointment as a Knight of the Portuguese order of the Tower and Sword. This award may not have come as a surprise to Wilson, never apt to underestimate his own merits, but it did surprise the Portuguese government. The Prince Regent's consent to Brigadier-General Wilson's acceptance of the knighthood was published in the *London Gazette* of 26 October 1811. When this reached Lisbon the secretary of the Portuguese Regency pointed out to Wellington that the government had not offered the honour to Robert Wilson. They had, however, proposed Brigadier-General John

Wilson and the two names had been muddled in the War Department. The upshot was that both Wilsons became knights but the Portuguese Regency can hardly have evinced much pleasure at having to grant an honour to a man who had consistently flouted their authority.[18]

In the same year he had tried to get a British medal for his Peninsular service. It had been decided that gold medals, large or small, or gold crosses should be given to officers commanding units or formations at the principal actions. Portuguese officers were eligible for these distinctions and Sir Robert applied for one to the Secretary for War who referred the question to Wellington. He replied that 'I have already had the honour of reporting my sense of the services rendered by Sir Robert Wilson while under my command and I see no reason why they should not be distinguished by the grant of a medal.' The problem was that Wilson had not been present at any of the actions for which medals were granted. He had been very close to Talavera but not close enough to qualify, as 'one of the rules is that an officer shall receive a medal for a particular action in which the corps to which he belongs has been engaged with musketry'. The Horse Guards were prepared to stretch a point and, although the Commander-in-Chief wrote to Sir Robert that 'Your services are too well known to need such a distinction', it was agreed that a special medal should be struck with, instead of the name of a battle, the inscription *Spain and Portugal*. It was unfortunate that the concession did not go far enough. When the medal was complete Wilson found that it was the small, field officer's, type and not the large, general officer's, medal. He declined to accept it and the authorities refused to grant the larger medal. Almost certainly they were wrong and this at least, among Sir Robert's multiplying grievances, was well founded. In the event he never received a British medal.[19]

Meanwhile the business of trying to get an appointment in Russia or Turkey dragged on. Part of the delay was due to Lord Wellesley's idleness, more was caused by the difficulties in finding someone to accept the embassy in Constantinople. Napoleon's occupation of most of the civilized world meant that most of

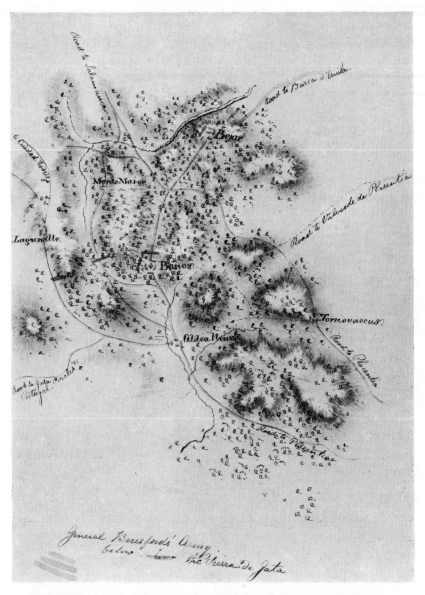

Road to Salamanca

Road to Barca d'Avila.

Bejar

to Cindad Rodrigo

Monte Maior

Road to Valverde de Plasentia

Lagunille

Buños

Tormovaccus

Aldea Neura

Road to Placentia

Road to Gata Coriegal

Road to Plasentias

General Beresford's Army
below the Sierra de Gata

5. Plan of the action at Baños attached to Robert Wilson's manuscript
Narrative of the Services of the Loyal Lusitanian Legion. The plan falsely shows
Marshal Beresford's Portuguese army as being close to the battlefield

6. Regular Cossacks. *Carle Vernet, 1814*

Britain's diplomats were unemployed, but few of them were prepared to accept appointment as Ambassador to the Sublime Porte. It was offered to Major Lord Burghersh, twenty-seven years old and a former ADC to Wellington, and when he refused it there was a rumour that Wilson was being considered. 'This', wrote George Jackson, himself an unemployed *attaché*, 'would be more extraordinary still. Sir Robert is a very gallant fellow, and a very pleasant one too; but he is too harum-scarum for a diplomatist.'[20]

It was not until March 1811 that the post was filled. Jackson commented, 'Constantinople is at last given to Liston. In point of seniority nobody can object, as Liston is in his seventy-third year, and the only cause for surprise is that he should wish the thing. But, they say, ambition is one of the last passions that leaves us; and then, his wife is not quite so old.'[21]

In fact, Robert Liston was only sixty-nine and had had a long, if unspectacular, diplomatic career. Brougham thought he had tolerable talents but Francis Jackson said that he was 'in every sense old for his work, and clings to a system and policy that are out of date'. He seems to have been an agreeable old man but he was the last person to have kept under control the officer who was appointed to be his military adviser, Robert Wilson.[22]

Sir Robert's appointment was not gazetted until December 1811, eight months after Liston was given his ambassadorship. Liston had not left England. In September a frigate had been detailed to take him out. His wife, his servants, and his baggage were embarked but the Marquess of Wellesley had not yet written his instructions and, after a short pause, the ship was allocated to other duties and the ambassador-designate, with his impedimenta, was put ashore. The New Year came and, on 16 January 1812, Wellesley resigned, leaving the writing of Liston's instructions to his successor, Castlereagh.

Wilson's terms of appointment were generous. He was made a brigadier on special service with rank and pay backdated to March 1811. In addition he received a special allowance of £1,000 a year, backdated to October, forage for five horses (from March 1811), and provision (9s. 6d. a day) for an aide-de-camp, although in fact Lieutenant Charles, who again filled this post, did not join him until January 1813. Wilson was given a contingent account for actual expenses and losses; the rate of exchange for the expenses was, insisted the Treasury, to be attested by a British consul or reputable merchant.[23]

Some Foreign Office eyebrows were raised at Sir Robert's appointment. Francis Jackson thought that it should have been realized that 'Wilson is, or would be, a spy of Opposition. As such, the intercourse he has with the Office ought long since to have been forbidden.' Castlereagh, however, contented himself with instructing Wilson that 'You are to consider yourself entirely attached to Mr. Liston's mission, and are to regulate your conduct by his orders, and with him alone to correspond.'[24]

The mission eventually sailed in HMS *Argus* on 8 April. Up to the last moment Sir Robert continued his commentary on events in the Peninsula. When news arrived in February that Wellington had recaptured Ciudad Rodrigo, whose loss Wilson had described as 'an irreparable mischief', he wrote that 'the capture of Ciudad Rodrigo does not, in my humble opinion, affect the war in Portugal'. Just before he sailed, he heard that the army was besieging Badajoz. The news appalled him and he dashed off his forecast to Lord Grey. 'The siege of Badajoz is so extraordinary an operation that I must refuse to believe in the undertaking. That Fort St. Christobal [the transpontine outwork of Badajoz] may be attacked is possible but that the Guadiana should be passed and battle be offered without a fixed bridge is to me an incredible phenomenon.' Before Grey received this effusion Wellington had taken Badajoz.[25]

In 1807 Wilson had written 'I *must*—I *ought* to abandon navigation. It is almost folly to contend with predominating fate.' It was the same in 1812. On the second day at sea there were 'fresh gales'; on the third he recorded, 'same weather: all passengers sick'. It was not until the sixth day, when they reached the Bay of Biscay, that he could say that the sea was 'more moderate, but still foul winds and the ship very uneasy. Mr. Liston, as his wife tells us, always plays the flute when he would charm HM

Ministers by the composition of his despatches.' The ambassador failed to charm the winds and it was not until 20 April that they reached Cadiz. They were greeted by the news that Badajoz had fallen and Wilson, with characteristic perversity, noted that this put the allied army 'in a dangerous situation'.[26]

Cadiz had been under French siege for two years but its situation made it all but impregnable to an enemy without command of the sea, provided that the garrison was staunch. The French had never dared to launch a serious attack on the defences. Wilson undertook a detailed survey of the place and pronounced that the city was 'exposed to great danger. A French attack with 30,000 men would inevitably be successful.'[27] He did not explain how 30,000 Frenchmen were to be assembled for such an attack or how they were to be transported across the water obstacles which were dominated by the Spanish and British navies. Eleven years later he was for a month to be commander of the Cadiz garrison. On that occasion he had to escape by sea before the garrison surrendered.

During his stay Sir Robert had a long conversation with Manuel la Peña, a commander remarkable, even among the Spaniards of his day, for his incompetence. His most famous feat was to hold 9,000 Spaniards back from the battle while Thomas Graham with 5,200 British and Portuguese defeated 7,000 Frenchmen on Barossa hill in 1811. Wilson found him 'a most sensible man. I satisfied myself that he had been a most injured officer, and time will convince the world of it.'[28]

After a week in Cadiz the ambassadorial party sailed on to Gibraltar, where Sir Robert considered the defences 'overrated', and, 'after experiencing the most perplexing weather', reached Palermo on 13 May. They were received by Lord William Bentinck, who doubled the roles of British Ambassador and Commander-in-Chief of the large British garrison which kept the French out of Sicily. Lord William had a most difficult post. The King of Naples and Sicily was an ineffective Bourbon but his Austrian wife, Queen Maria Carolina, the sister of Marie Antoinette, was a different proposition. She had been a close friend of Lady Hamilton and of Nelson, who had hanged a

Neapolitan rebel on his quarter-deck to please her. By 1812 the Queen loathed the British and, in particular, she loathed Lord William who made little secret of his ambition to introduce democracy on the Westminster pattern into Sicily.

Maria Carolina was delighted to meet Robert Wilson. As a Knight of the Order of Maria Theresa, he was, to her, almost a compatriot. At a long private interview she poured out her woes into his receptive ear. When he left the palace she appeared on the balcony, 'and on my bowing, she kissed her hand several times'.[29]

Wilson made a colourless report on the interview to Bentinck, claiming that his own part had been strictly neutral, but to Grey he echoed all the Queen's complaints about Lord William and added, 'I have come to the positive conclusion that we have embarked on an undertaking which will greatly increase our expenditure, render reinforcements necessary, and probably end in an avowed attempt to seize the island.' In his view Britain would have done better to take Corfu. He made no mention of the importance of Sicily as a naval base nor of the fact that, far from requiring reinforcements, Bentinck had a disposable force of 10,000 men which he was planning to send to the east coast of Spain. Wilson's letter to Grey ended, 'I trust your Lordship will not suppose that I have been influenced by any personal civilities or distinctions that I have received from the Court or Court party. I have been too much acquainted with, I may say familiarized to, the society of foreign sovereigns, not to have mastered the seductions of flattery.'[30]

Inevitably, Lord William learned, some weeks later, more of Wilson's interview with the Queen. He was justifiably angry and wrote to London, 'The Queen herself states that the language held by Sir Robert was that of disapprobation of the conduct of the British government. . . . [His] great object is singularity and his vanity knows no bounds. His opinions are always in opposition to those which happen to prevail. His address and forwardness enable him to do mischief. . . . With my consent he shall never put his foot in Sicily again.'[31]

On a less controversial note, Wilson was able to see the Twentieth Light Dragoons, 'whom I was delighted to greet; for really I have not only a personal attachment to several, but a strong *esprit de corps*'. What the regiment thought of their absentee lieutenant-colonel's *esprit de corps* is not recorded. Nevertheless, he found at Palermo an order from the Duke of York that a corporal and four dragoons should be attached to his entourage which, hitherto, had consisted only of Allen, his groom. 'They are fine fellows, and two of them went out to the Cape under my command.'[32]

Sir Robert reached Constantinople on 1 July. He had left the *Argus* before it entered the Dardanelles and had climbed Mount Ida and explored some supposed sites of Troy while Liston presented his credentials. He was greeted with two pieces of bad news. One was that the Prime Minister, Spencer Perceval, had been assassinated on 11 May. The other was that peace had almost been concluded between Turkey and Russia.

On public grounds, the second item was excellent. For Wilson it was a disaster, it 'made my presence on the Danube unnecessary'. He had counted on being able to act as a mediator, thus making it possible to achieve his overriding aim—to return to St. Petersburg. As it was, he found that 'only the boundary line on the Persian Frontier suspends the ratification of peace'.[33]

At the same time his determination to get to St. Petersburg grew more urgent. War between Russia and France was imminent. 'Our last account from Bucharest is of date of the 20th of June. War was then, according to recent advice from Poland, hourly expected.' It was not until 16 July that news reached Constantinople that French troops had crossed the Russian border on 24 June.

He pestered Liston to let him go to Russia but the 'ambassador thought that some decisive proceeding ought first to take place'. Wilson set about manufacturing one. The Russian ambassador, Italinsky, was persuaded to believe that Wilson could persuade the Czar that better terms could be obtained from the Turks if ratification of the provisional treaty of peace was delayed. Liston was converted and, on 11 July, agreed to let Sir Robert go. He had been sent to Turkey to assist in arranging peace between that country and Russia. Now he was to go to St. Petersburg to upset the terms already agreed.

He was in a fever to be gone. He detested Constantinople and thought it unhealthy. 'I wonder it is ever free from putrid diseases, for the bodies of the dead are not covered with more than a foot of earth, and one half of the city is occupied by cemeteries, which are the fashionable promenades.' Before he could leave he must have a passport and, although the Turks agreed to issue one, the death of the Sultan's only male child brought all government business to a halt; although, 'as he has four wives already pregnant, the loss of Prince Murad is not irreparable. . . . I could not sleep; my thoughts were in the most violent action. Until I reach Imperial headquarters, I shall be on tenter-hooks. I have transferred all my baggage into a pair of saddle-bags, so I may go *ventre-à-terre* if money, spurs and zeal can produce that pace.'[34]

He started on 27 July. 'The first hundred miles that I rode presented only a flat, naked journey; fifty of them ran along the sea-shore. The next two hundred and fifty were over a partially wooded country and through the Balkan mountains. . . . As I rode down the hills during the night at full speed, my horse pitched with the most furious velocity and turned completely over. Neither of us, however, were hurt and I have only been a temporary sufferer from a blow in the eye with one of the branches of the trees.'[35]

Sixty-eight hours' riding brought him to Turkish headquarters at Schumla (Kolarovgrad). It was, he wrote, 'an exertion beyond the strength of most men. My dragoons, indeed, executed the same undertaking but only one of them could pretend any rivalry with me.' He immediately went into conference with the Grand Vizier and, when it was over, two hours later, the Turk 'sent to my quarters twenty dishes; after which I was enabled to retire for rest, and might have slept for two hours had the fleas not tormented me'. Next there was a formal reception for the local notabilities and two more hours' conversation with the Vizier. 'On going away he gave me a very fine sword and a Persian shawl. I am now about again to mount, to the horror of my Janissary, who calculated on this night's rest.

'I quitted Schumla with delight, for it is the very hot-bed of plague: and connecting its physical and military imperfections, I think it ought to be called the headquarters of barbarism. As we approached the Danube, a most severe storm of lightning and rain suddenly broke over us. I was drenched to the bone before I could dismount, and when I did so, I fell to the ground in the dirtiest soil that could be selected by a man in a state of decadence.'

They reached the Danube at Rutschuk (Ruse) and, after sheltering from a second storm, they crossed the river in a small boat. The Russian commandant at Giurgevo (Giurgiu) received Sir Robert 'as a brother' and provided 'four hours entertainment', telling him that his men were under orders to march northward on the following day. Wilson preceded them in the commandant's carriage, leaving at midnight. On 1 August, 'at eight o'clock in the morning, after going at the most furious rate and over the rudest ground, with six horses tackled at every post, I arrived here [Bucharest] and waited on Admiral Tchitchagov with whom I remained for three hours.'[36]

It was somewhat improbable to find a Russian admiral commanding an army at Bucharest but Pavel Tchitchagov was an unusual man. He had been brought up in England and had married a Miss Proby at Paddington parish church. He spoke and wrote English fluently if without much accuracy. He had suffered imprisonment under Czar Paul but had been freed to command the Russian squadron which co-operated with the British in the Helder expedition in 1799. When Alexander came to the throne he appointed Tchitchagov Minister of Marine, an office he held until 1812.

His appointment to the south arose from the Czar's realization that war with France was inevitable and that he would need the troops which had been engaged in indecisive bickerings with the Turks for the past six years. Since 1806 the Russian Army of the Danube had been commanded by the veteran General Kutusov. They had overrun Moldavia and Wallachia, the area now covered by the eastern and southern parts of Romania. That had been the limit of their success. Kutusov could neither advance further nor reconcile the people of the occupied principalities to Russian rule, although for decades they had been begging the Czars to take them under their protection. Alexander decided to supersede him and, to the admiral's surprise, appointed Tchitchagov Commander-in-Chief on the Danube, Commander-in-Chief of the Black Sea Fleet, Governor of Moldavia and Wallachia, and Plenipotentiary to the Sublime Porte.

When he heard of his supersession, Kutusov patched up a peace with the Turks. It was a treaty which satisfied no one. Russia abandoned all her conquests except eastern Moldavia. Her troops were to be withdrawn to the river Pruth. 'It should seem that the Porte was of opinion it had been betrayed by its representatives signing the treaty, for the negotiator, Morusi, had his head cut off and the Grand Vizier was degraded and banished.'[37] When the admiral took over his command he found his army demoralized and occupied in looting the people they had liberated. They had no other means of subsistence although, by Russian standards, Kutusov had built up efficient supply services, which had managed to extract from the countryside three times as much as the army needed, but nothing was issued to the troops.

Tchitchagov quickly arranged the regular issue of rations, thus simultaneously restoring the discipline of the troops and persuading the populace that Russian rule was preferable to that of the Turks. The admiral, however, refused their pleas for his continued protection. His orders were to employ all the troops that could be spared against the French.

It was unfortunate that his ideas for doing so were unsound. He proposed to march due west from Bucharest, mobilize the Christian Serbs and Bosnians, seize French Dalmatia and Corfu and, from there, 'insurge Italy'.[38] This apotheosis of the 'indirect approach' would, he hoped, compel Napoleon to divert troops from Poland. He was prepared to admit that his plan would require the active support of the Turks who would have to agree to the arming of a million of their rebellious subjects. The admiral had a simple answer to this problem. If the Porte would not agree, he would make a start by marching on Constantinople where he would dictate terms more advantageous than Kutusov had been able to obtain.

Wilson believed that he had persuaded Tchitchagov to forgo this eccentric scheme and to march his troops directly to Russia's western front. At dinner on 2 August the admiral assured him that he would be moving north 'in a very few days, as I had assured him of the pacific intentions of the Grand Vizier and convinced him of the necessity of marching into Poland without loss of time. Thus I have begun my negotiations very auspiciously.'[39]

For the rest of his life Sir Robert asserted that it was his influence that released a large army to reinforce the Russians in Poland. It is probable that he believed this to be true, for Tchitchagov may not have told him that on that very morning he had received peremptory orders from St. Petersburg to take his whole disposable force, by way of the Dniester river, to the southern side of the Pripet marshes. There he was to assume command of the Third Army of the West which was blocking the road from Warsaw to Kiev.[40]

Wilson spent two days in Bucharest. He thought it would be 'a delightful city if the streets were not paved with logs of wood, which unhinge every joint as the carriage proceeds. I was quite racked, and all my saddle wounds re-opened, for it must be remembered that Russian carriages have no springs. . . . The women are very pretty and, if I may judge from my dinner today, Wallachia must be an Epicurean abode. I have seldom sat down to a greater variety, or to viands better dressed.'[41]

In Bucharest he met a gentleman from Yorkshire, Mr. Wyburn, 'greatly accomplished in languages, with good manners', who offered to accompany him to St. Petersburg. They set out on the morning of 3 August in a *kabitka*, a four-seater Russian carriage. 'Two of my dragoons at first rode, but afterwards got into the litter carts of the country.'

Wilson's usual breakneck speed was too much for the *kabitka*. 'At Fokchani [Focsani], the Moldavian frontier town, the forewheel gave way but Russian soldiers replaced it. The next morning at daybreak, the other fore-wheel, unable to withstand the shattering of the night, gave way, split into fifty parts. Happily we found a little open waggon which we took *bon-gré*, *mal-gré*, and a little car for the soldiers, as being larger than the post-cars. Thus we renewed our course over a dreary country; I think that for a hundred miles we did not see a single village.' Twice they were drenched by thunderstorms but they reached Jassy and crossed the Dniester at Khotim on 6 August. This was the Russian frontier but they were hurried through the quarantine station and reached Kamienetz (Kaments Podolsky) on the same day. There Allen, the groom, had to be left as he 'could sustain the journey no longer'.

On 9 August they came to Jitomar 'after a wretched journey, for the galloping of the horse filled our cart with filth, and the rain poured incessantly', but they reached Kiev for dinner on the following day and on the 14th in the morning they arrived at Smolensk, the Russian headquarters. 'I found General Bennigsen, Prince Galitzin and many others. No meeting could be more sincerely affectionate. I dined with Bennigsen.'[42] It had been a remarkable journey. They had covered almost twelve hundred miles in nineteen days, including their only rest, two days in Bucharest. On their travelling days they had averaged sixty miles.

Ostensibly the object of all this speed was to deliver despatches from Italinsky in Constantinople and Tchitchagov in Bucharest to the Czar and to urge him to delay ratification of the peace with Turkey. Alexander, however, was not with the army and a battle was imminent. Wilson handed the despatches over to Wyburn, his casual travelling companion, and established himself with the army. He scented battle and, what was equally to his taste, intrigue.

CHAPTER 6

Monsieur l' Ambassadeur des Rebelles

Neither the French nor the Russians had much reason to be satisfied with the first eight weeks of Napoleon's invasion of Russia. The Russians were distressed that so much of their territory had had to be abandoned. The French sought vainly for a decisive battle which would settle the war while they were still in touch with their supply depots in Poland and East Prussia.

The Russian plan had been simple. The enemy were to be allowed to advance for a hundred and fifty miles until they reached Drissa on the eastern bank of the river Dvina. There they had erected an entrenched camp which was to be garrisoned by 100,000 men of the First Army of the West. While Napoleon and his talented subordinates were puzzling out how to overcome this obstacle, they were to be encircled by the 48,000 men of the Second Army. This tidy scheme had been evolved by a Prussian Colonel, Ernst von Phull, a pedant who believed that warfare could be reduced to much the same rules as govern chess and who had managed to secure the confidence of Czar Alexander, a potentate much inclined to listen to the schemes of charlatans. Phull assumed that Napoleon would omit to guard his flanks and would keep his army stationary while its destruction was encompassed. He also overlooked the fact that Napoleon was employing 380,000 men on this part of the front while the Russians could oppose him with only 148,000.

When the First Army reached Drissa they found the entrenched camp sited in the wrong place and far too small for the garrison intended for it. They continued to retreat and the Second Army, poised for its encircling march, was lucky to escape from two French columns each of which outnumbered it.

A month later Wilson reached Smolensk as the two Russian armies were falling back on that city in some disarray. At regimental level, the problems were little more than the results of extreme fatigue and, as the Russians were the toughest soldiers in Europe, this was scarcely serious. In the high command there was open discord. In the army, as in all sides of Russian life, there was constant tension between the 'real' Russians and the 'foreigners', some of whom came from the western parts of the empire while others had transferred from the armies of their native countries. The 'real' Russians, who preferred a straightforward stand-up fight to any fancy manœuvring, bitterly resented the surrender of every inch of Russian territory and blamed the foreigners for all their misfortunes. Phull's fiasco at Drissa brought their xenophobia to the boil. It was primarily directed at the commander of the First Army.

Mikhail Bogdanovich Barclay de Tolly had been born in Livonia (Latvia) and was a Russian subject by birth. His family came of Scottish stock but was long settled among the Baltic Germans. Barclay had served for fourteen years in the ranks of the cavalry before receiving a commission, but had reached the rank of major-general by the age of forty-five. As such he had fought at Eylau and Friedland and he had later distinguished himself as a corps commander in Finland, fighting against the Swedes. In 1810 Alexander had made him Minister of War and, in the two years available to him, he had done much to make the Russian army fit to fight the French on equal terms. The infantry, cavalry, and artillery compared well with their opponents, but there were a number of defects which Barclay had not had time to rectify. There was no standardization of small arms. The troops facing Napoleon had muskets of twenty-eight different calibres.[1] The supply services were rudimentary. There was little effective staff work. Russian officers from all social backgrounds made excellent fighting leaders but few had the education and fewer still the application for administrative work.

For this the army had to rely on foreigners. Many of them, including Clausewitz, Scharnhorst, Wittgenstein and Phull, were Prussians, Bennigsen a Hanoverian, Arnfeldt a Swede.

Barclay was a competent and resolute general and might have retained the confidence of the army if he had seen the opportunity for even one offensive manœuvre in July and August 1812. The more the army retreated, the more Barclay became the focus of the discontent of the 'real' Russian generals, incited to disaffection by their close ally Bennigsen. Barclay's position had been difficult from the start. The Czar had not dared to make him commander-in-chief but put him in charge of the larger army and gave him the task of co-ordinating the movements of both. Thus he had to control the Second Army but could not give orders to its commander.

Prince Bagration, at the head of the Second Army, was, according to Wilson, 'gentle, gracious, generous and chivalrously brave'.[2] He was senior to Barclay in military rank and immeasurably superior in social standing. He disliked Barclay, resented his own quasi-subordination to him, and was in no hurry to comply with his suggestions. As a 'real' Russian (though he was in fact a Georgian), nothing would satisfy him but the fighting of major actions, whatever the odds. This was what he understood and his rearguard action after Friedland showed that he was an excellent battle general. He had no patience with Barclay's idea that Napoleon could only be defeated by being worn down by a prolongation of the war. Most of the senior officers sided with Bagration and, by the time the armies neared Smolensk, the two generals were barely on speaking terms.

When Wilson reached Smolensk on 14 August the first people he met were Prince Galitzin, who had left the army rather than serve under Barclay, and General Bennigsen, whose talent for intrigue greatly exceeded his talent for war. They soon converted Sir Robert to their view of Barclay's strategy. This was not difficult. Part of Wilson's instinctive sympathy for the Russians lay in his agreement with them on the desirability of fighting battles for the sake of fighting battles.

On the same day he met Bagration, who 'invited me to join

his army, and to live at his headquarters. He gave me a very fine horse to ride, equipped me with a greatcoat (for the nights are bitterly cold) and a Russian cap in case of a mêlée in battle, that I might be recognised.'³

The tension between the two army commanders was then at its height. Barclay had been persuaded to counterattack with both armies but, after a promising start, he heard that the French were marching to turn his right. He ordered a halt. This enraged Bagration who marched his army back to Smolensk and was thus out of touch when Barclay ordered the advance to be resumed. Meanwhile Napoleon was turning the Russian left with 175,000 men and, but for a dogged rearguard action by 10,000 men, might have reached Smolensk before either Russian army. As it was, 15 August found them both around the city.

Bagration was determined to fight to save the holy city of Smolensk. Barclay, knowing that they could only muster 130,000 men between them, ordered Bagration to retire under cover of the First Army. The main French attack was launched on 17 August. As soon as day dawned, Wilson 'accompanied the general into Smolensk. The action on the right soon commenced. I rode round all the posts with the general; but stopping to have a [horse]shoe fixed on one of the advances, I was, by another piquet deemed a French *parliamentaire*, and conducted, notwithstanding my remonstrances, to Count Siewers [commanding a Russian corps], who for a moment was under the same mistake. The action soon became serious. I was here, there and everywhere. Towards evening, however, I had the opportunity of being useful by inducing the general to put four battalions into the streets and by clearing the bridge; as I once had done before in the Polish campaign at Wehlau [see p. 40].'

It was not only in the fighting that Sir Robert made himself useful. He was doing his best to thwart Barclay's plan. 'In order to counteract the intention of General Barclay to quit Smolensk I was, about ten o'clock at night, obliged to mount again and enter the town to take the opinions of General Dokhturov and Prince Eugene of Würtemberg as to the capability of longer defence. The former said we had done *trop ou trop peu*; the latter engaged, with eight thousand men, to defend the city ten days, and begged me to assure the general of the necessity of further defence. I had at least a dozen letters from officers of rank on the subject as they thought I had access to and influence with the commander-in-chief that no one else had. Duke Alexander of Würtemberg [uncle of the Czar] with myself endeavoured to change the general's resolution. I cited Eylau, the preservation of Königsberg, &c. I proposed a sally with 10,000 men, whilst the Cossacks passed the Dnieper on the right and attacked the enemy's baggage and depots, greatly exposed: but in vain; the order to retire was given. The *sacred image* of the Virgin was removed, and before daybreak the town was completely evacuated.'[4]

The evacuation of Smolensk was the last straw for the 'real' Russians. Hetman Platov said to Barclay, in Wilson's hearing, 'You see, Sir, I wear only a cloak. I will no longer put on the Russian uniform. I consider it a disgrace.'[5] Wilson wrote in his diary, 'I cannot express the indignation that prevailed. The sacrifice of so many brave men; the destruction of an important town unnecessarily; the suspicion that Buonaparte directed the Russian counsels; the sight of the holy city in flames, &c. &c, worked strongly on the feelings of the Russians. I even, in this moment of disappointment and wrath, regretted the exertions I had made and the hazards I had run (for I had had my hair-breadth 'scapes) for objects which the general seemed to determine to be unobtainable.'[6]

Sir Robert did his best to add to the dissatisfaction. 'I sat and grumbled with the Duke of Würtemberg and repeated the same parts later in the day with Stroganov.' This did not stop him taking his full share in the rearguard actions. When Bagration was under desperate pressure at Lubino, Wilson rode at his side when, 'sword in hand, at the head of his staff, the prince galloped forward, rallying fugitives and crying out, "Victory or death! We must preserve this post or perish!", by his energy and example reanimating all. This gallant counter attack recovered a vital hill and thus, under God's favour, the army was preserved.'[7]

The dissident generals decided to send to the Czar 'not only the request of the army for a new chief, but a declaration in the name of the army "that if any order came from St. Petersburg to suspend hostilities and treat the invader as friends, in deference to the policy of Count Roumiantzov [Foreign Minister since Tilsit and suspected of pro-French leanings], such an order would be one which did not represent his Imperial Majesty's true sentiments and wishes, but had been extracted from his Majesty under false representations or external control; and that the army would continue to maintain his Majesty's pledge [not to make peace as long as a single Frenchman stands on Russian soil] and continue the contest till the invader was driven beyond the frontier."'

The demand for a change of command, for the dismissal of the chief minister, and the threat to disobey orders were, however respectful the language in which they were expressed, open mutiny. Since some of the petitioners, including Bennigsen, had been involved in the murder of the Czar's father, there was also an implied threat to Alexander's life, the more so since his brother and heir presumptive, the Grand Duke Constantine, was among the plotters. As Wilson remarked, 'The execution of such a commission might expose a Russian officer to future punishment.' It occurred to the generals that this difficulty could be circumvented by entrusting the delivery of the message to a non-Russian officer, to Wilson himself, 'under the circumstances of his known attachment to the Emperor, and his Imperial Majesty's equally well known feelings towards him'. Sir Robert accepted the task without hesitation.[8]

Before leaving the army, he set in train an experiment in political warfare. Since leaving London he had carried in his baggage leaflets supplied by the Spanish ambassador, the Duque del Infantado. They were addressed to the four battalions of Spaniards who were unwillingly serving in the *Grande Armée* and urged them to change sides. 'I distributed several hundred proclamations, and General Barclay agreed to leave several wounded Spaniards on the march with the proclamations sewed in their clothes, and with such verbal encouragement as, I hope, will produce a considerable defection from the enemy, if any

Spaniards or Portuguese survive [Buonaparte's] prodigal expenditure of them.'[9]

He set out from the army on 21 August, leaving behind one of his dragoons, 'being very ill with fatigue'. Two more dragoons went sick the following day and had to be entrusted to the care of Bagration. Accompanied only by the corporal and Baron Brincken, a Courlander, 'we travelled in the carriages of the post telegas, little four-wheeled carriages without any springs'. St. Petersburg was five hundred miles away and, as was Wilson's habit, they travelled night and day. When they had covered more than half the distance, they met, on his way to the front, Prince Kutusov, the grand old man of the Russian army who had been appointed to the supreme command. Thus half the purpose of Wilson's mission had been accomplished without his intervention. All that remained for him to do was to secure the dismissal of the Foreign Minister.

Mikhail Golenishchev-Kutusov was two weeks short of his sixty-second birthday. He came from the old aristocracy but his first commission had been in the artillery. Early in his career he had transferred to the light infantry where he had gained a great reputation for bravery. Twice he had been shot through the head by the Turks but, although he had lost an eye, his physique was unimpaired. In later years he had done himself more harm by an unrestrained indulgence in food, women, and champagne. By 1812 he was so stout that he could scarcely ride and had to move about his army in a small four-wheeled carriage. Wilson described him as 'a *bon-vivant*—polished, courteous, shrewd as a Greek, naturally intelligent as an Asiatic and well-instructed as a European—he was more disposed to trust to diplomacy for his success than to martial prowess, for which by his age and the state of his constitution he was no longer qualified.'[10]

The Czar, who had recently recalled him from the Danube for his laxity and inertia, distrusted him as an intriguer—'an immoral and thoroughly dangerous character'. It was the arguments of Count Rostropchin, the Governor of Moscow, which had convinced Alexander that only Kutusov could command the loyalty of the whole army and had forced him to place him above both Barclay and Bagration. Rostropchin's argument was true but, for all his bravery and determination, Kutusov was a less able commander than Barclay and, in the event, had to continue Barclay's strategy of retreat.

Kutusov and Wilson had an hour's conversation by the roadside. Wilson told him of the army's anger against Barclay and of the messages he was taking to the Czar. On parting, the general urged him to return to the army as soon as possible and added, 'I hope you intend to tell the Emperor all the truths you have told me.'[11] Sir Robert hurried on towards the capital, pausing on the journey only to consult with Count Panin, another influential member of the conspiracy against the Czar's father.

On 27 August, when Wilson reached St. Petersburg, the Czar was absent. He had gone to Åbo (Turku) in Finland to meet the Prince Royal of Sweden, formerly Napoleon's Marshal Bernadotte, in the hope of concluding a Russo-Swedish alliance. The British ambassador had accompanied the Czar and, armed with a subsidy of a million pounds, was hoping to persuade the Prince Royal to accept Norway, then a Danish possession, as compensation for Finland, which the Russians had seized in 1809 and were determined to retain.

Lieutenant-General the Earl of Cathcart, Ambassador and Military Commissioner to Russia, would have been scandalized if he had known of the message Wilson was bringing to Alexander. Cathcart did not approve of his subordinates acting on their own. One of his *attachés* wrote, 'His lordship is accustomed to direct the whole of affairs himself, from the most important to the most trivial. He keeps every paper himself. No archives of this embassy exist.' Wilson, with his unrestrained tendency to act on his own erratic initiative, was the last man Cathcart would wish to have on his staff. Where Wilson was mercurial, his lordship, who in his youth had been called to the Scottish bar, moved with massive deliberation. Castlereagh's brother wrote, 'Lord Cathcart takes two days to consider a despatch and two days to write one, and he never begins to think until other people have finished.'[12]

For all his slowness, Cathcart was an excellent ambassador. He spoke Russian fluently, having been brought up in St. Petersburg when his father held the embassy. He had the absolute confidence of the Czar. In what may have been a unique gesture of confidence in an allied ambassador, Alexander, when Moscow was threatened by the French and the end of the war imminent, gave secret orders that, if he should be forced to surrender, the Russian fleet 'should be put at the command of the British ambassador, and that the Minister of Marine should conform to any instructions Lord Cathcart might give for removing the fleet to England, to be at the disposal of the Prince Regent as soon as possible'.[13]

Cathcart may have had an inkling of what Wilson intended. Two letters had reached him since Sir Robert left Smolensk. In the first he had written that the dismissal of Roumiantzov 'is universally required'. In the second, he asserted that 'General Barclay does not possess the confidence of the army. I am certain that he is not making a war of manœuvre upon any fixed and pre-arranged military system, but a war of marches without sufficient arrangement and method to avoid a serious misfortune. . . . The state of affairs is too desperate to admit of any attempt to enforce the maintenance of his authority.'[14]

Any ambassador would be alarmed to know that one of his nationals was acting as the spokesman of a group of dissident generals in demanding of the sovereign to whom the ambassador was accredited, the dismissal of his commander-in-chief and his foreign minister. If Cathcart did realize what was afoot, he underestimated the speed at which Wilson travelled. Arriving in St. Petersburg twenty-four hours behind the Czar, Cathcart found Sir Robert setting out to dine at the Imperial table. All he could do was hurriedly to urge discretion. Wilson described the conversation as 'rather remarkable and unexpected' and complained that it made him half an hour late for dinner. The Czar was not perturbed. He 'would not suffer me to kiss his hand, but took me in his arms and kissed me repeatedly.'[15]

Discretion was not one of Wilson's outstanding characteristics but it did restrain him from reporting his interviews with the Czar in his journal, which was posted at intervals to his wife in England. He wrote only, 'It is impossible for me to record anything that passed on political subjects. It would have been well on many interesting accounts if I could have immediately transacted all with the Emperor that I wished to do; but Lord Cathcart's arrival tied my tongue on some matters, and diplomatic etiquettes have again, as heretofore, interfered with great national interests to their prejudice.'[16] His only account of the interviews comes from his *Narrative of Events during the Invasion of Russia*, written thirteen years after the meetings (see Note at end of chapter).

He was surprised at how well the Czar was informed about feeling in the army. He even knew of Platov's refusal to wear uniform. He asked whether 'Marshal Kutusov would be able to restore the subordination?' Wilson could only reply that Kutusov, 'whom I had met going to the army, was fully aware of the temper in which he would find the army; that I had thought it my duty to communicate to the marshal the facts with which I was acquainted, and that the marshal had conjured me to conceal nothing from his Imperial Majesty. I earnestly implored his Majesty to bear in mind that the perilous state of his empire, which might justify patriotic alarm, from the gravity of its cause, extenuated a trespass on authority instigated by the purest motives, and intended for the permanent preservation of that authority itself; that the chiefs were animated by the most affectionate attachment to the Emperor and his family; and if they were but assured that he would no longer give his confidence to advisers they mistrusted, that they would testify their allegiance by exertions or sacrifices which would add splendour to the crown and security to the throne under every adversity.'

If Alexander was able to unwind this verbal cocoon, it must have been clear to him that he was faced with an ultimatum. Wilson recalled that 'during this exposition the Emperor's colour occasionally visited and left his cheek. When Sir Robert had terminated his appeal, there was a minute or two of pause, and his Majesty drew towards the window, as if desirous of recovering an unembarrassed air before he replied. After a few struggles, however, he came up to Sir Robert Wilson, took him by the hand, and kissed him on the forehead and cheek, according to the Russian custom. "You are the only person", then said his Majesty, "from whom I could or would have heard such a communication. In the former war you proved your attachment towards me by your services, and entitled yourself to my most intimate confidence; but you must be aware that you have placed me in a very distressing position—*Moi! Souverain de la Russie!*—to hear such things from anyone! But the army is mistaken in Roumiantzov: he has not really advised submission to the Emperor Napoleon; and I have the greatest respect for him, since he is the only one who has never asked me for anything on his own account, whereas every one else in my service has always been seeking honours, wealth or some private object for himself and connections. I am unwilling to sacrifice him without cause: but come again tomorrow—I must collect my thoughts before I despatch you with an answer." '[17]

That night Wilson wrote in his diary, 'I have been playing a bold and high part on this stage. I have been the organ of the Russian army and nation, and, I hope, one of the best friends that a sovereign ever had in a foreigner. But supposing all I now propose now succeeds, I shall ever have to regret that the irresolution of British counsels so long kept me in a state of inactivity.'[18]

At their interview next morning the Czar cheerfully greeted Sir Robert as *Monsieur l'ambassadeur des rebelles* but continued, 'I have reflected seriously during the whole night upon our conversation and I have not done you injustice. You shall carry back to the army pledges of my determination to continue the war against Napoleon whilst a Frenchman is in arms on this side of the frontier. I will not desert my engagements come what may. I will abide the worst. I am ready to remove my family into the interior, and undergo every sacrifice. If necessary I will let my beard grow down to my waist and eat potatoes in Siberia; but I must not give way on the point of choosing my ministers: that concession might induce other demands, still more inconvenient and indecorous for me to grant. Count Roumiantzov shall not be the means of any disunion or difference—everything shall be done to remove uneasiness on that head; but done so that I shall not appear to give way to menace, or have to reproach myself with injustice. This is a case where much depends on the *manner of doing it*. Give me a little time—all will be satisfactorily arranged.'

Alexander asked Wilson to return to the army in a few days' time and authorized him 'to interpose with all the power and influence he could exert, to protect the interests of the Imperial Crown in conformity with [the Czar's pledge not to make peace], whenever he saw any disposition or design to contravene or prejudice them'. Sir Robert was, in fact, to be the Czar's personal representative at headquarters. It gave him the opportunity to make his views known both to the generals and to the Czar on all matters, knowing that both sides would have at least to listen to him. It was the position he had always craved. He was to have great influence but no responsibility. 'I have,' he wrote in his journal, 'if successful, gained a greater victory over Buonaparte than if I had preserved fifty Smolensks, nay driven him beyond the Vistula.'[19]

He stayed a week in St. Petersburg and dined several times at the palace. He also called on Madame Narishkin, the Czar's mistress, 'but this is the only visit I paid her, as I do not choose to let persons think I owe my influence to her favour'. He presided at a dinner given by 'the English gentlemen here' to celebrate the news of Wellington's great victory at Salamanca (22 July). He arranged for his book on the campaign of 1806–7 to be translated and published in Russian, German, and French. For £36 he 'picked up a beautiful Gobelin picture which I am sending to England. I think it extremely valuable, though perhaps a little *too natural* for a family drawing room.'[20]

Lord Cathcart, without enthusiasm, sanctioned his attachment to the Russian army. In view of the Czar's known predilection for Wilson, the ambassador had little choice. All he could do was to stipulate that Sir Robert should go in a strictly military capacity, with no 'public character'. In the fullness of time this was reiterated by Castlereagh, who insisted that Wilson should confine himself 'to points of military detail, and not engage in measures of independent diplomacy'. The Foreign Secretary had been distressed to learn that Sir Robert had recently sent a message to the Emperor of Austria threatening that the British government might 'cease to regard the interests of his empire' if he supported France 'beyond what was necessary to avert any immediate evil'. Castlereagh's letter of appointment to Wilson was distinctly unenthusiastic.[21]

On 12 September Cathcart and Wilson attended 'the ceremony in the church of Alexander Nevsky on the baptism day of the Emperor. After the service Prince Gorchakov read a despatch from Marshal Kutusov announcing the defeat of Buonaparte at a great battle. The recompenses of the Emperor were then proclaimed. Two hundred thousand roubles (two shillings each) to Prince Kutusov: twenty-five roubles to each soldier.'[22]

The Czar's bounty to his soldiers was amply justified by their bravery but, as Wilson was later to learn, Kutusov's despatch was 'not correct, nor candid'. The battle of Borodino (7 September) had been a defeat for the Russians. During the day the French had lost 30,000 men and the Russians 40,000 and, eventually, some key Russian positions were lost. Kutusov drew the army back to a new position a thousand yards in the rear. This did not prevent him reporting that 'The enemy has in no part gained an inch of ground. Remaining at night masters of the field, so soon as I shall have recruited my troops, supplied my artillery, and augmented my forces by reinforcements from Moscow, I shall see what I can undertake against the enemy.'[23] This despatch was a piece of imaginative fiction, for Kutusov knew little of the state of his army. He had spent the day well to the rear, 'surrounded by champagne bottles and eating delicacies'. Tactical control had been left to Barclay and Bagration, who co-operated no better than might have been expected from two generals who were not on speaking terms.

On the evening of the battle Kutusov declared, 'Tomorrow I shall place myself at the head of the army and drive the enemy, without further ado, from the holy soil of Russia.'[24] Next morning he held a Council of War and proposed to withdraw towards Moscow. Bennigsen, as Chief of Staff, opposed a further retreat, an attitude very different from that which he had displayed when he had held supreme command after Eylau and Friedland. No other voice opposed the marshal. Bagration had been seriously wounded.

Although at this Council Kutusov had declared his intention of fighting another battle in the near future, he laid it down that 'The loss of Moscow does not mean the loss of Russia. I see my first duty as the preservation of the army.' He was, in fact, adopting Barclay's policy of overextending the French and, in so doing, he sacrificed the popularity he had had with his fire-eating subordinates. Robert Wilson turned against him but, more importantly, he gained the enmity of Count Rostropchin who, not long before, had been insisting on his appointment to the supreme command. Counting on Kutusov's pledge to fight another battle, Rostropchin assumed that he would have three days in which to organize the evacuation of Moscow and the destruction of the city 'by a general and municipally regulated conflagration', for which he, as governor, would give the signal by setting fire to his own two magnificent palaces. When the army retreated through Moscow without further fighting and with the French at their heels, all Rostropchin could do was to remove all the fire engines. As it happened, this was enough. Moscow caught fire without municipal regulation and, fanned by a strong wind, it burned for six days. The governor never forgave the marshal for thwarting his grand gesture.

Kutusov was right in his appreciation. He saw, as Barclay had seen, that the deeper Napoleon committed his army the more desperate their situation would become. The French army still numbered over 100,000, more than enough to win another set-piece battle, but Napoleon was 500 miles from his base and he could only reinforce his army by drawing on the forces guarding the long narrow corridor which formed his lines of communications. The Russians had lost heavily but there was no limit to the number of recruits they could raise and, as the French communications were extended, they became more and more vulnerable to attack by irregulars. Autumn was drawing on and if Napoleon could not force a decision within weeks he would be forced to choose between retreating and starving. As long as the

Russian army was in being the French could not forage widely. If he could not build up a stock of food, Napoleon could not win.

Kutusov was a poor organizer and a second-rate battle commander, but he had strategic insight and infinite determination. He showed his quality when Moscow was evacuated. Barclay recommended a retreat to Nizhni-Novgorod (Gor'kiy), 250 miles to the east. Kutusov refused to break contact. He wheeled the army south and then west, taking up a position on the river Pakra, twenty-five miles south of Moscow and covering the roads to Kaluga and Tula, the empire's two great arsenals. Behind him lay almost infinite supplies of food and recruits and it was across his front that Napoleon must march if he decided to retreat. The initiative passed to the Russians. It was several days before the French, preoccupied with the burning city, established with any certainty where their enemies had gone.

After a final dinner with the Czar, Robert Wilson left St. Petersburg on 15 September accompanied by his dragoon corporal and a Russian orderly. In the forlorn hope of restraining his wilder excesses, Cathcart had attached to him Lieutenant and Captain Lord Tyrconnell, First Guards. The Czar had attached Baron Brincken to Sir Robert as a Russian ADC, but his uniform of the Hussar Guards was still in the hands of the tailor and the baron had to follow later.

'My mode of conveyance was improved, for I now had a carriage with hind springs, which broke in some degree the violence of the wooden roads. We travelled unremittingly night and day until we reached Tver [Kalinin] a hundred and twenty wersts* from Moscow, where we heard of the fall and firing of the city.' Having to travel by side roads and keep at least thirty miles from Moscow, they 'had great difficulty in procuring horses. The weather added to our inconveniences, as the rain poured for at least three days.' They reached headquarters at Krasnoi Pakra on 22 September, having covered seven hundred miles in seven days.

Kutusov affected to be delighted to see Sir Robert and gave him a room in the headquarters mansion, 'an apartment rather

* A werst = 3,500 feet, roughly $\frac{2}{3}$ mile.

more calculated for summer than for autumn'. He also lent him two of the Czar's riding horses, while his old friend Platov 'gave me a beautiful Cossack horse, which was very acceptable'. Another general gave him four draught horses for his carriage and Prince Galitzin provided a cow to ensure his milk supply. Prince Bagration was dying of gangrene from his Borodino wound. Wilson went to his bedside and told him of the Czar's promise to continue the struggle till the French were driven from the country. 'He pressed my hand convulsively and said, "Dear general, you have made me die happy, for then Russia will assuredly not be disgraced."'[25]

Note. Wilson left two accounts of the part he played in the Russian campaign, neither of which is wholly satisfactory. The journal he kept at the time, supplemented by his letters, is to some extent restrained by his knowledge that it would almost certainly be examined by the Russian censor. He became less inhibited by this consideration as the campaign moved away from Moscow.

The second source, his *Narrative of the Events during the Invasion of Russia*, was not written until 1825 (and not published until 1860) and is tainted with hindsight. For example, in August 1812 Wilson was asserting that unless Roumiantzov was dismissed, 'the Emperor's government, nay his person, is in danger'. In 1825, knowing that Roumiantzov had remained in office until 1814, he wrote that he told the Emperor that the minister's removal was 'not a *sine qua non*'.

I have tried to steer a middle course between these two versions, checking, where possible, with other versions of Wilson's doings.

CHAPTER 7

Advance from Moscow

Napoleon had hoped that, when he reached Moscow, he would receive proposals for peace. Instead he found that his army and its communications were surrounded by a flexible cordon of Cossacks and irregulars and that a powerful Russian army was stationed, quietly menacing, twenty-five miles to the south of the city. At an early stage he had to give an order that no French force of less than 1,500 men should move on the Moscow–Smolensk road. On 27 September Robert Wilson wrote, 'Every day since we have been here, prisoners in parties of fifty, and even of a hundred, have been brought in, chiefly wounded. In five days at Krasnoi Pakra, thirteen hundred and forty two were delivered to the commandant at headquarters. Of course, many more are killed; for such is the inveteracy of the peasants that they buy prisoners of the Cossacks and *put them to death*. Two guns have been taken by the peasants; vast quantities of baggage ... and some of the [French] Guards— of whom two squadrons were taken—told me that they had been obliged to blow up a convoy of sixty powder waggons, rather than suffer them to be a prize.' Among the prisoners were seventeen Spaniards. 'I gave them seven pounds among them, as they were naked, and sent them to St. Petersburg.'[1]

When he had been in Moscow six days, Napoleon started suggesting peace talks in letters to the Czar and other members of the Imperial Household. He received no answers. Soon he would be forced to reach a decision. The French army had no winter clothing and if they attempted to stay in Moscow until the spring it would be a question of whether they froze to death before they starved. If the Russians would not make peace, the French were faced with the choice between retreat and fighting their way to the more temperate fertile Ukraine. The Russians were gaining in strength, the French army was shrinking, and unless a decisive battle could be fought in the near future, Napoleon would not have the strength to get to the Ukraine. As the Russians had shown a great reluctance to accept battle, the only rational course would be to retreat, but Napoleon would not accept the logic of the situation. A tame retreat with a much reduced army would make him the laughing-stock of Europe and bring into the open underlying disloyalties in France and among his unwilling allies. He decided to seek another battle.

In this decision he had powerful but unwitting allies in the Russian high command. Bagration was dead and Barclay was soon to resign his command, but a strong and vocal party, led by Rostropchin and Bennigsen, were demanding that a battle should be fought. Wilson, of course, supported them. Kutusov was determined to keep his army intact. He knew, as Wellington had known at Torres Vedras two years earlier, that, sooner rather than later, the French must retreat. There was no purpose in losing thousands of men in a battle which, at best, would drive the enemy to adopt a course which they would have to follow even if no battle was fought. If, on the other hand, the battle was lost, Russia would be defenceless. This attitude the fire-eaters thought defeatist. They put it about that the old marshal contemplated an agreement with the enemy.

The French cavalry found the Russian position on the Pakra on 26 September and reported that earthworks had been constructed. This suggested to Napoleon that Kutusov was prepared to make a stand and he sent two corps, with another in support, to attack the position. Kutusov instantly withdrew to a stronger position at Tarutino on the Nara river. The earthworks were Bennigsen's creation and Kutusov took no interest in them. He knew that he could safely retreat further than the French could afford to advance.

A strong rearguard under Miloradovich remained on the

Pakra. Bennigsen, as chief of staff, proposed that it should counterattack. He was dismissed from his post and Miloradovich was ordered to retire. The fire-eaters were scandalized. One evening Rostropchin, Bennigsen, and other generals, with Wilson and Tyrconnell, were bivouacked round a camp fire. 'Rostropchin prevented all sleep with his bitter complaints against Kutusov, declaring that he would never forgive the marshal.' As Miloradovich retired, he struck out at a French corps trying to creep round his flank. Wilson urged the marshal to reinforce the rearguard and strike at the French force, 'which I saw was only a parade corps'. Kutusov refused.[2]

Marshal Murat, leading the French advance, probed the Tarutino position on 4 October and there was sharp fighting. Sir Robert was with the Russian advanced posts and brought up two light guns to an enfilading position. He might have done more had he not been mistaken for a Frenchman and arrested. At the end of the day Murat retired about two miles.

Next day Napoleon resumed his diplomatic offensive. He asked Kutusov to meet one of his aides-de-camp, Count Lauriston, between the outposts of the army. Kutusov agreed but Bennigsen and the fire-eaters raised a storm, calling Wilson into their counsels. They asserted that Napoleon had proposed a convention 'for the immediate retreat of the whole invading army from the territory of Russia'. This was an invention as Napoleon had only written that Lauriston would speak '*des affaires très importantes*'. He hoped for a short truce in which he could evacuate his more seriously wounded.

Bennigsen and Rostropchin declared that Kutusov would agree to a convention and 'required' Wilson to prevent his doing so. Wilson was told of 'the resolve of the chiefs, which would be sustained by the army, not to allow Kutusov to return to the army if once he quitted it for this midnight interview. They wished to avoid extreme measures, but their minds were made up to dispossess the marshal of his authority if he should inflexibly persevere.'[3] Six weeks earlier a similar cabal had sought to put Kutusov in command of the army; now they threatened to dispossess him. In each case Wilson was their catspaw.

He felt it was 'a duty from which he could not shrink with honour'.

Sir Robert waited on the marshal, taking with him the Czar's uncle and brother-in-law and one of the imperial aides-de-camp. He put forward the mutinous proposals of the generals and threatened, on his own account, to send couriers to Constantinople, Vienna, London, and St. Petersburg to denounce the marshal's treachery. There is no record of Kutusov's thoughts on being accused of treachery by a foreign officer whose experience of command was small and unsuccessful, but he recognized the strength behind Wilson's threats and agreed to meet Lauriston only in his headquarters.

When Lauriston arrived, 'the strictest forms of etiquette were preserved'. Kutusov was accompanied by Wilson and Prince Wolkonsky, ADC to the Czar, but, after some formal greetings, Lauriston and the marshal withdrew out of earshot. Wilson could only see 'that the conversation was very animated on the part of the marshal by his gestures'. Kutusov later told him that 'Lauriston proposed a truce, saying that "Nature herself would, in a short time, oblige it." The marshal told him that he had no authority on that head. Lauriston continued, "You must not think we wish it because *our* affairs are desperate. Our armies are nearly equal in force. You, it is true, are nearer your supplies and reinforcements, but we also receive reinforcements. Perhaps you have heard that our affairs are disastrous in Spain?" "I have," said the marshal, "from Sir Robert Wilson, whom you just saw leave me, and with whom I have daily interviews."

'"General Wilson may have reasons to exaggerate our reverses. We have indeed received a check [the battle of Salamanca] by the *bêtise* of Marshal Marmont and Madrid, *en attendant*, is occupied by the English, but they will soon be driven out; everything will be retrieved in Spain by the immense forces marching thither." He then denied the burning of Moscow by the French army, adding, "It is so much at variance with the French character, that if we take London we shall not fire it." In about an hour Lauriston withdrew.'[4]

By coincidence, Marshal Murat, Napoleon's brother-in-law,

sent in a flag of truce on the same day. He complained that he had been shot at and described the circumstance as 'a breach of convention'. He was met at the outposts by Bennigsen who, considering his objections to Kutusov meeting Lauriston, showed a singular lack of discretion. No conversation of importance took place, the most significant remark being Murat's observation, '*Ce n'est pas un climat pour un roi de Naples*', but the dissidents maintained that the fact that Murat had referred to 'a breach of convention' meant that a secret convention must exist. Once again they turned to Wilson. His right leg had been trapped by an overturned droshky that morning and was badly cut and swollen, but the generals insisted that he drag himself from his bed to call on the marshal and extract from him an oath that no convention existed.[5]

Murat continued to act as if a truce had been agreed. His forward units, which were grouped round Vinkovo, kept only the most casual guard. Reluctantly Kutusov sanctioned an attack upon them. On 18 October three Russian columns advanced. One attacked the French in front while the other two tried to turn the flanks and Cossacks swarmed round Murat's rear. Unfortunately the infantry columns were composed largely of recruits and a long approach march in darkness resulted in chaos in some divisions. Wilson could use neither boot nor stirrup and his 'wounds burned like the effects of hot sealing wax', but he rode with Bennigsen on one of the flanking columns. The attack started well. Surprise was complete and Murat, woken by firing close at hand, lost all his baggage and silver plate. There was, however, an escape route still open for the French and Bennigsen sent Sir Robert to ask Kutusov for more troops. The marshal refused, seeing that if both sides sent reinforcements a major battle must develop. Murat escaped with the loss of 4,000 men killed and captured and thirty-eight guns.

Napoleon had already issued orders for the evacuation of Moscow. The battle of Vinkovo induced him to advance his timetable by twenty-four hours. On 19 October his stepson, Eugène de Beauharnais, led his Italian corps out of the city to the south-west, as the advance guard of the *Grande Armée*. Behind them streamed an endless procession of troops, 'waggons, carts, droshkys and chaises, often laden with booty. Whereas most officers owned a cart, the generals had half a dozen. Supply officers and actors, women and children, cripples, wounded men and the sick drove in and out of the throng; countless servants and maids, sutlers and that sort of person accompanied the march. . . . The great congestion of waggons and troops poured through the fields in three wide columns. Inexhaustibly they seemed to press out from the ruins of Moscow, and the heads of these columns vanished far away on the horizon.'[6]

Kutusov had been right. Napoleon had been extruded from Moscow without a battle. Wilson saw the situation differently. He believed that the marshal had been timid and dilatory. Only one incident relieved his gloom. On 18 October, the evening before the retreat started, 'the Cossack chiefs fêted me with all their luxuries, amusements, honours, &c. The enemy were not distant more than six hundred yards, and grouped to hear the music. The singers gave me their famous boat song, and the enemy having recognized my vessel, the answer to the hail was, "She is loaded with Spanish victories."'[7]

When Eugène marched out of Moscow he took the Kaluga road and the Russians assumed that it was an unusually strong foraging expedition: 15,000 men were sent against them. Wilson, although 'my leg is not yet well', rode with them expecting that they would be able to 'effect a *coup-de-main* against a corps of ten thousand Frenchmen'. While the Russians marched on an interception course, further information arrived. Eugène was being followed by heavy columns of troops. It was not until the evening of 23 October that Russian headquarters learned that Moscow had been evacuated. Meanwhile their detached corps had swung southwards and was marching parallel to Eugène, striving to reach the river Luzha before him. At Maloyaroslavets there was a position where the enemy could be delayed until the main Russian army could arrive and block their retreat.

Bad staff work slowed the Russians and their advance guard reached the town on 24 October in 'the greatest confusion'. The leading Italians were already across the Luzha but all was not lost. Two regiments of cavalry charged in Maloyaroslavets and drove the enemy back to a deep ravine leading down to the bridge. The horsemen could go no further but on a hill above the ravine was Wilson, who had 'gone upon the right flank of the town and perceived, as day dawned, a large body of the enemy descending the lofty hill on the [far] bank of the river to pass the bridge and enter the town; this dense body was flocking forward as if quite at ease and quite unconscious of any opposition being designed to the passage.' He galloped back, caught up a battery of light guns and led it 'to an elevation which he had already selected for its site, and opened its fire almost within grape-shot of the mass. At the first discharge there was a general halt, on the second a wavering, on the third a total dispersion, and every one flew forward or scrambled up the hill to get out of reach of this unexpected cannonade. The movement of the advanced guard was thus checked and nearly an hour gained before [Eugène] could arrive in person, bring up his artillery, and re-establish order: an essential hour for the Russians.'[8]

The battle for Maloyaroslavets raged throughout the day with neither side being able to consolidate a hold on the town. Other French corps closed up behind Eugène's while the French could see, to the east, dark masses moving towards them as the main Russian army approached from Tarutino. Napoleon rode up the hills on the north bank of the Luzha and watched the situation through his spy-glass. He was all but captured by a Cossack patrol. He saw that he would have to commit the whole army if he was to force the river line. It would be another Borodino but with the enemy in a stronger position. This could be the decisive battle he had sought all through the summer, but now he could not afford to accept the challenge. His first concern must be to get the army to Smolensk where there were depots of food. He had hoped to reach it by a more southerly road than that by which he had advanced, since the direct road had been swept clear of provisions and fuel. Now he gave orders to march north and regain that road.

At almost the same moment Kutusov also ordered a retreat.

The generals pressed him to throw in the whole army but he saw no point in fighting an unnecessary battle. The fire-eaters rose in their wrath and Wilson wrote, 'The Russians accuse *one person* of being deficient in example; in addition to the heavy charges which can be brought against him for ignorance in the conduct of the troops, for sloth, for indecision of counsels, for panic operations and "for a desire to let the enemy pass unmolested", Marshal Kutusov affords a memorable instance in a chief of an absence of any quality which ought to distinguish a commander.'[9]

He went so far as to remonstrate with the marshal against the retreat, and this time Kutusov had had enough of this impertinent foreigner. He replied, coldly, 'I prefer giving my enemy a *pont d'or*, as you call it, to receiving a *coup de collier*: besides, as I have told you before, I am by no means sure that the total destruction of the French emperor and his army would be such a benefit to the world; his succession would not fall to Russia or any other continental power, but to that power which already commands the seas, and whose domination would then be intolerable.'[10]

Wilson's interventions into Russian military politics were a source of great concern to Lord Cathcart in St. Petersburg. Even more, the ambassador was worried by Sir Robert's habit of writing down his impressions and posting them to England, apparently oblivious of the fact that they would be read by the Russian censor. 'His Lordship said that you seemed to be as great a dasher in your letters as with your armies, and if any of those letters had been opened it would have been very serious.'[11] At this stage Cathcart had a reluctant admiration for his unwanted Military Correspondent. One of the attachés wrote, 'Wilson, with all his faults, has certainly great merit. His lordship gives him full credit for the judgment of Buonaparte's plans. You must know that Kutusov was inclined to think that the French wanted to penetrate into the fertile southern provinces. This Wilson could not be brought to believe.... The sanguinary contest at Maloyaroslavets confirmed Kutusov in his opinion. At this Wilson lost all patience. The enemy then did what Wilson would have it they intended to do—they retreated. Thus Kutusov let them slip.'[12]

What neither Cathcart nor Wilson realized was that Kutusov was following a plan laid down, under the Czar's direction, in St. Petersburg. When Wilson had first met Alexander in 1807 he had noted that he displayed great knowledge of the geography of his empire. This he now put to good use. Traditionally the place for barring the road to Moscow or, as in this case, the road from Moscow to the frontier, was the so-called River Gate. This gap between the rivers Dvina and Dnieper, with Vitebsk to the north and Smolensk to the south, was a corridor about eighty miles wide. Although the two great rivers could be used for securing the army's flanks, it was not an ideal defensive position as there was no geographical feature across the gap on which a defence could be based. It was also the station of Napoleon's main reserve, 25,000 men under Marshal Victor. Alexander's plan called for the French to be pinned against the river Beresina, a hundred and seventy miles west of Smolensk.

The *Grande Armée* had set out on the retreat with more than 90,000 men effective in the ranks. It was falling back on more than twice that number who were guarding the flanks of their corridor. Kutusov's army had 100,000 infantry apart from cavalry and 20,000 Cossacks. Two other Russian armies could be brought into play. In the north was General Wittgenstein with the corps which had covered St. Petersburg, reinforced by men whom the treaty with Sweden had released from Finland. Wittgenstein's task was to drive in the French northern flankguard and then block the gap between the Dvina and Beresina rivers. In the south was the Third Army of the West, reinforced by men from the Danube and commanded by Admiral Tchitchagov. They were facing a large Austrian army and a corps of Saxons under the French general Reynier. The Austrians were showing little enthusiasm in support of Napoleon and their attention was to be diverted by a raid far to the south. Tchitchagov's task was to march on Brest-Litovsk, drive the Austrians and Saxons back to Warsaw, leaving a covering force to hold them in check. Then, with 30,000 men, veterans of the Turkish wars, Tchitchagov was to skirt the western side of the Pripet marshes and 'occupy Borisov and the course of the Beresina; fortify all points defensible so that the enemy, pursued by our main army, may be checked at every step in his retreat'.[13]

Kutusov's part in the plan was a passive one. He was to follow the French, harrying them as much as possible without getting involved in heavy fighting. His time would come when the enemy found their retreat blocked on the Beresina. Then the marshal would act as the hammer to the admiral's anvil.

Kutusov chose to march on a road parallel to and to the south of that used by the French, with a flankguard, 20,000 men under Miloradovich, between the main army and the enemy. The direct harassing of the enemy was entrusted to Hetman Platov and his Cossacks supported by a single division of infantry. This unspectacular parallel march did not appeal to Kutusov's bellicose subordinates or to Robert Wilson. In fact the marshal had no alternative. Feeding the Russian army was always a problem and to attempt to do so on a road already gleaned twice by the French would have destroyed Kutusov's army. As it was, the dearth of supplies was so great that his army lost half its effective strength before it reached the Beresina.

Such battle casualties as occurred were due to Miloradovich, who either did not know or did not want to know Kutusov's intentions. At every opportunity he hurled his corps at the French, causing heavy casualties on both sides. Wilson's instincts were to be where the fighting was but, for ten days after Maloyaroslavets, he stayed at headquarters, importuning Kutusov to attack the French. He made no impression. On 4 November he decided 'to wait no longer with the main army which had wearied itself with wandering: I therefore took three Cossacks and my dragoons' and, accompanied by Baron Brincken, now free of his tailor, set off to join Miloradovich. As they rode they heard gunfire ahead. Sir Robert instantly abandoned the road and set off at a gallop across country. He rode straight into a bog. 'My led horse first plunged in; and I and my own horse shared the same fate immediately afterwards: I was in a hole, many feet deep, but supported myself with my arms; with some difficulty I was extricated, but wet to the breast; the horses required more exertion and time, but they were saved.' As a consequence, he was somewhat late for the battle of Vyazma.[14]

The battle was brought on by Miloradovich's attempt to cut off the French rearguard, Davout's corps, while Platov attacked the rear. 'The French manœuvred steadily, but the Russian cavalry charged and cut down to a man several detached columns of infantry.' Davout's corps was rescued by Eugène's Italians, who turned back and counterattacked, but, just as the Frenchmen's safety was assured, their morale snapped and they ran in panic for the rear. Davout claimed that the panic had been started by 4,000 stragglers 'belonging to all the regiments of the army, who will not move with regularity; on the slightest attack on the part of the enemy they fly and endanger the steadiness of my columns.' This may have been true but it was a great shock to the French when this corps, reputed to be the steadiest in the army, broke in the face of the enemy. 'The French, obliged to give way incessantly for twelve wersts, blew up a number of powder waggons, and abandoned carriages, cars and baggage of all descriptions and all his wounded who could not walk. The route and fields were covered with their ruins.'[15] The French loss was 8,000 men that day.

For once, Wilson took no part in the fighting. As soon as he saw the situation he turned his horse and galloped back to Kutusov, begging him to join in the fight or, at least, to send 'a division of cavalry with some flying artillery [which] must embarrass the enemy, and might perhaps achieve a *coup-de-main* in his rear of influential importance. The marshal only replied "The time is not yet come."' Wilson was so angry that he demanded a courier's passport so that Baron Brincken might travel to St. Petersburg. The threat was clear. Wilson intended to tell the Czar that the marshal was betraying Russian interests. Kutusov was quite unmoved and signed the passport immediately. Sir Robert wrote in his journal, 'The conduct of the marshal makes me wild.'[16]

Vyazma marks the beginning of the disintegration of the *Grande Armée*. It was also the day, although Wilson's diary does not mention the fact, that the first snow fell. Two days later,

6 November, heavy falls set in. Up to that point the French could comfort themselves with the belief, promulgated by Napoleon, that they were making only a limited withdrawal, that they would winter at Smolensk, with its stocks of food, and, in the spring, would march on St. Petersburg and finish the war. Now they were beginning to discover what the Russian winter was like and to realize the size of the enemy forces moving against them. They heard that Wittgenstein had captured Polotsk and was across the Dvina, that Tchitchagov had taken Brest-Litovsk, that Victor's corps, on which they were retreating, had had to be sent north to prop up that flank. Above all, they heard frightful stories of the savagery of the Russian peasants.

On 13 November Wilson tried to describe the fate that was overtaking the *Grande Armée*, though he admitted that 'no pen can truly convey the image'.

The naked masses of dead and dying men; the mangled corpses of ten thousand horses, which had, in some cases, been cut for food before life had ceased, the cravings of famine at other points forming groups of *cannibals*; the air enveloped in flames and smoke; the prayers of hundreds of naked wretches, flying from the peasantry, whose shouts of vengeance echoed incessantly through the woods.

At Vyazma, fifty French, by a savage order, were buried alive; but these terrible acts were minor features with comparatively little protracted suffering. I will cite three or four of the more painful incidents that I witnessed. A number of naked men, whose backs had been frozen while they warmed the front of their bodies, sat around the burning embers of a hut. Sensible at last to the chill of the air, they had succeeded in turning round, when the fire caught the congealed flesh, and a hard burnt crust covered the whole of their backs. They were still living as I passed.

Sixty dying naked men, whose necks were laid upon a felled tree, while Russian men and women with large faggot-sticks, singing in chorus, with repeated blows struck out their brains in succession.

A group of wounded men, at the ashes of another cottage, sitting and lying over the body of their comrade which they had roasted and the flesh of which they had begun to eat.

A French woman, naked to her chemise, with black, long dishevelled hair, sitting on the snow, where she had remained the whole day, and in that situation had been delivered of a child, which had afterwards been stolen from her.[17]

Wilson's diary was sent home to his wife by instalments and was circulated among his friends. It was the first news to reach England of the disaster that had overtaken Napoleon. After two decades of French victories, many found a French defeat hard to believe. More doubted the tales of Russian atrocities. Francis Jackson wrote from Brighton, 'Sir Robert Wilson's wife, who is here, tells numberless stories from her husband's letters. But Wilson's stories are not to be received as pure gospel. He does not, I think, deliberately mis-state, but his imagination runs away with him, and his enthusiasm makes him see things in a different light to that in which more matter-of-fact minds perceive them.'[18]

His reputation was different in Russia. Francis Werry wrote from the embassy, 'the Russians tell me Wilson is in the hottest part of every action; he charges with the Cossacks, who call him brother. He gets into *mêlées*, scours the country; and at night I verily believe never sleeps, for he writes folios of despatches in which he introduces all kinds of matter. He is an astonishing fellow. By dint of lecturing, Lord Cathcart, however, keeps him in order, and he is certainly incalculably useful.'[19]

Napoleon's advance guard reached Smolensk on 8 November to find that Victor's corps had made great inroads into the stocks of food. The issue of the remaining supplies was mismanaged. The Imperial Guard, leading the retreat, were issued with rations for fourteen days. The rearguard got nothing. No guards had been mounted on the storehouses and vast quantities of food were looted; 1,000 cattle, grazing unguarded near the city, were seized by Cossacks. In the first half of November the *Grande Armée* was down to 49,000 men, half the number that had left Moscow. The Imperial Guard, which had scarcely fired a shot since entering Russia 47,000 strong, could muster only 16,000. The Polish corps was reduced to 800, the Westphalians to 700. Eugène's hard-fighting Italians still had 5,000 but they had left Poland in June with 49,000.

Nobody believed that they could winter in Smolensk. Tchitchagov was moving on Minsk and Oudinot's corps had to be despatched to secure Borisov, where the main road crosses the Beresina, before the admiral could reach it. In the north Victor could barely hold Wittgenstein on the Ulla river. If the *Grande Armée* was to escape they must move fast. Kutusov's main body was only twenty miles south of Smolensk on 13 November. On the previous day the first French divisions marched out of the city. The rearguard left on the 15th.

The French retreated in four blocks with a day's march between each. The Russians could not resist the temptation to try to destroy them in detail. Miloradovich cut the road in front of the Imperial Guard at Krasnoye on 15 November. He was brushed aside. Next day he ambushed the Italians but Eugène escaped, though with only 3,000 men. The French rearguard, 15,000 men of the corps of Ney and Davout, presented a target that even Kutusov could not resist. He announced, according to Wilson, that 'He would no longer act the part of Fabius, but draw the sword of Marcellus.' The sentiment may have been Kutusov's but the words were the words of Sir Robert.

Kutusov was not slow to realize that he had underrated the opposition. Napoleon and Eugène turned back to rescue the rearguard and, as soon as he knew that the emperor was present, Kutusov called off his attack. It was one thing to pick up two corps cheaply, quite another to risk a general action. Davout's corps escaped but Ney's was cut off. That was not the end of the matter. *Le brave des braves* set off on a circuitous route and rejoined Napoleon at Orsha, forty miles to the west. At Smolensk Ney's corps had consisted of 6,000. He reached Orsha with 900.

Wilson was bitterly angry with Kutusov for breaking off the action. 'He is *a sad old rogue, hating the English* connection, and basely preferring to independent alliance with us a servitude to the canaille who govern France and her fiefs.'[20] To Sir Robert, fighting a battle was an end in itself.

In the intervals of 'getting into *mêlées* and scouring the country', Wilson was dreaming of ways in which he could settle the affairs of Europe. 'If I were sent during the winter to Vienna, with full powers on a given basis, I am sure that not a Frenchman would be in arms in Germany by this time next year. I am not an under-taker to court a mission likely to fail, although I assign, perhaps, no solid reason for my success.' Two days later he saw himself at the head of a British corps on the Russian front. 'I have asked for twelve hundred British dragoons, six hundred chasseurs and a brigade of horse artillery for the next campaign. If the British government grants my request, I shall erect on that basis a force of some consideration. Platov alone will give me six regiments of Cossacks. Of Germans I may have any number, and such additional Russian regular forces as my object may require. Once in the field, such a force will be no insignificant feature.'[21] London's only reaction to this fantasy was to transfer him from the Twenti-eth Light Dragoons to the Twenty-Second (10 December 1812). His new regiment was serving in India and he never saw them before they were disbanded in 1818.

While Wilson was dreaming of the command of polyglot corps, the campaign moved to its climax. Tchitchagov took Minsk on 16 November, capturing a huge depot of supplies. Five days later he reached the Beresina at Borisov, beating Oudinot to the town by the narrowest of margins. As the Russians probed the east bank, the French swept down on them. Instead of fighting in a prepared position behind a river line, the admiral found himself involved in an encounter battle. His bridgehead was lost but his engineers succeeded in burning the bridge. It was six hundred yards long and there was no other that the French could use. Tchitchagov dug in and there was nothing the French could do to molest him.

The epic of the French crossing of the Beresina is not part of Wilson's story. He was with Kutusov's army, five days' march behind the French and in poor condition for fighting. Their supply was in chaos and they were no better equipped to resist the winter weather than were the enemy. Wittgenstein harried the French unmercifully but Tchitchagov's reserves were lured away to the south while the French crossed on improvised bridges at Studianka, nine miles north of Borisov. When Kutusov's men reached the river on 1 December, the French rearguard had been gone for two days, destroying their bridges behind them. Although he had been reinforced by the corps of Victor and Oudinot, Napoleon marched westward for Vilna and food with only 25,000 men, many of them unarmed. On 5 December he quitted his army and set off for Paris to raise fresh troops.

Wilson believed that Napoleon had been able to extricate 45,000 men from the Beresina trap and that, when he had collected his flanking corps, he would be able to bring 135,000 men against the Russians. This, in his opinion, made the campaign a major Russian defeat and he railed against Kutusov for not pushing his men forward faster. How the army could have marched faster he did not explain. By his own account, a greater pace would have been impossible. 'During these last marches the Russian troops, who were moving through a country devastated by the enemy, suffered nearly as much as the French did from want of food, fuel and clothing. The soldier had no additional covering for the night bivouacs on the frozen snow; and to sleep longer than half an hour was probable death. Firing could scarcely ever be obtained; and when obtained the fire could only be approached with very great caution, as it caused gangrene to the frozen parts; but as water itself froze at only three feet from the largest bivouac fire, it was almost necessary to burn before the sensation of heat could be felt. Above ninety thousand [Russians] perished. One of the chief causes of these losses was that the trowsers becoming worn by the continued marches in the inner part of the thighs exposed the flesh, so that the frost struck into it when chafed, and irritated it with virulent activity. . . . It often happened that a sentinel died at his post. The case of one soldier deserves to be mentioned: he was employed in carrying a load of wood; his hands, nipped by the frost and cleaving to the faggot, dropped from his arms.'[22]

Sir Robert did not feel the cold. 'When in the air I defied the cold for I even took off the great coat I had been accustomed to wear in order that it might be repaired, and walked about, with the thermometer at 19 degrees, in my jacket without any waistcoat.' His unfortunate dragoons 'are all chilled to the bone and I am obliged to procure them sheepskin coats'.[23]

He was 'in very low spirits indeed' when they reached Minsk

on 7 December. 'Although I got a good quarter, alas! I could find no wood for the stoves and that night and this morning I was in splendid misery. It was near ten o'clock before I could get a fire lighted in a chimney and the air was afterwards so severe that water froze at a distance of three feet from a wood blaze that in England would have scorched intolerably at twelve feet.' He was disgusted with Kutusov's continued refusal to fight a battle and 'greatly mortified' at Castlereagh's 'not noticing his services at Bucharest and Schumla and in not taking any notice of the heavy expence he is under, and of the great loss he has sustained by the exchange'.[24]

His vanity betrayed him a week later. He was riding in 'a frost of twenty degrees and a very biting wind. I had scarcely gone a werst, before a Russian carter roared out to me to stop and made the most anxious signs to me to dismount. I had no sooner done so than he filled his hands with snow and rubbed my face violently. I followed his efforts, but the frost had so deadened the nose and right cheek that very little effect was perceptible for some time, and the carter actually moaned over me as if I was his own child. At length I felt blood return, and with much pain. It was impossible for me to brave the inclement air any more that day, and I got into a calash that was passing.'[25]

On that day, 14 December, Marshal Ney, the last man of the invading army, recrossed the Niemen and left Russia. He was 'wearing a brown coat. He had a long beard. His face was black and seemed to be burnt. His eyes were red and glistening. He said "I am the rearguard of the *Grande Armée*. I fired the last shot on the bridge at Kovno [Kaunas] and threw the last of our weapons into the Niemen."' The strength of the *Grande Armée* was 400 infantry and 600 dismounted cavalry.[26]

CHAPTER 8

Disenchantment

Robert Wilson learned of the birth of his thirteenth child on 16 December 1812 and, the following day, rode into Vilna (Vilnyus) 'along a road covered with human carcasses, frozen in contortions of expiring agonies. The entrance to the town was literally choked with dead bodies of men and horses, tumbrils, guns, carts, &c, and the streets were filled with traineaus carrying off the dead that still crowded the way. . . . The dead, however, are to be envied. Yesterday I saw four men grouped together, hands and legs frozen, minds yet vigorous, and two dogs tearing at their feet.' It was not only the French and their allies who died, for the Russian army was in little better shape. The British mission lost the Earl of Tyrconnell, who died of exhaustion and was buried in Vilna, his body being escorted to the grave by two companies of the Czar's Guards. Wilson, who was chief mourner, still affected not to feel the cold. 'Since leaving Moscow I have always ridden without a rag of additional clothing other than my blue great coat, except in heavy snow, when I have put on my Cossack bourka. I confess that there is some vanity in this deviation from general practice, but it is, in its effect, beneficial.' He was prepared to admit that his quarters were chilly—'a magnificent summer palace, but a winter ice-house; no fire-place and only one stove; so that there are eighteen degrees of frost in the room where I am obliged to sit and rest at night.'[1]

On the day of Tyrconnell's funeral, 22 December, the Czar arrived in Vilna to decide on the future of the campaign. With the invader cleared from Russian soil there were many in the army, not least Prince Kutusov, who favoured halting on the frontier.

The French were unlikely to make another assault on the empire and what they did in Germany was none of Russia's business. Sir Robert, who was anxious to see the Russians march to Paris, intensified his vilification of the old marshal, accusing him of lethargy, incompetence, and cowardice. He circulated a joke, attributed to Platov, that 'it would be a good historical representation to draw his Serene Highness fast asleep in his droshky, actively pursuing Buonaparte'. In his diary he wrote, 'Had I commanded ten thousand, or I might say five thousand men, Buonaparte would never again have sat on the throne of France.'[2]

His campaign became so blatant that the Czar found it necessary to speak privately to him but, as with his other interviews with the Emperor, Wilson did not put his account of it on paper until 1825. 'On the morning of the 26th December, the anniversary of the Emperor's birthday, Alexander sent for [me] and said, "General, I have called you into my cabinet to make a painful confession; but I rely on your honour and prudence. . . . I know the marshal has done nothing he ought to have done—nothing against the enemy which he could avoid; all his successes have been *forced* on him. He has been playing some of his old Turkish tricks, but the nobility of Moscow support him, and insist on his presiding over the national glory of the war. In half an hour I must therefore (and he paused for a minute) decorate this man with the Great Order of St. George, and by doing so commit a trespass on its institutions; for it is the highest honour, and therefore the purest, of the empire. But I will not ask you to be present —I should feel too much humiliated if you were there; but I have no choice. . . . He is an old man, therefore I would have you show him suitable courtesies, and do not refuse them when offered on his part."'[3]

The accuracy of this report must be doubtful. Alexander was a strange man but it seems unlikely that he would express himself in such terms, which were suspiciously similar to the terms Wilson himself had been using, about the commander who had just liberated the empire. It is even more unlikely that he would have used them even to his favourite foreigner, a man who, as he must have known, was wildly indiscreet. Possibly something of the sort was said but, as Wilson failed to realize, the kernel of the interview was in the last sentence—a plea for Wilson to show common courtesy to Kutusov. The Czar realized that his friend's careless conversation was making the task of commanding the army even more difficult. Sir Robert failed to take the hint. That evening the marshal gave a ball in the Czar's honour. It was 'attended by about thirty ladies, several very handsome; and those who were not so had all the attractions of their country— variety, figure, taste in dress, and grace of movement.' Wilson refused to dance until the Czar 'came up twice to me and noticed my forbearance, in a manner that admitted of no longer non-compliance with his expectation ... I danced the Polonaise, Parade, Promenade and one country dance.'[4]

His lack of discretion also caused concern to Lord Cathcart, still in St. Petersburg, who repeatedly remonstrated with him about 'those letters in which political matter, and circumstances of most delicate and secret nature are intermixed with intelligence of the operations'. To make matters worse Wilson was in the habit of sending his letters by the hand of Russian officers, and 'you are aware that all officers who arrive from the army are con-ducted to Count Arakcheyev, who has orders to take charge of all the letters they bring with them. ... You must feel that it is more than an officer's commission is worth to disobey positive orders on this subject. ... Every letter that I have received from you, except the last, has been sent to me by one of the Emperor's aides-de-camp. ... In future, I must beg you, as you now belong to this mission, you will confine your publick correspondence to the transmission of the official reports of military proceedings.' Cathcart wrote to Castlereagh that 'Sir R. Wilson was very imprudent on the subject of the Commander-in-Chief. Unfor-tunately opening letters is not confined to one office and Prince Kutusov's family and friends deeply resented Sir R. Wilson's interference. It is difficult to keep Sir R. from dabbling in politicks, but I flatter myself I have given sufficient warnings against it.'[5]

His Lordship flattered himself in vain. Wilson continued to ignore the possibility of censorship. The only difference was that his private letters contained more abuse of Cathcart. He wrote to the Duke of Gloucester, the King's nephew, that 'in the British counsels at this court not only talent and energy are strangers, but even truth is proscribed, however confidentially communicated.' In his journal, which was also sent through the post, he wrote that 'In private life Lord Cathcart may be, and indeed is, an excellent gentleman and an honourable man, and in the field a good executive cavalry officer, but he has defects in his nature and habits which disqualify him from any public station in which a man is charged with high public interests. . . . [He] will not transmit any information contrary to the official state-ment of the marshal with a long name and unjustifiable fame.'[6]

Meanwhile Napoleon was supervising the assembly of a new *Grande Armée* to fight in Germany. He planned to make it 600,000 strong by anticipating the conscriptions of 1814 and 1815. His immediate weakness was in troops to hold his eastern front while the new army was mustered. His allies began to forsake him. On 30 December the Prussian general Yorck von Wartenburg, who had been besieging Riga, took his 18,000 men over to the Russian side. On 26 February 1813 the King of Prussia made a secret agreement with the Czar and, in mid-March, declared war on France. Before that time the Austrians had retired within their own frontiers and declared their neutrality. The French covering force fell back to the Elbe. Warsaw and Berlin fell to the Russians. It was 10 February when Wilson reached Warsaw, and he wrote that 'for the first time since I left St. Petersburg on the 15th September last (a hundred and fifty nights), shall I have pulled off my clothes at night, or slept in a bed.'[7] The Cossacks swarmed ahead of the Russian armies. Two hundred of them raided Ham-burg and so alarmed the French commander that he evacuated the city. Davout, ordered to recapture it, evacuated Dresden in order to have enough troops for the task.

The eastern allies were also short of troops. On 1 February Wilson wrote, without exaggeration, that 'The Russian army is reduced almost to nothing; I am sure in the whole line there are not 60,000 effectives now. One battalion of Guards musters 200 men.'[8] The Prussians were making great efforts to raise an army but, for the time being, only Yorck's 18,000 were fit for the field.

As for the third ally, Sweden, the Prince Royal was moving his troops forward with agonizing slowness while he waited to see how the campaign would go.

Napoleon planned to hold the allies on the line of the Elbe while his striking force swung round their southern flank through the Thüringer Wald. He left Paris on 14 April and set up his headquarters at Weissenfels, south-west of Leipzig, at the end of the month. He had 145,000 men in hand and was faced with only 68,000 Russians and Prussians. There had already been some inconclusive skirmishing, and Wilson wrote on 25 April that Kutusov 'has had a glimpse of the enemy, and is taken ill very opportunely. Perhaps it is a stratagem to get rid of the responsibility.' The marshal had died of typhoid on the day before Sir Robert passed this uncharitable opinion. When he heard of his death his comment was, 'He died most opportunely for his fame.'[9]

The allied command passed to Count Wittgenstein, whom Wilson described as 'this accomplished general and honest soldier. He is really a man without guile: confident but not presumptuous. ... He seems one of those enterprising, straightforward characters who by their courage and their patience extricate themselves from difficulties which would baffle, if not ruin, better tacticians.'[10] What Sir Robert meant by describing the general as enterprising and straightforward was that he was willing to bring on a battle whatever the chances of victory. On 2 May he tried to outflank a French force twice as strong as his own at Lützen and was defeated for his pains. It was a hard-fought day and Wilson was in the thick of the fighting. 'It was my good fortune, aided by Colonel [Neil] Campbell and my aides-de-camp Charles and Brincken, to rally the Prussians as they were flying from Glogau and extending panic through the Russians; to enter with them sword in hand, and carry the village, which was maintained until night.'[11]

It was a gallant exploit which resulted in Wilson being awarded the order of the Red Eagle of Prussia, but he cannot have made much contribution to allied unity if he went about repeating the comment he made in his journal. 'I was quite unhappy to see the Prussians slaughtered from mismanagement. They are fine material, but they require exactly what has been done with the Portuguese—the loan of British leaders to train their own.'[12]

After Lützen the allies retreated, leaving Dresden to the French. Napoleon's pursuit was much hampered by his shortage of cavalry, but on 19 May he attacked his enemies at Bautzen. It was another bitterly contested battle in which the French lost more than 13,000 men, making their losses more than 40,000 during the month. The allies, whose losses were even heavier, retreated in fairly good order leaving Breslau (Wroclaw) to Napoleon.

At Bautzen Wilson secured a height which he described as the key to the position of the advance guard by bringing up a Russian battalion and battery which had begun to retire. 'We advanced at the head, caps in hand, and accompanied with loud cheers. The enemy fell back, but again we were obliged to retire by fresh succours sustaining the fugitives. Again and again we rallied and charged; and finding about forty Prussian lancers, we dashed in among the enemy's infantry, while our own pressed forward to help our inferiority. The enemy threw their fire upon us before they gave way, and in flying singed us; but we were revenged.'[13]

This exploit brought Wilson another honour. On 27 May the Czar 'ordered a grand review of the troops in camp near Jauer. His Imperial Majesty went along the line, and was received with enthusiasm by the soldiers. Observing a favourable moment when he was surrounded by his generals and staff officers, and in front of the troops, his Imperial Majesty called Sir Robert Wilson to him, and addressed him in the following gracious speech: "Sir Robert, I have duly appreciated the services, gallantry and zeal which have distinguished you throughout the war: in testimony of which I have determined to confer on you the third class of the Order of St. George;" and then, as if desirous of doing it in the most gratifying manner, the Emperor directed General Augerausky to take the cross from his neck, and he delivered it to Sir Robert Wilson.'[14]

The pleasure Wilson derived from receiving this promotion (he had received the fourth class of the order in 1807) was lessened by the presence of the man who wrote that description of the scene. This was Major-General the Hon. Sir Charles Stewart, who had been appointed Minister and Military Commissioner to the Prussian court. He had many advantages over Sir Robert. He was a year younger and a rank senior. He was Castlereagh's half-brother and had spent three years as Wellington's Adjutant General in the Peninsula. He was partially blind from a wound, had a defect in his hearing, and Sir John Moore had declared that he was 'a very silly fellow'. Wellington liked him but did not think highly of his brains, remarking that 'Castlereagh had a real respect for Charles's understanding, and a high opinion of his good sense and discretion. This seems incomprehensible to us, who knew the two men, but the fact was so.'[15]

Stewart and Wilson were friends but they were too alike to work successfully together. Both men had abundant charm, both had the same nonchalant bravery, both had inordinate confidence in their capacities as field commanders, and both preferred a dashing career in the field to the hard grind of staff-work. At the beginning of 1813 Wellington had written to Sir Charles, 'although it might be more agreeable to you to take a gallop with the hussars, I think you had better return to your office.'[16] It was obvious to Wilson that there was only room for one *beau-sabreur* among the British officers on the eastern front and that Stewart had more advantages with which to sustain the role.

Making the best of the position, Wilson appealed to Stewart to rescue him from Cathcart's increasingly irksome control and to attach him to his own staff. 'This arrangement would be advantageous to all parties, but personally it would terminate a very unpleasant situation in which I now find myself.' This request embarrassed Stewart, who sent a friendly but non-committal answer to Wilson and wrote to Castlereagh, 'I have been attacked already by my friend Wilson. I believe that Cathcart and he have had many differences; but Wilson does not give me a great proof of friendship by asking me, *immediately* on my arrival to separate him from Cathcart, who must take such a measure on my part extremely ill. I shall throw complete cold water on this application.'[17]

The defeat at Bautzen had thrown the allied command into disarray. The Prussians wished to concentrate for the defence of Berlin; the Russian generals favoured a retreat into Poland. Wittgenstein was removed from the chief command and the succession was in dispute between those discarded warhorses Bennigsen and Barclay de Tolly. The alliance was on the point of collapse when it was rescued by Napoleon. On 1 June he proposed an armistice which was agreed three days later and lasted, having been extended once, until the middle of August. His explanation was that 'my lack of cavalry prevents me from striking decisive blows and Austria is adopting a hostile attitude'.[18] It was, apart from his invasions of Spain and Russia, the worst mistake he ever made.

The whole future of the eastern alliance now hung on the attitude of Austria. Wilson was confident that she would remain neutral and mocked Cathcart's more hopeful view. 'He still sees the Austrian army with the *feldzeug*, or laurel-sprig, in their caps, descending from the Bohemian mountains, and forcing with their bayonets the boundaries of the French empire. So did he dream on the very day on which the armistice was signed. I shall leave the British ambassador to his dreams.' On 24 July Wilson was even more convinced that Austria would not be a belligerent. On 11 August he wrote, 'There is not one person—Russian, Prussian, or English—who is not satisfied (Lord Cathcart only excepted) that Austria never seriously intended war.'[19]

On the following day Austria declared war against France. The supreme command of the allied armies was given to the Austrian Prince von Schwarzenberg. He was not a great general but he was an excellent co-ordinator, an essential qualification as he had not only to persuade three national army commanders to conform to his plans but to suffer the presence of the Emperors of Austria and Russia and the King of Prussia at his headquarters. After the war Blücher toasted him as 'the Commander-in-Chief who had three monarchs at his headquarters and still managed to win the war'.[20]

Charles Stewart suggested that Wilson should be attached to the Austrian army. Cathcart reluctantly agreed since he had no alternative. A senior officer had to be sent to Schwarzenberg's headquarters and Sir Robert, who had been promoted, by seniority, to major-general during the armistice, was the only one available.

In the renewed war the allies had a numerical advantage. Napoleon could deploy 373,000 men in Germany. The combined armies of Austria, Prussia, Russia, and Sweden could put 435,000 men in the field. They planned to use their main striking force to capture Dresden, which the French had turned into a fortified camp. Napoleon drove them away and inflicted 25,000 casualties on them; Schwarzenberg led them on a hazardous retreat through the Erzgebirge. But the subordinate French commanders suffered a series of heavy defeats. Oudinot was defeated at Gross-Beeren; Macdonald was routed on the Katzbach river; Vandamme's corps was almost destroyed at Kulm (Chlumec); the Prussians overwhelmed Ney at Dennewitz. By the second week in September the French had lost 75,000 men and 250 guns. Napoleon, after some hesitation, decided to retire on Leipzig. The allies followed slowly without giving any appearance of unified direction. Believing that his homogeneous army would be able to defeat his unco-ordinated opponents, Napoleon decided to stand and fight a decisive battle at Leipzig in mid-October.

When the allies had attacked Dresden, Wilson 'remembered what I owed to Austria, England and myself' and, when the Austrian stormers were reluctant to leap over the parapet of a redoubt, 'I dismounted, climbed the palisades, with extreme difficulty reached the crest of the parapet, sprang on it, took off my cap and gave three cheers. . . . My cheers were answered by all around me of all ranks, and instantly hundreds mounted and manned the redoubt.' At Kulm, 'I was enabled to lead a charge with several squadrons of Austrian cavalry, into the flank of the enemy on retreat.' Almost more to his satisfaction was a chance to escape from Lord Cathcart. On 2 September a newly appointed British ambassador to Austria reached allied headquarters at Töplitz.

The new envoy was George Hamilton Gordon, 4th Earl of Aberdeen, later to become the least memorable prime minister of the nineteenth century. His qualifications for his new post were that, being an orphan, he had been brought up in the household of William Pitt, and he was president of the Society of Antiquaries. His diplomatic experience consisted of refusing the embassy to Sicily in 1807 and that in St. Petersburg in 1809. He had been persuaded to take the post in Vienna because his wife had recently died and his friends were unanimous in thinking that some occupation might take his mind from his grief. Metternich called him 'the dear simpleton of diplomacy' but Mrs. Arbuthnot was to say that he was 'more pompous than wise'. Henry Fox wrote that he 'never opens his mouth but to contradict sarcastically and insolently'.[21]

Robert Wilson deployed his considerable charm to captivate the twenty-nine-year-old earl and to bring him to the view that he, Wilson, should be attached to his embassy as an independent military commissioner. Realizing that Aberdeen was susceptible to flattery, he wrote to him on 5 October, 'I find Metternich is really a very sincere admirer of yours. He says . . . that there is a frankness, purity and desire to embrace the general interests in your views which he has never met with before.'[22] He may well have been reporting the Austrian chief minister correctly. Prince Metternich had his own designs on the 'dear simpleton' and saw him as a means of changing British policy to suit Austrian interests.

Aberdeen, who had dressed himself in the red coat of the colonel of militia which he had once been, was plied with prophecies on the forthcoming actions. As 300,000 allies closed round 190,000 French, Wilson foretold disaster. On 10 October he wrote, 'Be assured that Buonaparte has great means as well as great skill. . . . I would rather be in his position than ours.' He was slightly more optimistic on the following day. 'We may beat the enemy, but it will not be with his tail towards the kennel of France.' On the 12th the earl was told, 'The more I see of Buonaparte, the more I calculate his means, so much the more am I convinced that we shall be wrong in fighting a general action.' Two days later, 'You will never keep the coalesced armies together', and on the 15th, the day before the battle started, 'I have never been an advocate of the enterprise. . . . If I had commanded I would have forborne from action.'[23]

Napoleon was completely defeated at Leipzig. The battle lasted three days and on 18 October Napoleon broke free with only 100,000 men, forcing his way to the Rhine. The allies had 47,000 casualties but their booty included 15,000 prisoners, 325 guns, and 900 ammunition waggons. They had also, apart from some isolated garrisons, liberated Germany.

Wilson's part in the battle is obscure, though it cannot be doubted that it was both active and gallant. Writing a month later, Lord Aberdeen said, 'His services in the field have been most conspicuous; on the 16th at Leipzig, the day was saved by the brilliant conduct of the Austrian cavalry under Nostitz, which Schwarzenberg declares to be chiefly owing to the intelligence and able dispositions of Wilson.'[24] The background to this incident appears in neither the account of Charles Stewart nor in Wilson's journal. Certainly he did not believe in the completeness of the victory and told Lord Grey that the French loss 'has been much exaggerated' and that Napoleon had retired across the Rhine 'with 80,000 effectives, independent of Kellermann's corps and the stragglers which might be expected to join them'.[25] The fact was that only 56,000 exhausted and for the most part unarmed men completed the retreat into France.

During the battle Napoleon had sent a captured general to the allies with suggestions that he was prepared to discuss peace. Metternich ignored the proposal at the time but three weeks later he took it up on the basis that France should retire behind her natural frontiers. Aberdeen agreed to this basis although he knew it was contrary to his instructions. France's natural frontier on the east was the Rhine and almost the only constant point in British war aims since 1793 was that Belgium and, in particular, Antwerp should not be in French hands. The ambassador's agreement had partially been the result of his revulsion from war after seeing the battlefield at Leipzig. Another reason was the flattering attentions of Metternich, of whom he wrote to Castlereagh, 'Do not think [him] such a formidable person. Depend upon it, I have the most substantial reasons for knowing that he is heart and soul with us.' The third factor was the advice of Wilson who, as soon as he heard of the French proposals, wrote, 'I have no hesitation in giving my vote for peace on the terms Buonaparte offers.'[26]

Aberdeen's gullibility almost cost him his embassy. It certainly cost Wilson any chance he may have had of obtaining 'an independent situation'. His chances were in any case small since a Military Commissioner had already been appointed in London. This was Lieutenant-Colonel Lord Burghersh, who had been Aberdeen's contemporary at Harrow. Although he was junior to Wilson, everything else was in his favour. His father, Lord Westmoreland, was in the government, having been, with one short break, Lord Privy Seal since 1797. Burghersh had sat in the House of Commons, as a government supporter, since 1806, although he had taken time from his parliamentary duties to serve for two years in Sicily. More recently he had spent two years in the Peninsula being, for some of that time, ADC to Wellington. That general's stock was high at allied headquarters since the news had arrived of his victory at Vitoria which ended the Bonaparte kingdom of Spain. Any connection of Wellington's was highly regarded, and Burghersh had not only been his ADC but had married his niece, Priscilla Wellesley Pole, who accompanied him to Germany. He was a talented amateur musician who, ten years after Leipzig, was to found the Royal Academy of Music, but his prime virtue was that he was wholly dependable. He was as brave and charming as Wilson but without Sir Robert's penchant for intrigue.

Aberdeen was anxious to continue to enjoy Wilson's advice and suggested that Burghersh should be sent to the subsidiary theatre of Italy where French and Austrian armies faced each other in total immobility. He pressed this view on Castlereagh. 'Schwarzenberg and Metternich have frequently spoken to me on this subject; the first has written to me in the most pressing manner, the latter has told me that he has it in command from the Emperor to express his sense of the great services of Wilson, and to state his wishes that he should continue to serve with the army.... From [Wilson's] intimate knowledge of the Russian and Prussian armies, and the great respect invariably shown to him by the Emperor of Russia and the King of Prussia, he is able to do a thousand things which no one else could. . . . I am perfectly persuaded that there is no man in existence who unites in the fourth part of the degree, the love and admiration of the three armies.'[27]

Cathcart disagreed and wrote to the Foreign Secretary that Sir Robert 'has exerted himself in every way, and not very prudently, to obtain the appointment at the headquarters of the Austrian army, and in this view has completely gained the confidence of Lord Aberdeen, having persuaded him that he can govern the Commander-in-Chief and the headquarters at least of the other allies. . . . His intrigues in a lower rank would be ridiculous because they are very little concealed, but in his rank and with reference to mine, they are highly indecent. His distinguished conduct in the field and his good qualitys gain him the affection of everybody, and mine in particular, but when his inclination to intrigue and party leads him to interfere with the service, I am compelled to check it because it may go to dangerous lengths. . . . It is well known that he would readily carry an order to the mouths of the enemy's batterys, but it will be as readily believed that he will guide Prince Metternich in conducting the administration of the Austrian government as that he will influence the military plans of the Austrian generals. I have reason to think that he has asked a great person [the Austrian Emperor] to have him kept at headquarters. There are also reasons for thinking that such a request would not be wholly disregarded.'[28]

Castlereagh settled the matter brusquely by writing to Aberdeen, 'If Sir Robert Wilson has the confidence of all other countries, he wants that of his own.'[29] Wilson was to go to Italy without further argument. He set out at the New Year, solaced by promotion in the Order of Maria Theresa, the Russian campaign medal for 1812, and an effusive letter from Schwarzenberg.

Sir Robert reached Austrian headquarters at Vicenza on 14 January 1814. Marshal Bellegarde, he said, received him as a brother and at first his situation seemed tolerable. 'The more I see of the marshal, the more I esteem him. All about him are of good *ton*, and every Austrian who presents himself but augments the number of my well-wishers.' The opera at Vicenza 'is tolerable. The music when the trumpet joins is exquisite.' The ballet was more questionable. He admitted that it was 'marvellous [but] a naked Pict would, I am sure, blush at the exhibition. The finest gauze, with a few silver spangles on it, alone covers any part of the person. And what portion? One inch above the ceinture, and six below. When in motion, the whole collects into the breadth of a ribbon.' Three weeks later, at Verona, he was complaining that 'all the performers had mammoth legs'.[30]

Despite the ballet and the good *ton*, Wilson was bitter: 'I cannot obliterate recollections, or forget that I am removed from a field where I had some personal influence in the great interests of the world. I avoid, nevertheless, as much as possible, these recollections for they exasperate me and make me feel violently, until I am sometimes tempted to act violently.' The main object of his bitterness was Lord Castlereagh who had arrived at Imperial headquarters a few days after Wilson left them. 'It is fortunate I did not wait the arrival of a certain person. I never could have brooked that presence.'[31]

The war in Italy was at a very complicated stage. Four armed protagonists were in the field. Bellegarde and Eugène Beauharnais, Napoleon's Viceroy of Italy, faced each other across the Mincio river, but to the south was King Joachim of Naples, better known as Marshal Murat and Napoleon's brother-in-law. On the day before Wilson reached Vicenza, Austria had made a treaty with Murat, recognizing his kingdom of Naples in return for his armed assistance against Eugène. Lord Aberdeen had agreed to the recognition but this made very difficult the task of the fourth protagonist, Lord William Bentinck, who was still ambassador to Sicily and commander of the British troops on the island. London had agreed that he might conclude an armistice with Murat but forbade him to recognize his kingship. Such recognition would have been, in any case, difficult for him to concede since Lord William was accredited to King Ferdinand of Naples and Sicily, who was in no doubt who was King of Naples. Bentinck's refusal to recognize Murat naturally offended the marshal but also upset Bellegarde, who had grounds for believing that the British were betraying their Austrian alliance.

Lord William had a difficult hand to play and he added every complication that he could devise. On 10 March he disembarked at Livorno with a mixed force of British, German, Sicilian, and Neapolitan troops. Not only did he land wearing the red cockade of the Neapolitan Bourbons but he permitted one of his Neapolitan battalions to carry on its colours the slogan 'Italian Unity'. He thus succeeded in giving the maximum of offence to Murat and to the Austrians who were, with British approval, seeking to restore their dominion over northern Italy. As Wilson remarked, 'Austria may say "Defend me from my friends, and against my enemies I will defend myself." Austria will always believe that we landed to declare war against Murat, or we should not have disembarked Neapolitans.'[32]

Sir Robert managed to be present at what little fighting was going on. On 8 February 1814 Bellegarde made a half-hearted attempt to cross the Mincio at Vallegio, and Wilson's habit of snatching up whatever troops happened to be nearby and leading them into battle almost proved his undoing. 'Two orderlies and myself went forward to head, as I thought, some Austrian *tirailleurs*, that I might dislodge the enemy's right from a house. The *tirailleurs* ran as I approached, and we all went on together until we came upon the reserve mass. It was then that I saw the French eagles in their caps. I called out to the orderlies, who were a little behind, to save themselves. All endeavoured to catch at me. The officers cried out "Surrender!", others cried "Fire!" and in the confusion I wheeled round, clapped spurs to my horse and ran the gauntlet. The shot flew like hail and the falling sticks of the mulberry-trees covered me and my horse, but contributed to his panic and speed. The Austrians, when I rejoined the line, did not believe it was myself.'[33]

Bentinck employed Wilson to negotiate with Murat, believing, no doubt, that they were birds of a feather. Against his will Sir Robert came to admire the marshal-king. 'His dress is singular. Hair curled in Roman coiffure—two ringlets dependent on each shoulder. Blue uniform coat, red pantaloons, yellow shoes with spurs; sword with three pictures in the handle. His countenance martial, his manners soft, his conversation easy and intelligent. We had more than an hour's very interesting conversation on past military events, particularly those relating to the Russian campaign.... In the evening I was at the dinner table with Murat. The banquet was according to all the rules of perfect gastronomy. The master's manner was very gracious. It was impossible for Lord Chesterfield to have done the honours better.'[34] Wilson was soon convinced that 'Murat's case is a very good one'.

As reports came in from the main front, now on the French side of the Rhine, Wilson selected the most depressing items and recorded them in his journal. Time and again he noted that Blücher had been defeated and, on 9 February, he wrote that Wellington had been 'obliged to fall back on St. Jean-de-Luz', a piece of information which, if it had any basis in fact, must have referred to the early hours of the battle of the Nive two months earlier. When he heard that the eastern allies proposed to march on Paris his pessimism knew no bounds. 'I deny the power to get there.... Although the allies are within sight of the capital, I do persist that the expedition will end in disgrace and disaster. ... The Leipzig manoeuvres succeeded because the [French] line of communication was weak and extensive; but it is madness to repeat the experiment against Paris, where all is reversed.'[35]

The allies entered Paris on the last day of March and, a few days later, Napoleon was exiled as Emperor of Elba. From that moment Wilson became a Bonapartist partisan. Napoleon's 'conception of the French Empire, his conquest of every capital in Europe, are lofty memorials, but his intention to re-establish Poland, with the creation and nurture of the kingdom of Italy, are magnificent traits of policy and intelligence which will secure him immortality, and prevent his offences and faults from being dwelt upon by future generations.'[36]

He urged the Foreign Office to embrace the cause of Italian independence. 'Independence is the unequivocal demand of the men of letters, the army and the people.' He told Lord Grey that 'The political existence of Italy must be preserved if we wish to avoid a long series of sanguinary calamities. No power can suppress the action of that will, supported by the zeal, the talents and the courage of the Italians. This is not the age when the partial interest of thrones can be preferred to the justifiable pretensions of the multitude.'[37] It seems that the machinations of his friends the Emperors of Austria and Russia had, in his opinion, little to do with the fact that Italy and Poland were not to be independent kingdoms when peace was made. It was the malign influence of the British government, of Castlereagh in particular, that was thwarting the 'justifiable pretensions of the multitude'. 'I feel that I ought not to serve such a government as ours, especially after the affront of my removal from the grand army.'[38]

Two months after the war ended he started for home, meeting Castlereagh's letter of recall on the road. In France he called on the Czar, who was returning from a visit to England. He was pleased to find that Alexander shared his own poor opinion of the British government, and wrote to Grey that if the Czar's 'sense of the national worth of England did not surmount his prejudices against its government, I should much fear that his future policy would be rather at variance than in unison with British objects'. Wilson was not to know that Grey had met Alexander in London and had thought him 'a vain silly fellow ... but quite royal in having all the talk to himself, and of vulgar manners'.[39]

Wilson's impression of Paris was no more favourable than that he had formed thirteen years earlier. 'I entered Paris without respect; I shall quit it, I am confident, with contempt.' An English-woman who met him in the city wrote that he seemed 'very good-humoured, but such a decided Englishman, and so loaded with prejudice, I wonder why he leaves England. When I spoke of the grandeur of Paris, he said he did not know; the generality of the streets were so narrow and dirty, that he should think more of *Swallow Street* ever after.'[40]

When he reached England at the end of July he found his financial position greatly straitened. His pay as a major-general on the staff and his allowance of £1,000 a year from the Foreign Office had ended with his recall. He was not even still lieutenant-colonel of the Twenty-Second Light ,Dragoons as an overdue reform had established that general officers should be paid as such even when not on the staff but that, in return, they should surrender their regimental rank. As a major-general he would, in the future, receive twenty-five shillings a day. In place of his regimental commission he was given an unattached commission as lieutenant-colonel which could be sold when he retired. Legally this was a just settlement but he felt aggrieved since, regulations notwithstanding, a regimental commission would sell for more than one that was unattached.

He was even more aggrieved by the reorganization of the Order of the Bath. Several officers junior to him became Knights Commander but, owing to the way the new statutes had been framed, Wilson was not eligible. Neil Campbell met him 'grumbling at not being included in the K.C.B. and openly expressing his resolution never to serve again. No officer can receive this order unless he has received at least *five* medals.'[41] Wilson had been awarded only one British medal, and that he had refused to accept (see p. 88). He petitioned the Duke of York for an exception to be made in his case but the Duke replied that while he 'was impressed by the merits of your zealous and distinguished services . . . [he] had to regret that the principle of limitation under which the Order of the Bath has been extended did not admit of your name being included as this limited time did not embrace a period when you were materially employed with the British army.' Undeterred, Sir Robert asked the Duke to recommend him to the Prince Regent for the colonelcy of a regiment of cavalry. This was an optimistic request even for a man of Wilson's self-esteem. He was a major-general of one year's standing and it was rare even for a lieutenant-general to be given a colonelcy of cavalry. The Duke replied that he would be most happy to bring his name under the Prince Regent's consideration.[42]

In mid-March 1815 news reached London that Bonaparte had escaped from Elba. Wilson scarcely disguised his pleasure and told Greville 'that the Parisians were delighted at the return of Napoleon, and great satisfaction and gaiety prevailed'. He returned to his self-appointed task as military adviser to the

Opposition, and on 7 June Neil Campbell, the man who allowed Napoleon to escape, saw him in the lobby of the House of Lords 'prompt Lord Grey during one of his speeches, and upon his returning again his lordship asked for Sir Robert's despatches [to be laid before the House]'.[43]

No call came for Sir Robert to join the allied army assembling under Wellington to defend Brussels. He spent his evenings among his Whig cronies at Brooks's. He was there on the evening of 21 June and 'demonstrated satisfactorily to a crowded audience that Boney had 200,000 men across the Sambre and he must then be in Brussels. He read a letter announcing that the English were defiling out of the town by the Antwerp Gate: when the shouts in the street drew us to the window, and we saw the chaise and the eagles.'[44]

Outside in St. James's Street, Major the Hon. Henry Percy was taking despatches to the Prince Regent, who was attending a ball at 16 St. James's Square. His hostess remembered how 'the first quadrille was in the act of forming, and the Prince was walking to the dais on which his seat was placed, when I saw every one without the slightest sense of decorum rushing to the windows, which had been left wide open because of the extreme sultriness of the weather. The music ceased and the dance was stopped; for we heard nothing but the vociferous shouts of an enormous mob who had just entered the square, and were running by the side of a post-chaise and four, out of whose windows were hanging three nasty French eagles. In a second the door of the carriage was flung open and, without waiting for the steps to be let down, out sprang Henry Percy—such a dusty figure—with a flag in each hand—pushing aside every one who happened to be in his way, darting up stairs, into the ballroom, stepping hastily up to the Regent, dropping on one knee, laying the flags at his feet, and pronouncing the words "Victory, Sir! Victory!"'[45]

Waterloo had been won; Mrs. Boehm's ball had been ruined but Sir Robert Wilson retained his belief in his own gift of prophecy. Less than a month after Waterloo he wrote to Lord Grey, 'If Buonaparte survives a few years, he will see his triumph in the re-establishment of his dynasty.'[46]

CHAPTER 9

Errant Knight

Although Wilson had left Paris with contempt, he could not keep away from the city. At the end of the year Hobhouse saw him dining there with two Poles and Lord Byron, and a year later he was back with his wife and eldest daughter, announcing that 'I am going to lead a philosopher's life and devote myself to the occupations or idle habits of retirement. I am sure that metaphysicks are less wild than politicks.' None of his friends was deceived and Lord Hutchinson wrote, 'I do not see what business you have in Paris. You will get yourself into some scrape or other.'[1]

Hutchinson was right. Sir Robert had hardly reached Paris before he threw himself into the campaign to secure a pardon for Marshal Ney who, having betrayed Louis XVIII during the Hundred Days, was tried by his peers and shot on 7 December. Sir Robert's ally in this campaign was the twenty-eight-year-old Michael Bruce, the wastrel son of a banker. He had spent the war years in travel, including a long spell as the lover of Lady Hester Stanhope. He had been in France during the Hundred Days, leading a busy social life including a flirtation, or possibly a more intimate relationship, with Madame la Maréchale Ney. An opinionated young man, his politics were a combination of a muddled idealism and a passionate conviction in the correctness of his own ideas. Neither he nor Wilson bothered to conceal their low opinion of the government of the restored Bourbons and their activities became the object of constant, if inexpert, police supervision.

The two became interested in another object of restoration

vengeance. This was Antoine-Marie, Comte de Lavallette, a long-standing friend of Napoleon who had been Postmaster General during the Empire. Unlike Ney, he had betrayed no one and had gone into retirement during the first restoration and resumed his post during the Hundred Days. The death sentence pronounced against him was widely unpopular and it was said that King Louis would gladly have pardoned him had it not been for the opposition of his reactionary supporters. On 21 December 1815, the eve of the date set for his execution, Lavallette escaped from prison by changing clothes with his wife and walking out on the gaoler's arm. Paris was combed for him but no trace was found as he had taken refuge in the Ministry of Foreign Affairs.

Once his friends had accommodated him in this unlikely sanctuary, they could think of no way of smuggling him out of the country. One of them turned for help to Michael Bruce, and he called in Wilson. Sir Robert embraced the idea with enthusiasm and, said Lavallette, 'made quite a military operation out of the business'. He decided that the fugitive should be dressed as a British officer and cross the Belgian frontier by the Valenciennes road, one much used by the British army. Bruce, being a civilian, could do little to help with this plan beyond paying the expenses, and a third conspirator had to be enlisted. Their choice fell on Lieutenant and Captain John Hely-Hutchinson, First Guards, who was on the staff of the army of occupation. A nephew of Wilson's old friend, Lord Hutchinson, he was an idle, easy-going man of twenty-six. He took little interest in politics but was, according to Bruce, 'the best-natured man in the world and always ready to do a generous action'. A story was current, probably without foundation, that he was the lover of Lavallette's sister.[2]

Wilson applied to the British embassy for two passports. One of these was in the name of Major-General Lewis Wallis, Wilson's brother-in-law, the second husband of Frances Bosville, and a half-pay officer of long standing. The other was made out for a Colonel Lestock, a name chosen, said Wilson, because it was 'not preceded by Christian names'. The ambassador, Sir Charles Stuart, was an old friend of Sir Robert's and granted the passports

without question, but at the Ministry of Foreign Affairs, where
the documents had to be countersigned, a secretary asked who the
colonel was. He was satisfied with the information that he was
the father of Admiral Lestock.

An apartment in the Rue de Helder was rented in the name of
Colonel Lestock and Hely-Hutchinson was installed as the tenant.
As soon as he was in residence, a message was smuggled to Lavallette telling him that he should wear 'no moustaches and an
English wig; my beard to be shaved very clean after the manner of
the officers of that nation'. At 8 p.m., dressed in the grey-blue
great coat of the Guards and 'with boots several sizes too large so
that I could hardly walk in them', he left the Ministry and drove
in a *fiacre* to the Rue de Helder. It was well for his peace of mind
that he did not know that the judge who had presided at his trial
lived on the second floor, but Wilson thought that he was 'sufficiently disguised to pass without remark in the apartment of an
Englishman'.

'When I reached the first floor, I saw before me a tall gentleman
with noble features: it was Sir Robert Wilson. He introduced
me to two persons who were expecting me in the parlour;
one of whom I recognized as Mr. Bruce whom I had occasionally
met in the previous winter. Mr. Hutchinson, to whom the apartment belonged, was a captain in the English Guards. He received
me in a friendly fashion and we seated ourselves round a bowl of
punch. Our conversation turned on public affairs and we talked
with as much ease and freedom as if we had been in London.
After sitting for about an hour Sir Robert and Mr. Bruce rose
and the former, taking me by the hand, said "Be up tomorrow
by six o'clock, and be very careful about your dress. You will
find here the coat of a captain of the Guards which you must put
on. At eight o'clock precisely I shall expect you at the door."'

Next morning Lavallette went down to the street in Guards
uniform and concealing a pair of double-barrelled pistols. He
'found Sir Robert in full dress, seated in a very pretty gig. Mr.
Hutchinson soon appeared on horseback, and we set off', Hutchinson riding close to Lavallette's side of the gig so as to conceal
him as much as possible. Behind rode Wilson's servant with a led

mare. It was Sir Robert's intention that 'in case of any embarrassment, we should mount these horses in order that we might act
more freely and gain in expedition'.

The first, and most hazardous, part of the operation was to
pass the barrier at Clichy where their passports had to be examined.
Lavallette remembered that 'as I was wearing the regimentals and
cap of the Guards, the English soldiers we met saluted us. Two
officers we saw on the road appeared much surprised at seeing
Sir Robert with one of their comrades they did not know, but
Mr. Hutchinson went up to them and talked to them as we were
approaching the barrier.' Wilson wrote that 'I passed the barrier
at a moderate pace; the gendarmes looked earnestly at us but the
presenting of arms gave Lavallette the opportunity of covering
his face while returning the salute. When we got through the
barrier, Lavallette pressed his leg against mine, and when we
were out of reach of observation his whole countenance appeared
enlightened by this first favour of fortune.'

While the horses were fed and watered at La Chapelle, the
passengers had to alight as it would have drawn attention had
they stayed sitting in the gig. 'When we approached the inn we
saw four gendarmes standing in front of the door. Sir Robert
went up to them: they separated to let us pass and Mr. Hutchinson got into conversation with them to divert their attention.'
Back in the gig, Wilson 'observed some grey hairs projecting
from under the brown wig worn by Lavallette. Fortunately I
had scissars with me and I performed the part of his *friseur* on the
road.'

Compiègne was the next staging post and there they were
entertained by Ensign John Fennell, ADC to General Brisbane.
Fennell did not know the identity of his mysterious guest and
was somewhat reluctant to assist since 'his existence depended
on preserving his situation'. Wilson had some doubts about
involving the young man in the affair, 'but the case was too important to stop at that consideration, and I encouraged the hope
that a day would arrive when it might be possible for me to
acknowledge this service'.

The gig was abandoned at Compiègne and the travellers

changed into Sir Robert's coach which had left Paris empty on another road to divert suspicion. 'I caused the lamps to be lit, as well to show the road, as to make it appear that we were under no apprehensions; and having taken leave of our friends, we set out, well armed, and prepared to make resistance if we experienced any obstacles.' There was no need for pistols but there was an anxious moment at Valenciennes, the last town before the frontier. They reached it at 7 a.m. and 'the postmaster told us to go and have our passports examined by the captain of gendarmerie. "You forgot, I suppose, to read who we were," said Sir Robert calmly. "Let the captain come here if he chooses to see us." The postmaster felt how wrongly he had acted and, taking our passports, he went himself to get them signed. As it was a very long time before he came back, I began to be tormented by anxiety. Suppose the officer came to verify the signatures and to apprehend me. Fortunately the weather was very cold, it was scarcely daylight and the officer signed the passports without getting out of bed.

'At last, we reached the frontier. I was saved! I pressed the hand of Sir Robert and expressed to him, with deep gravity, the extent of my gratitude. But he, keeping up his gravity, only smiled without answering me. About half an hour later he turned to me and said, in the most serious tone possible, "Now, pray tell me, my dear friend, why did you not like to be guillotined?" I stared at him in amazement and made no reply. "Yes," he continued, "they say that you had solicited as a favour that you might be shot."'

Sir Robert left Lavallette at Mons and drove rapidly back to Paris, reaching the capital sixty hours after he had left it.[3]

Lavallette's escape was a blow to the prestige of the Bourbon government but it was not a serious blow. It may well have come as a relief to the King and some of his ministers that an internationally unpopular death sentence did not have to be carried out. It is hardly credible that the Ministry of Police would not have a shrewd idea of how the escape was managed and who was responsible. However, to search for proof would risk a useless diplomatic embarrassment and the government was content to let the matter lie.

They had reckoned without Sir Robert. He wrote a long letter to Lord Grey giving all the details and including the names of all concerned, not even omitting the unfortunate Fennell. This letter was, to save postage, franked by the unsuspecting ambassador and sent through the public mail although it was common knowledge that letters were censored in France and that Wilson himself was under police surveillance.

With a signed confession in their hands the French authorities had no alternative to arresting the conspirators. Sir Robert and Lady Wilson were in bed when, at 7 a.m. on 13 January 1816, the police arrived at his house in the Rue de la Paix. They searched his papers and took him to the Prefecture. Bruce and Hutchinson were arrested at the same time.

Wilson spent two days in solitary confinement before he was brought before an examining magistrate. Then he made a speech announcing that he 'did not propose to resist the laws of France but that there were laws of nature and common equity'. The magistrate committed him to La Force prison from where he wrote a diatribe to the Minister of Police asserting that 'when the Bastille was stormed and won, Europe did not rejoice in the capture of a state fortress but in the destruction of a system that vitiated the public law of nations and was pernicious to the liberties of every country.' He went on to accuse the minister of having shamelessly abused his powers and of being 'an individual who is destitute of any feeling of a man of honour'. Tactfully, and probably truthfully, the minister returned this document with the explanation that it was illegible.[4]

The British ambassador, who had every reason to be angry with Sir Robert, had written to assure him that he would do 'whatever depends on me to get you out of this scrape', but Wilson's speech to the magistrate and his letter to the minister prompted Sir Charles to remind him that 'You are amenable to the law of France for a transaction which took place in France and during the time you were under the protection of the French law.' This gentle remonstrance infuriated Wilson, who accused the ambassador of having delivered the three conspirators 'bound hand and foot to the tyranny of a lawless government'.[5]

Wilson's arrest, as he may have intended, was a source of great embarrassment to the British and French governments. Both saw a Franco-British understanding as the main guarantee of peace in Europe after twenty years of war. The restored Bourbons were not popular in England but nobody could see an acceptable alternative. To the British government, as to the French people, Louis XVIII was *Louis l'Inévitable*. Lord Liverpool's cabinet was prepared to go to great lengths to support his authority. On their side the French were doing all they could to minimize damage to their relationship with London.

The chief minister, the Duke of Richelieu, called on the Duke of Wellington, commanding the army of occupation, immediately after the arrests. Wellington raised no objections except in the case of Hely-Hutchinson who, being on the staff, had immunity from French arrest. He made a formal protest on that point but added that, had the French asked for Hutchinson to appear in court, he would, according to his usual practice, have surrendered him. He disclaimed all responsibility for Wilson and Bruce, who were not under his command.[6] The Duke was, in fact, extremely angry, the more so since Wilson had carried out his stratagem by using British uniforms. As he remarked later in life, 'A sort of fabulous Englishman is not to be permitted to go about the world bullying, smuggling and plundering as he pleases.' Wilson may have had a moral justification for his act but there is no doubt that he saw himself as 'a sort of fabulous Englishman' who was above all laws of which he disapproved.

In London the French reaction was conciliatory in the extreme. The ambassador called on Castlereagh and offered 'to leave the extent of punishment entirely to us, and even to be sent home to be punished as we thought proper'. The cabinet did not feel able to accept this offer and, in consultation with Wellington, decided to let matters take their course, provided the French did not press the charge of constructive treason, which would carry the death sentence. They also decided to let Wilson think that they were doing nothing to help him, for, 'if Sir Robert were aware that the

British government interfered decidedly to save their lives, he will so presume upon it as to conduct his defence in a way to set the French government at defiance, and thereby degrade it in public estimation.'[7]

It was April before the trial began. The prisoners were represented by Maître Dupin who had been Ney's counsel, and his defence of Wilson consisted largely of praising his gallantry in war and reciting the acts of kindness he had done to French prisoners during the Russian campaign. There was little else he could say as his client's letter to Grey furnished all the evidence that any prosecution could want. On the third and final day, Wilson and Bruce spoke in their own defence. Miss Berry, who was in court, said that Wilson spoke first 'and very well, except for his *extra bad* pronunciation; however, everybody seemed to excuse that, and the speech had considerable effect, and I think deserved it; for it was manly, soldierlike, to the point and temperate. . . . Bruce *peroréed* with much contemptuous affectation. . . . Hutchinson wisely thought proper to say nothing.'[8]

The jury was out for less than an hour and inevitably brought in a verdict of guilty. Each defendant was sentenced to three months' imprisonment, the term to start from the first day of the trial, 22 April. This meant that, including the time since their arrest, they would have served six months, a light sentence in the circumstances. They served their time at La Force prison in 'a small, wretched room, about eight feet by twelve, dirty and felonious, with two small windows, one looking into a court where a parcel of ragged prisoners were playing at fives, the other into a sort of garden where others were loitering away their listless vacuity of time'. Bruce and Hutchinson had to share a room. Wilson had one of his own.[9]

As soon as sentence had been pronounced, the British authorities started to consider what should be done about Sir Robert. He had been guilty of both civil and military offences under British law and, at a court martial, a charge of 'conduct unbecoming an officer and a gentleman' could hardly fail. The British view was that his real offence lay in obtaining two false passports through his friendship with the unsuspecting ambassador. As

7. Czar Alexander, Emperor Francis, and King Frederick William giving thanks on the battlefield of Leipzig. Prince Schwarzenberg is mounted on the left of the sovereigns. *Anonymous gouache by an eye-witness*

8. Sir Robert Wilson, 'Sir John Ely Hutchinson', and Michael Bruce in the 'exercise yard of La Force prison, 1816.
A contemporary French print

Miss Berry wrote, in a splendidly insular passage about the trial, 'Luckily for him nobody touched the *really* bad part of his story—the having obtained passports under a positively false pretence, and for two non-existing persons—so that he was not obliged to defend himself on the only indisputable point in English eyes. In those of French truth and probity it was *nothing*; not worth adverting to, even by their magistrates.'[10]

In one quarter there was no doubt about what should be done. A message arrived at the Horse Guards saying that 'The Prince Regent wholly disapproves not acting against Sir Robert Wilson by *dismissing* him.'[11] The government view was that it would be a mistake to let Wilson become a martyr, thus stirring up a political storm which would disrupt Anglo-French relations. The Duke of York, who had been Wilson's patron for twenty-two years, also advised against harsh measures. It was decided that a public reprimand would be sufficient.

On 10 May 1816 the Duke of York issued a General Order, to be 'published to the army at large', expressing the Prince Regent's 'high displeasure that an officer of his standing in his Majesty's service should have been so unmindful of what was due to his profession as well as to a government under whose protection he had voluntarily placed himself. . . . His Royal Highness cannot admit that any circumstances could justify a British officer in having obtained, under false pretences, passports in feigned names from the representative of his own Sovereign, and having made use of such passports for himself and a subject of his Most Christian Majesty, under sentence for high treason, disguised in a British uniform, not only to elude the vigilance of the French authorities, but to carry him, in such disguise through the British lines.' Hutchinson was included in this censure, though in more moderate terms, and was dismissed from his post on the staff in France.

Wilson and Hutchinson were lucky to have escaped with their commissions, but Sir Robert preferred to represent the General Order as an incident in the campaign of denigration which Castlereagh and his colleagues had been waging against him since 1812. On his release from prison, he called on the Duke of York and offered to tell him, in confidence, the names of several highly placed Englishmen who had been involved in the Lavallette affair. This was nothing but malicious mischief-making and when challenged by Sir Charles Stuart, who suspected that his might be one of the names Wilson had in mind, Sir Robert fell back on generalities about 'party persecution'.[12]

When the news that Wilson had got himself into a scrape first reached England, there was widespread disapproval. Thomas Grenville wrote in January, 'I am convinced from all I hear and see that this business of Wilson's is generally execrated throughout the country . . . even Brougham admitted that it is to be *deplored*.' Grey warned Wilson that 'the general feeling in this country is decidedly hostile to everything connected with the French revolution or Buonaparte, and that everything which might proceed from a motive favourable to either would be very severely judged.'[13]

During the trial British opinion swung behind the defendants, largely from a widespread feeling that it was an impertinence on the part of the French to imprison three Englishmen. By the time Sir Robert returned to England, he found himself a hero of the Opposition and widely acclaimed as the defender of the rights of true-born Englishmen. Since the Duke of York's censure made it improbable that he would be employed again as a major-general, his thoughts turned to politics. He had disregarded two of his father's last injunctions—not to join the army and not to marry before he was thirty-five; he could follow the third and 'make Parliament the object of a patriotic ambition'.

Inevitably he joined the Opposition. From his early years his friends had been Whigs and he believed that the Tory government had slighted and underrated him. However, the Opposition, as was inevitable in a party which had been out of office almost continuously for thirty years, was in great disarray. On one wing were the great Whig Lords, such as Grey and Grenville, who were almost indistinguishable from their Tory counterparts and little less conservative. On the other were radicals, like Sir Francis Burdett and Henry Brougham, who were in favour of a sweeping reform of the whole political system but were far from agreeing on what to put in its place. Between these two extremes were numerous factions, united only in believing themselves to be the rightful political heirs of Charles James Fox.

Wilson had attachments on both wings of the Whig party. He had for years been a friend of both Grey and Burdett, but it was to the left of the party that he gravitated, joining a political club called the Rota, of which Burdett was the leading spirit. Another member, John Cam Hobhouse, wrote that 'We dined together once a fortnight during the sitting of Parliament, read essays, concocted plans of reform, framed resolutions to be moved in parliament, and drew up addresses for parliamentary candidates. We were all parliamentary reformers, but we were by no means agreed as to the extent or general character of the change which ought to be made in the representative system. The term radical, used as a substantive, had not come into use, but was commonly applied as an epithet; and I recollect that the member of our society who in those days seemed determined with nothing short of reform was [Robert Wilson].'[14]

It is very difficult to determine what, if any, political beliefs Wilson held. He believed in the reform of parliament but never made up his mind how much reform was desirable. He saw himself as the champion of the underdog—a role that appealed to his sense of chivalry. He was opposed to the established government, at least until 1827, because he felt himself deprived of his due share of honours and appointments. Above all, he liked calling attention to himself. Deprived of the chance to become a public idol for his military service, he determined to make such a nuisance of himself that authority would have to take notice of him. He acted as a radical until he had become a feature of public life. Then he retired into liberal Toryism and abandoned politics.

In 1818 he fought the election as a Radical in Southwark, a borough which, by the standards of the time, had a wide franchise. The vote was held by all those who paid scot and lot, a number estimated in 1816 as 'about 3,000',[15] but the main electoral force was the mob and the mob supported the radicals. The sitting members were Charles Calvert, who had held the seat since 1812, and Charles Barclay. The latter, who had first been elected in

1815, was the principal brewer of the borough and, for family reasons, had the support of the strong local Quaker interest. His re-election should have been certain had he not, in 1818, voted with the government in a debate on the Corn Laws. This was enough to make his name anathema to the mob.

Wilson stood on a vague programme of reform, much abuse of ministers, especially Castlereagh, and an extensive rehearsal of his military services. Polling started on Thursday 18 June and at the end of the day Calvert had 427 votes, Wilson 338 and Barclay 228. That evening all the candidates made speeches from the hustings but Barclay was shouted down, as he had been throughout the campaign. On Friday, Calvert went far ahead with 1,313 votes to Wilson's 923 and Barclay's 734. It was becoming clear that only brave men voted for the brewer and anyone who was prepared to mount the hustings and declare a vote for Barclay was certain to be pelted with mud, and might suffer a rougher fate. Saturday's poll, with one day to go, made Calvert unassailable with 1,932. Wilson had 1,377 and Barclay only 1,090 but, before his words were drowned by the howling of the crowd, he was heard to declare his confidence in eventual victory. Over the Sunday he had second thoughts and when the poll re-opened on Monday his withdrawal was announced and Calvert and Wilson were declared elected. In a speech to his cheering supporters, Sir Robert said that he was overcome with gratitude. He compared his situation to that of a French grenadier whom he had discovered dying of cold and hunger during the retreat from Moscow. He had given him his last crust of bread but the Frenchman had declined it, saying, '" I cannot brave [*sic*] it; I was prepared for anything but kindness", and thereupon expired.'[16]

The stress he had laid, throughout the election, on his military career led the *Quarterly Review*, in a review of his latest book, *A Sketch of the Military and Political Power of Russia in the Year 1817*, to comment, 'Sir Robert is, we believe, not unacquainted with an officer of high rank and of considerable reputation as "an able partizan" who thought fit to enliven a period of inaction during the Spanish war by despatching to headquarters a false report of a victory gained by the corps under his command.'[17] This obvious reference to the action at Baños gave Wilson to address an Open Letter to the electors retelling the story of the battle and quoting Marshal Ney to prove that it had been a victory for Wilson.

Having reached the House of Commons, Sir Robert found it a far from ideal place for the display of his talents. As usual, he ignored the advice of his friends. Lord Grey had urged him not to 'begin by a set speech on a large or general question, and do not speak at all for some time, but observe well all that is said by others and try yourself in some strict discussion, or some simple point of business, and more especially in a committee where you have the right of reply, and greater freedom of explanation than can be allowed you in the House. In short, let your audience have an impression of your diffidence in yourself.'[18]

Grey had many illusions about Wilson and he must have been the only man of his acquaintance who credited Sir Robert with having any diffidence in himself. Parliament met on 14 January 1819 and on the 26th Wilson rose and delivered himself of a speech on the evils of paper currency. As a gesture to diffidence he opened by saying, 'I do not pretend, Sir, to discuss the subject of finance as a professor of arithmetic—I am little versed in mathematics', but his speech was long and full of hyperbole. Henry Fox wrote 'Sir R. Wilson made his maiden speech, (a complete failure, though his friends tried to gloss it over) on finance—a bad subject in bad hands.' Greville said that he 'had failed lamentably'.[19]

Having started speaking in the House, he continued to do so although Hansard's reports of his speeches are punctuated by comments such as 'coughing and other marks of impatience' and, for some of his wilder oratorical flights, 'loud laughter'. In his first ten weeks in the House he spoke on twenty-one occasions (apart from shouted interjections) and filled $36\frac{1}{2}$ columns of Hansard. There was no subject on which he did not feel impelled to give his opinion. The conduct of the Member for Limerick during the election had him speaking on seven occasions, but he also spoke on the Westminster Hustings Bill, the claims of British subjects in France, the Vote of Thanks to the Marquess of Hastings, duties on coal, and the Friendly and Parochial Benefit Societies Bill. Naturally he spoke on the Mutiny Bill, urging that flogging should be retained for the army although it should be used only as a last resort. He also opposed the proposal to abolish trial by battle on the grounds that depriving an accused man of the chance of meeting his accuser in single combat was an infringement on individual liberty. He was not widely supported.

He became known as a parliamentary bore. One MP wrote that he 'has spoken, as was expected, flippantly, rashly and feebly and is of no importance. If ministers had made him a KCB, and would have the sense to distinguish his military from his political merits, they would get quite the whip hand of him.' Another said, 'You know how little I am absent from a debate, but when Sir Robert Wilson rose I began to think that my own dinner would be better than anything I could gain from his speech.'[20]

He was not an easy political ally. The Duke of Bedford, one of the Whig grandees, believed that the party 'owe all our misfortunes to a little faction at Brooks's consisting of Brougham, Sir Robert Wilson, Sir F. Burdett and Duncannon. Each has his own views and it is no difficult matter to surmise by what their views are directed.' Even to the 'little faction at Brooks's' Sir Robert's views were unpredictable. He consorted with radicals but he declared in the Commons that 'He was no radical; he objected to the vote by ballot, and thought it inconsistent with universal suffrage, because, if it existed, many of the institutions he had sworn at the table to defend could not be maintained.' He was a reformer but looked for only 'such reform as was suitable to the moral and intellectual advancement of the age'.[21]

More alarming to men of all parties was his increasing attachment to the Bonapartist cause. The *Quarterly Review* declared that he advocated bringing Napoleon back to France as the only security against a Russian domination of Europe, adding, 'There are some spirits so strangely constituted that, though zealous and able allies in the hour of danger, they cannot bear to witness a too complete success to the cause in which they have laboured. If we desire to retain their friendship we must submit to be always in need of their help, since the first moment of our triumph will be the last of their goodwill.'[22]

Certainly Wilson's opinion of the French emperor had changed as soon as his military power was broken. From having referred to him in the contemptuous Italian form of his name, Buonaparte, Sir Robert became a devoted propagator of the Napoleonic legend, collecting relics of the great man. Napoleon's friends and staff made a point of visiting Wilson when they came to England and he helped to bring the exiled emperor's supposed grievance to the notice of the British people. When General Gourgaud, on his return from St. Helena, landed in England and was arrested as an undesirable alien, Wilson sprang to his defence in the Commons. When Count Bertrand, Napoleon's executor, was brought to court at Bow Street accused of having misappropriated the emperor's death mask, Wilson told the magistrate that 'he had never witnessed a more flagrant piece of injustice practised on an individual than this, and it was more disgraceful that it should be practised on a foreigner'.[23]

So great was the mistrust inspired by Sir Robert's Napoleonic activities that the Secretary for War thought it worthwhile preserving an anonymous letter in French which said that 'Mrs. Wallis, Wilson's sister, has a son who is an officer in the regiment at St. Helena. She is confident that the young man will help Buonaparte escape. If this is true, he should be recalled immediately.'[24]

Wilson's view of the Bourbons had changed correspondingly since 1807 when he had noted the 'quick eye and countenance of benignity' of Louis XVIII. Now he described the French royal family and their supporters as 'a faction contemptible in its numbers and odious in its conduct'. This did not stop him making frequent visits to Paris where his friends included General Savary, who had been Minister of Police at the time of the murder of the Duc d'Enghien. The Freemasons of Paris gave Wilson a dinner at which he was toasted as *'le philosophe et le citoyen du monde'*, but when Lady Ossultone crossed to France on a rough sea in an open boat with Mr. Lambton and Wilson, she was 'very ill received by the King of France who said to her "*Quand on voyage en si mauvais compagnie on mérite d'être noyé*".[25]

In 1820 the Prince Regent became George IV and Wilson's relationship with him continued to deteriorate. With his radical allies, he was in the forefront of the Queen's supporters when the King tried to divorce her and to exclude her name from the prayer book and to prevent her attending the coronation. In February 1821 Charles Arbuthnot, 'in coming from the House of Commons, fell in with a knot of radicals who were determined to keep up the ferment in the country until they had got the Queen's name in the Liturgy. Sir Robert Wilson said they (he himself not having a guinea) meant to raise a subscription, that should get 30 or 40,000£ and would push it to all extremity. Mr. Arbuthnot said . . . what would they do if they failed? To which Sir Robert said "Oh! if we we fail, our game is gone." '[26]

To the radicals, the Queen was only a pawn in their political game, a handy weapon with which to attack the King and harass the ministers. It is unlikely that any of Wilson's friends felt much personal sympathy for Caroline. Her squalid intrigues at home and abroad sickened people of all parties even more than her husband's unedifying amours. Wilson, who had a strong puritan streak, could not have enjoyed her constant swearing and scratching. After her undignified attempt to force her way into Westminster Abbey during the coronation, she lost much of her support from her most potent ally, the London mob, and it seemed that the radicals' game was indeed gone until, on 7 August 1821, she died at Hammersmith.

Sir Robert was in Paris, dining with Count Orloff, when he heard the news of her death two days later. He decided to return to England immediately, a step to some extent justified by the fact that his son Henry was one of the Queen's equerries. He reached London on 12 August to find the funeral arrangements in chaos. The only point on which everyone was agreed was that she should be granted her wish to be buried in her native Brunswick.

The King was travelling to Ireland and had no intention of returning for the obsequies. Croker remarked that His Majesty was 'indeed gayer than it might be proper to tell'. He sent orders that the body should be sent down the Thames and embarked in a frigate at the Nore. The Admiralty had only one frigate available, HMS *Glasgow*. She was at Spithead and 'it was at that time blowing a gale of wind at *west* so that there was no chance of getting her to the Nore'. On Admiralty advice the cabinet decided that the embarkation should take place at Harwich, though it is not clear why it should not have been arranged for Portsmouth.[27]

The advantage of Portsmouth would have been that the funeral procession would not have had to pass through or near the radical stronghold of the City of London and, as soon as it was known that the destination was to be Harwich, the Common Council started to plan a grand popular demonstration of grief, knowing that it would annoy the King and embarrass the ministers. They issued instructions for 'the different bodies that may attend on foot to join in the procession' and for 'such persons as purpose attending in mourning coaches or private carriages' to form up at Hyde Park Corner. They sent a deputation to the Prime Minister to inquire the time at which the Lord Mayor should attend at Temple Bar to receive the procession. Lord Liverpool replied that the Lord Mayor need not trouble himself as the cortège would be going by the New Road (now Marylebone Road) to Romford and would not enter the City.

The Queen's adherents were determined, nevertheless, that the hearse should pass through the City, and tried to enforce their determination in two ways. On the one hand the Queen's executors, Dr. Lushington, MP, and Mr. Wylde, a lawyer, were to assert their supposed right to regulate the funeral. They started by complaining that the government was conducting the business in a hole-and-corner fashion, while inconsistently objecting that there was no need to provide an escort of Household Cavalry. If the executors were unable to exert control, a further set of plans was made. The roads were to be blocked so that it would be physically impossible for the procession to go any way except through the City. Robert Wilson was later said to have made this plan but he denied responsibility and his denial can be accepted, since the timing of his return from France left him little time to do the work involved. He did, however, meet Lushington and Wylde

at Brooks's Club on the evening of 13 August and it is probable
that he knew of the plan even if he did not make it.

Next morning he dressed in civilian clothes, adorned with the
star of the Black Eagle of Prussia, and borrowed 'a little, handsome, chestnut horse' from Alderman Matthew Wood, MP for
the City and an ardent supporter of the Queen.[28] He set off from
South Molton Street at 5 a.m. and, about an hour later, reached
Brandenburgh House, where the Queen had died and which
stood close to the river about a quarter of a mile downstream
from the present site of Hammersmith Bridge. There he found
the executors, most of the radical members of parliament, Sir
George Nayler, Clarenceux King at Arms, who was attended by
a herald, and 'Mr. Bailey, of Mount Street, Grosvenor Square
who had been appointed [by the government] conductor of her
Majesty's funeral'. A squadron of the Royal Horse Guards,
commanded by Captain Everard Bouverie, a veteran of Vitoria,
Toulouse, and Waterloo, with their standard, was drawn up in
front of the house. 'The helmets of the officers were partially
covered in black crepe.'

The first act of what was to be a tragic farce was played when
Wilson and the other notables were summoned into one of the
state rooms where Sir George Nayler, in his state dress, stood at
the foot of the coffin. Once they were assembled, Lushington
made a formal protest at the high-handedness of the government
in pre-empting the funeral arrangements. To this Mr. Bailey replied, 'Very well, Sir; I shall discharge my duty firmly and, I
trust, properly.'

At half-past seven the hearse was brought to the front door.
It was 'rather a small one, and surmounted by a profusion of
black plumes: on each side, the royal arms, quartered with those
of the Brunswick family, were emblazoned in scarlet and gold'.
Immediately behind, in a mourning coach, rode Sir George
Nayler, who had on his knee 'a cushion about two foot long and
one foot wide—black velvet, edged with a gold fringe, and a
large gold tassel at each of the four corners'. On the cushion was
the Queen's crown.[29]

Wilson asked permission for himself and his friends to ride

beside the hearse but this Nayler would not permit, insisting that all mourners on horseback should ride behind the twelve mourning coaches which carried members of the Queen's household.

Before the procession moved off, the executors made another protest to Bailey and demanded to know the route the procession was to take. The undertaker replied that it was to go along what is now Kensington High Street and turn left 'by Kensington gravel pits, near the church'. This would take them up the present Church Street to the Bayswater Road which they would use as far as Tyburn Turnpike (slightly to the east of Marble Arch), where they would turn north on the Edgware Road until they came to the New Road, which led through the fields to Islington. Beyond that they would take the City Road and Old Street.

No untoward incident occurred until the head of the procession reached Kensington church. When the leading file of Horse Guards tried to turn up Church Street, they found the way barred by a mass of carts, waggons and carriages. There was a long halt during which Wilson and his friends remained at the rear. He heard rumours that the troops were attacking the barricades but, rightly, he discounted them. It is clear that the barricades came as no surprise to him. When an hour had passed and everyone had been soaked by a torrential shower of rain, he said to Joseph Hume, MP for Aberdeen, 'Let us move forward and see what is the matter.'

They rode up to Captain Bouverie at the head of the procession and Sir Robert 'entered into conversation with him, and said "I understood that a message had been sent to the Earl of Liverpool, for the purpose of ascertaining whether or not the procession should be allowed to pass through the City. That I thought this would be the best way to settle the question, for the undertaker did not seem to have any powers, and certainly none which would justify the interference of the military." Captain Bouverie answered "That he considered himself in command of a guard of honour, and he did not feel it his duty to interfere without an express order."' He added that the crowd had seized a baggage waggon belonging to the Foot Guards on its way to Windsor and had incorporated it in their barricade. He thought it his duty to extricate it but Wilson, according to his own account, persuaded the people to release the waggon, which they did 'very good-humouredly'. At this moment the cortège started to move again, heading due east for Hyde Park Corner.[30]

The order to move on had been sent by the Prime Minister who entrusted it to Sir Robert Baker, Chief Magistrate at Bow Street, who arrived on a troop horse. He had been told that the procession was on no account to go through the City but that it should turn into Hyde Park by the Kensington Gate. Baker was accompanied by a squadron of Life Guards and other detachments of that regiment were sent to secure the other gates into the Park which, in those days, was surrounded by a high brick wall surmounted by iron railings. Two companies of the Foot Guards, with the regimental pioneers, were also ordered 'to move towards the line of march for the purpose of removing all obstructions'.

When Kensington Gate was reached it was found to be blocked by the crowd. Captain Oakes of the Life Guards suggested clearing a way into the Park but Baker refused. Unaccountably he also declined Oakes's suggestion that the cortège should enter the Park through Knightsbridge Barracks. Baker had made up his mind to go up Park Lane.

Most of the trouble during the rest of the day stemmed from this decision, for at Hyde Park Corner was a mass of men, some of them deputations from 'Benefit Societies with banners and bands of music', summoned to the spot by the Common Council of the City, while more of them were the raw material for a mob. Moreover, when the Corner was reached, Baker found that the entrance to Park Lane was blocked as firmly as Church Street had been. There was another long halt during which Baker was approached by several aldermen who impressed him with the dangers of trying to avoid the City. The magistrate lost his nerve and agreed that the procession should go by Piccadilly, Pall Mall, and Charing Cross. With the leading division of the Blues he started down Piccadilly and there was great excitement and some cheering in the crowd. It was not until Baker reached the bottom of the dip that he realized that the hearse was not following. Mr. Bailey had refused to allow it to go down Piccadilly, saying that his orders to use the New Road were peremptory. He was supported by Captain Oakes.

There was another lengthy pause during which further orders, of the same purport as the earlier set, arrived from Downing Street carried, on another troop horse, by Mr. W. W. A. White, a magistrate from Queen Square. He reached the hearse but could not communicate with Baker, since a hostile section of the crowd had isolated the leading Horse Guards in Piccadilly. White decided to force a way up Park Lane and sent a detachment of Life Guards to remove the barricade. 'Upon this the mob gave a loud and deep shout, and mud and missiles flew at the soldiers from all directions. Many of them, as well as of the crowd were badly wounded.'[31]

Seeing this, White changed his mind and ordered Hyde Park Gate, immediately to the west of Apsley House, to be opened. This was done by the Life Guards, using the flats of their swords against the crowd who were yelling 'Piccadilly Butchers!' and 'Murderers!' As soon as the procession was through, the gates were slammed shut and the hearse set off up East Carriage Drive at a trot while the mob raced on foot parallel with it up Park Lane. Grosvenor Gate, half way up, was secured by Life Guards who were pelted with stones 'and several were struck on their caps and faces'. Constable George Avis, who had just arrived on the scene, saw 'one man dressed like a smith with an apron continue throwing after the rest had desisted and crying out to the soldiers, 'Bloody murdering rascals!'

When the head of the truncated procession emerged from Cumberland Gate, which stood on the site of Marble Arch, they found themselves in a cul-de-sac. On their left the southern end of Edgware Road had been barricaded with carts by the mob; on their right a double line of Life Guards blocked Tyburn Turnpike, at the entrance to Oxford Street. As soon as the hearse emerged, the mob slammed the gate behind it, but this was soon reopened by soldiers and constables. White gave orders for the Edgware Road to be opened and a dismounted party of the Life Guards, covered by a double line of horsemen, moved across to start the work under a shower of stones.

It was on the turnpike side that the real trouble happened. Thirty yards of railings from the top of the park wall were torn down and, with brickbats and stones, were used as missiles against the soldiers guarding the turnpike. Simultaneously the mob rushed at the hearse and tried to turn the horses' heads towards Oxford Street. The Blues, who throughout confined themselves to their escort duties, drove the mob off without trouble. The shower of missiles continued and Constable Avis saw 'two men dressed in black come from the corner of Cumberland Street toward Cumberland Gate with a piece of a large flag stone and throw it at a Life Guardsman which knocked him off his horse, the people crying out *Murder him*, but some said let the bugger go. I was struck by a brickbat or stone on the back part of the head.'

So far the troops had behaved impeccably. Even Opposition accounts concede that 'the forbearance displayed up to this point was highly praiseworthy',[32] but the pressure on the Life Guards at the turnpike was becoming intolerable Several were unhorsed, many suffered severe bruises, and some broken bones. Next day thirty-seven of them had to go to hospital and one was so severely injured that he had to be discharged from the army.[33] Already angry at the insults they had suffered, the soldiers began to be split into small groups, surrounded by a huge and hostile mob. Some were frightened, drew their pistols and fired. Most of the shots were fired into the air but a carpenter was killed and a bricklayer mortally wounded.

Robert Wilson was riding at the rear of the procession when shots were heard. Brougham, riding beside him, asked what the noise was. 'Oh,' he said, 'it is a noise you are not used to. We are in fire.' He started to ride to the scene although Joseph Hume, by his own account, said, 'For God's sake, Sir Robert, don't let's go there.'[34]

'On passing the Gate, I saw the hearse in the middle of the street with the Blues steadily formed round it, but the Life Guards in great confusion, similar to that which occurs when cavalry are suddenly thrown back or unexpectedly checked in some deployment. . . . I rode forward to the advanced group, and asked them by whose orders they were firing. They said "They had no orders, but that they had been ill-treated." I put the question to another party, firing towards the turnpike gate, who were in equal disorder and I received a similar answer. A pistol shot, fired from behind, passed so near my face that I thought the skin was grazed. I turned round immediately to the man who I conceived had fired, when I saw two or three men re-loading their pistols. I immediately said, "It is quite disgraceful to continue firing in this manner."'[35]

At this moment Mr. White the magistrate rode up. He had been supervising the dismantling of the barricade but was severely rated by Wilson for not attending to the officer commanding the troops. While they were talking, Captain Oakes arrived and Wilson handed the magistrate over to him, advising him to guard him with a dragoon, lest he slip away. Oakes had been an officer in the Twenty-Second Light Dragoons while Sir Robert was lieutenant-colonel but Wilson did not know him. He asked Oakes if he had given any order to fire. Oakes replied that he had not but when Wilson began to make suggestions, which sounded very like orders, the captain replied, 'Sir Robert, I know you perfectly well, but I can enter into no discussion with you at present. I shall do my duty and my men will do theirs.'[36]

By this time the crisis was over. The firing had stopped once it had achieved its purpose of making the mob retreat. The barricade had been removed and the cortège moved up Edgware Road at what Brougham described as 'a brisk pace'. Sir Robert took his place at the rear. He claimed all the credit for stopping the firing. It is doubtful how much he actually achieved, particularly as his statement quoted above infers that there was much more shooting than actually occurred. The fact that two ranks of soldiers firing pistols at point-blank range into a mob only caused serious harm to two men suggests that few shots were actually fired other than in the air. The officers, who had given no orders to fire, would have done everything they could to stop the shooting, even if only for the sake of their own careers. The troopers, though some of them had been frightened, would soon calm down—re-loading a horse-pistol was a trying business—and would realize the risk they were running by firing without orders. The shot fired close to Sir Robert's head may well have been a deliberate attempt to frighten him away. The soldiers were angry at his interference and he admitted in the Commons that his language was violent—'but I beg the House to recollect the circumstances which were occurring at the time'.[37]

The procession had a respite as it trotted up the Edgware Road and turned right along the New Road. For a time it seemed that all would be well, but the conductors had underrated the preparations made by the Queen's adherents. At the corner of Tottenham Court Road (where Warren Street Station now stands) they were faced with yet another barricade. As a triumphant radical wrote, 'Every waggon, cart, coach and vehicle of whatever description was seized, or rather spontaneously seemed to go and form itself into parts of a dense mass, extending the whole width of the road, and almost 100 yards in depth.'[38] By this time a company of the Third Guards and another of the Grenadiers, with the pioneers of both battalions, were available to clear the obstacle. Unfortunately Sir Robert Baker had rejoined the procession. He and Mr. White wrangled over what was to be done. White, supported by the officers, urged the removal of the barricade. Baker, as the senior magistrate, would not agree. He sent the Foot Guards back to barracks and led the cortège down Tottenham Court Road. He made one last attempt to avoid the City by turning down Francis Street (now Torrington Place), but finding this also barricaded he resigned himself to going down St. Giles High Street and into the Strand. At Temple Bar the Lord Mayor, who had kept his carriage standing ready at the foot of the Mansion House steps throughout the day, met the hearse with all due ceremony. The procession moved through the City in an atmosphere more suitable to a jubilee than a funeral. Wilson rode in the rear until Ilford was reached, when he turned his horse's head and trotted back to Brooks's.

CHAPTER 10

Transformation Scene

It was reported to the King that, at the Queen's funeral, 'the mob had attained a triumph, as they conceived it to be, over the government and the military'.[1] There was no doubt that the government had suffered a humiliating and unnecessary defeat and unfortunately the only member of the cabinet who would have been equal to the situation had been abroad. The Duke of Wellington's view was that 'if I had determined to send her by land and round the City, I would have taken care to occupy the roads in such a manner that the procession could not have been stopped. After all, I don't see why she should not have gone through the City if she had to go at all by land.'[2] As things stood, the government had had the worst of all worlds and had been made to look foolish into the bargain.

The cabinet was anxious to strike back at those who had fomented the trouble, but there was not much that they could do. They dismissed Sir Robert Baker, whose vacillations had made a bad situation worse, and they ignored the conclusions of two coroners' juries which had brought in verdicts of murder and manslaughter against unknown Lifeguardsmen after directions which were grossly biased against the soldiers. The prosecution of at least one alderman was contemplated but no proceedings were started, as, although the obstructions to the hearse were clearly pre-planned, the chances of collecting enough evidence to convince a court were slim.

The man who was most exposed to punishment was Robert Wilson. As a general officer his conduct at the funeral had undoubtedly been 'unbecoming to an officer and a gentleman', not least because it was known that it was the King's wish that as few people as possible should attend. Wilson's efforts to persuade Captain Bouverie, while still in Knightsbridge, to lead the cortège through the City, contrary to his orders, were open to a charge of incitement to mutiny. To address, abuse, and give orders to soldiers not under his command at Cumberland Gate also laid him open to serious charges. Nor could he look to the Horse Guards for support. Only the friendship of the Duke of York had saved his commission after the Lavallette affair and now the Duke's patience snapped. He wrote to the Secretary for War, 'Nothing could be more impudent or infamous than Sir Robert Wilson's conduct on 14th August, and I for one am not sorry that he has at last given a fair opportunity of freeing the army of a person who has long been a disgrace to it.'[3]

Wilson was not slow to realize the dangers of his position and told a friend that 'he was in a scrape and wished to be advised how to get out of it'.[4] His first step was to call on the Duke of York, only to find that he had gone to Brighton. The Military Secretary received him but declined to read his private account of the incident or to receive 'any communication otherwise than officially and in writing'. At the end of a twenty-minute interview, Wilson dictated a message to the Duke saying that 'he understood that there were many calumnious misrepresentations afloat in regard to the part he took in the proceedings of the 14th August; but as no official communication had been made to him on the subject, and as he learned from [the Military Secretary] that he had not been instructed by the Commander-in-Chief to make any to him, he did not feel he was called upon, or that he could with propriety notice them in any representation to his Royal Highness, but that he feels at all times able to refute them.'[5]

There were indeed many 'calumnious misrepresentations afloat'. Signed statements, attested under oath, poured into government offices about Wilson and anyone else connected with the affair. Many of them were demonstrably untrue; more were highly improbable. It was said that Sir Robert first heard of the Queen's death 'at a dinner in Paris at which were assembled thirty French officers; and that when the communication was made, I used an expression which outraged the feelings of all present.' He was accused of attending a dinner given by a Mr. Youde, a tavern-keeper at Hammersmith, 'and had, there and then, planned all the obstructions to the funeral'. A deposition was lodged at the Home Office saying that 'I had been seen with a pewter-pot in my hand encouraging the people to pull up the pavement and offer obstructions to the funeral'.[6]

Most of this Wilson could and did deny, but the military offences remained. The Life Guards were particularly bitter against him and a sheaf of complaints from men in the ranks was sent to the Commander-in-Chief. To confirm their authenticity Wellington rode down to Knightsbridge Barracks and interviewed the complainants. 'I find they are all old soldiers of most unexceptionable characters; and in every way deserving of credit.'[7]

To make matters worse, Wilson sent a memorandum to the King, who was still in Ireland, through Lord Hutchinson (now Lord Donoughmore). This again was a military crime since, although any serving officer may petition the Sovereign, he may only do so through the proper channels.

The cabinet decided to have done with Wilson without further ado and to proceed through the Royal Prerogative. On 18 September the *London Gazette* published the decision:

War Office, September 17th 1821

MEMORANDUM. The King has been graciously pleased to remove Major General Sir Robert Wilson from his Majesty's service.

Three days earlier the Duke of York had written to Wilson, 'Sir, I have it in command from his Majesty to inform you that he no longer requires your services.'[8] As Sir Robert had taken himself off to Paris, this letter did not reach him until 20 September and he had already seen the announcement in the *Gazette*. He wrote to the Duke requesting a court martial and drawing attention to his twenty-nine years of service and the fact that he had 'purchased every commission except the junior one'. A court martial was refused.

Wilson's dismissal caused a political commotion among the radicals and even the more orthodox Whigs. They regarded him as a political liability but saw that he would be a useful stick with which to beat the government. A subscription was put in hand to compensate him for the £5,300 he had lost with his commission as a lieutenant-colonel. John Lambton (later 1st Earl of Durham), who told Creevey that '£40,000 was such an income as a man might jog on with', sent £500, but other contributors were few and far between. The electors of Southwark affirmed their confidence in their member at a public meeting and the Dover Lodge of the Order of Modern Druids sent him a song composed in his honour by Brother Mayne, 'an honest tradesman and an independent mind'.[9]

None of these effusions caused ministers much concern. Nor were they disturbed when, in February 1822, Wilson moved for the papers concerning his dismissal in the House of Commons. In one of his longest and windiest speeches he tried to justify his actions at the funeral by denying some of the more unlikely rumours which were circulating about his conduct.

Lord Palmerston, Secretary at War, led for the government and outlined the points which had induced the cabinet to advise the King to dismiss him. The first was that he had continued to ride in the procession after it had been driven off the route which the King, speaking through his ministers, had prescribed—that by continuing 'with a number of persons engaged in illegal proceedings, and opposing the legitimate orders of the King, his master, he was guilty of a direct and gross insult to the Sovereign whom he served'.

Secondly he had 'acted in a manner calculated to promote military insubordination—officer that he was—holding a commission but not having authority on that occasion—by addressing either the soldiers or the officers who were employed at the time, and who were responsible for the manner in which they performed their duties. It was an act of great military insubordination to address troops under such circumstances at all: but the language in which, by the hon. gentleman's own admission, he addressed them, highly aggravated the character of his military offence. . . . The hon. gentleman—a general officer—knew, or ought to have known, that by the rules and disciplines of the army, he was guilty of a great breach of those rules and that discipline by interfering with soldiers in the discharge of their duty.'[10]

Palmerston's case was unanswerable, and although Wilson's political friends did their best for him there was little they could say except to make the most out of his part in stopping the firing. They also claimed that the Prerogative had been misused by dismissing an officer without trial. That that horse would not run was promptly established by the Marquess of Londonderry (until recently Lord Castlereagh) by quoting a judgement of the most respected Whig lawyer of the time. 'The King', Lord Erskine had said, 'is the acting party here. He is at the head of the army and the grounds for his decision cannot be questioned in any court of law; and whenever his Majesty dismisses an officer, whether of the highest or the lowest rank, he loses all benefit from his situation, according to the articles of war; and this every soldier must know when he enters the army.' To clinch the argument, Londonderry produced a paper giving the names of 212 officers who, in the last ten years, had been removed without trial and without questions being raised in Parliament. When the House divided, Wilson's motion collected only 97 votes against 199 for the government.[11]

The breaking of his military career did not inhibit Wilson as a Member of Parliament. He continued to speak frequently in the House, his subjects including the vexed question of whether roasted wheat was, or was not, a 'breakfast powder' and whether letters written to MPs by prisoners should be subject to censorship. He also moved, unsuccessfully, a motion which would have enacted that licences for public houses should not be granted in respect of premises owned by brewers. He still had friends in all parts of the political spectrum and the Duke of York was prepared to forgive his old *protégé* sufficiently to give his son, Henry Wilson, an ensign's commission without purchase in the Fifty-Fourth Foot, despite the boy having been an Equerry to the late Queen.[12]

Even when he was forty-six, Sir Robert showed no signs of settling down. Denied military employment in his own country, he looked for adventure in the armies of other countries. Spain's colonies were in revolt against rule from Madrid and Lord Cochrane urged him from Chile to 'come to South America and leave behind the insuperable evils of the old corrupt and still degenerating world'. The idea appealed to him. Cochrane, he reflected, 'has the start, but South America presents a sufficient field for more than one Quixote. . . . The transfer of intellect, spirit of enterprise and indignant feeling will electrify the western hemisphere with a Promethean fire.'[13]

His friends advised him against the expedition. Lord Donoughmore wrote, 'Surely you are not going to rush into so mad a scheme. Recollect that you are not young. I confess that nothing makes me so melancholy as to see a friend who in despight of the progression of years, is resolved to continue young.' Lord Cochrane, he added, 'is a dull dog'.[14]

Cochrane and Wilson had much in common. Both were able publicists and impossible subordinates. Cochrane had been dismissed not only from the Royal Navy but from the House of Commons for being implicated in a Stock Exchange swindle. His constituents at Westminster promptly re-elected him. Perhaps feeling that Cochrane would be an uncomfortable fellow-Quixote, Sir Robert decided to help the South Americans from Europe, and went to Paris to act as an intermediary between the Colombians and Madrid. The French deported him as soon as they realized what he was doing but, in the fullness of time, he received a medal from Peru and the thanks of independent Chile.

Another opportunity of fighting soon arose on more familiar ground. When the French had finally been driven from Spain in 1814, Ferdinand VII had been restored to the throne of his ancestors. He immediately revoked the Constitution of 1812 and restored the Inquisition and absolute rule until a military revolt in 1820 forced him to readopt the constitution. Liberal ministers governed in Madrid but a 'royalist' army maintained an ineffective presence in north-eastern Spain. Despite British protests, Louis XVIII resolved to rescue his Spanish cousin and, on 6 April 1823, a French army led by the Duke of Angoulême but commanded by Marshals Oudinot and Moncey again crossed the Pyrenees.

The Whigs cried out for British intervention and even Canning, who had been Foreign Secretary since Castlereagh's death, confessed, 'I do not deny that I had an itch for war with France.' Wellington, however, pointed out that Britain was in no state to embark on another Peninsular war. Post-war economies had reduced the army to a position where 'we have not men to perform the necessary duties in England nor a battalion nor even a company to relieve or reinforce a post'.[15]

Robert Wilson was, of course, an advocate of intervention. He declared in parliament his hopes that he 'would have the satisfaction of knowing that the day could not be far off, if the war was protracted, when the standard of Spain would be united with the standard of England; because it was impossible that the people of England could submit to this timid and inglorious neutrality.'[16] He himself would not contemplate neutrality. He would take service with an Iberian army despite the Foreign Enlistment Act of 1819. He did not regard the Act as a bar to him since, when it had been debated, he had opposed it, describing it as 'an unjust, impolitic and most degrading measure. Unjust because it was opposed to the generous feelings of this country; impolitic because it retarded the progress of freedom in other nations.'[17]

One factor prevented him from going immediately to Spain. In January 1823, two months before the French invasion, he had received from the Portuguese *chargé d'affaires* a verbal invitation to succeed Beresford in command of the Portuguese army. This was a consequence of the Portuguese revolution of 1820 in which a liberal constitution had been accepted by King John on his return from a fourteen-year exile in Brazil. Wilson would have accepted this offer without hesitation were it not that, having once given the invitation, the Portuguese would not answer any letters about the appointment.

Lady Wilson, who had been blind for several years, was seriously ill, but Sir Robert decided to go to Galicia to size up the situation before moving on into Portugal. He sailed on 22 April.

He landed at Vigo to enthusiastic cheers on 1 May. 'Our reception has been the most gratifying that Englishmen ever received in any country and our presence here is doing all the good I anticipated.' The cheering was understandable since he was careful to put about the story that Britain was certain to intervene and that, when 5,000 British troops land, 'we will not only save Gallicia and the Asturias . . . but terminate the Spanish war south of the Ebro'.[18] He made a tour of Coruña, Lugo, and Orense, but what he found was far from gratifying. There were two Spanish armies in Galicia. Their commanders, Generals Morillo and Quiroga, were reluctant to co-operate and determined not to take the offensive. The Spaniards made Wilson a general, cheered him, fêted him, and composed poems in his honour. They ignored all his proposals to attack the French.

He decided to move on into Portugal and reached Oporto overland on 1 June. His timing was unfortunate. He had only been there for three days when a counter-revolution broke out. The constitution was overthrown and absolute monarchy re-established. A new junta was formed and summoned Sir Robert to appear before it. He slipped out of the city and made for Braga, but there the new regime was even more popular. He was surrounded by a mob which insisted that he cry 'Long live Absolute Monarchy'. He refused and would have been torn to pieces had not thirty veterans of the Loyal Lusitanian Legion intervened to rescue him. He was sent to Oporto under escort and imprisoned for a week before it was decided to deport him. He was marched to the Minho river, guarded like a common criminal, and sent over the frontier.

Back in Vigo on 14 June he found that there was no change for the better. Before leaving he had announced that 1,000 British volunteers would shortly arrive, but none had appeared. The attempt to recruit them had caused a stir in England. The King was reported to be 'in a great fuss about the efforts made to raise troops to send to Sir R. Wilson'.[19] None reached Spain except Count Lavalle Nugent who arrived at Cadiz complete with the uniform and horse furniture of a Spanish general.

There was no military activity in Galicia until, on 9 July, Morillo's army marched away to the south to make their peace with the French. Pablo Morillo, whose record in the earlier war was surpassed by no Spanish general, realized that 1823 was not

1808. He wrote to Wilson that 'From the first days of the invasion there could be no doubt that the people detested the war and greeted the French as liberators. . . . I cannot continue to fight without object and in opposition to the whole nation.'[20] Quixote Wilson would not admit that the Spaniards, led by their priests, preferred the incompetent absolutism of their royal family to well-meaning plans for their welfare. They had opposed the French in 1808–14 because they had removed the Bourbons. Now they supported their old enemies who were marching to restore the Bourbon power.

Sir Robert was in Coruña in mid-July when the French besieged the town. He received a musket ball in the thigh and was sent by sea to Vigo. The garrison of Coruña was not far behind him and soon Vigo was under siege. Wilson was put on board a British schooner, the *Nassau*, which was on its way to Gibraltar. He wrote to London urging the government to occupy Vigo and Coruña to save the honour of the Constitutional Party.[21]

His troubles were not over on the sea. A Portuguese warship boarded the *Nassau* as she sailed south. They searched the ship and behaved with studied rudeness to Sir Robert, making him so angry that he resigned his knighthood of the Tower and Sword. The government in Lisbon was not distressed since they had never intended that he should have the honour.

He reached Gibraltar on 16 August. The governor was Lord Chatham, elder brother of William Pitt and a man chiefly renowned for his lethargic conduct of the Walcheren expedition of 1809. He reported to London that 'Wilson has nearly recovered from his wound, and talks of going to Cadiz, but I suspect does not like to run the risk of being taken. It appears from his conversation as if he thought he should serve the cause more by intrigue and his talent for negotiation than by the sword. I wish he were gone home, but as he is a British subject, and disclaims being in any shape in the Spanish service, I can do nothing with him.'[22]

Chatham introduced his unwelcome guest to Sir William A'Court, the British Minister to Spain, who had moved to Gibraltar when the Spanish government, dragging their reluctant king with them, had taken refuge in Cadiz. On 21 August Wilson and A'Court had a long conversation at the end of which Wilson, always prone to believe what he wanted to believe, maintained that A'Court had agreed to act as mediator between the French and the Spaniards and to give 'the guarantee of England for a representative system against foreign aggression'. As he wrote in his journal, 'The British government, once engaged as a constitutional mediator, will find itself obliged either to procure an honourable and advantageous peace for Spain, or to oppose her enemies in arms.' He set off for Cadiz to break the good news to the Spanish government. It was not until 10 September that A'Court heard what had been pledged on his behalf, a course of action directly contrary to his instructions and his inclinations. He immediately denied that he had authorized any such *démarche* and declared that he would have no further dealings with Wilson. Unabashed, Sir Robert replied that 'the question at issue is one that now rests upon the credit due to the affirmation of the respective parties.'[23]

In Cadiz, Wilson was welcomed with enthusiasm. Even Ferdinand VII, acting under duress, 'raised him from his knees and told him that such was not the posture for a patriot and a hero like him and *one* of his best *friends*'.[24] The Cortes were genuinely glad to see him and, on 12 September, appointed him to command the defences of the city. It was the greatest command he had ever held but, on the day he received it, an English newspaper reached him telling him that his wife had died three weeks earlier. 'I saw in an instant all my hopes destroyed, all my dreams vanish.'[25]

There was nothing to cheer him in his new command. The garrison was dispirited and anxious only to surrender. The French started to bombard the city on 24 September and Wilson realized that, although the French artillery was at its extreme range, the place was bound to fall. He set a magnificent example of bravery and activity but he knew that it was hopeless. He devoted himself to trying to secure a compromise between the king and the Cortes. The king, whose word was less dependable than any man living, promised an amnesty 'in amplest form' to the *liberales*. Wilson then resigned his command and made for Gibraltar. Ferdinand, true to his reputation for perfidy, issued an order for Wilson's arrest and, backed by the French army, imprisoned all the *liberales* he could secure.[26]

It was 27 October before Sir Robert could obtain a passage home and, when the steamship *Walsingham* eventually took him, he had one of his usual stormy voyages, taking two weeks to reach Falmouth. Another blow awaited him. The sovereigns of Austria, Prussia, and Russia were angered at his support of the Spanish 'rebels' and stripped him of all the honours they had given him. This had the effect of bringing public opinion in England to his support. Many who detested his actions and opinions thought he had been hardly treated. Canning, whose neutralist policy he had done his best to wreck in Spain, paid him a handsome compliment in the Commons and it was noticeable that men of all parties continued to address him as 'Sir Robert' although his only remaining claim to the title was the Turkish Order of the Crescent.

Heartened by this swing in opinion, Wilson started a campaign to have his military rank restored. Progress was slow but, by 1825, it was believed that the Chancellor of the Exchequer was supporting him. Hearing this, the Duke of Wellington wrote to Lord Liverpool, 'expressing in the strongest manner his sense of the impropriety of showing any favour to Sir R. Wilson. He remarked upon his having assisted Lavallette to escape, disgracing by doing so his character as a British officer, upon his conduct at the Queen's funeral which caused him to be dismissed, and upon his subsequent conduct in going to Spain contrary to law and the King's proclamation, for which he could be punished by law if the legal proof could be obtained. The Duke concluded by saying he could not be a party to such a step which would injure the character and discipline of the army and which Sir R. Wilson had done nothing to render himself deserving of.' There the matter rested but, in the next year, Wilson enlisted the support of his old friend Sir John Cradock, now Lord Howden, to plead his case with the Duke of Wellington. Wellington agreed to see Wilson but told him that he could not recommend his restoration although he would not oppose it if the King and the Duke of York agreed to it. He recommended Sir Robert to write to the King asking for reinstatement as an act of grace and favour. George IV, however, was inexorable. He sent for the Duke and told him to let Wilson know that his letter had been received but that he had no answer to give to it.[27]

In Parliament there were signs that Sir Robert was veering away from his radical friends. He appalled them in 1825 by supporting a government motion to increase the army by 9,000 men, although he made a gesture towards them by adding that he 'looked upon a standing army as an excrescence forced upon us by foreign pressures, and not the natural growth of the British constitution'. However, when Joseph Hume complained of the size of the garrison of Gibraltar, Wilson snapped that if his honourable friend thought that the Rock could be defended by 4,000 men 'he had never looked at it with the eye of a soldier or the knowledge of an engineer'. Palmerston, speaking for the government, was so taken aback by this unexpected support that he thanked Wilson as 'the hon. and *gallant* member', though no government supporter had referred to him as gallant since his dismissal. This did not stop Wilson from voting to reduce the expenses of the Royal Military College, always a Whig bugbear.[28]

Wilson's greatest contribution to the House of Commons had been his intervention on 17 April 1823, just before he set out for Vigo. The occasion was a violent quarrel between his friends Brougham and Canning. Brougham had accused the Foreign Secretary of exhibiting 'a specimen, the most incredible specimen, of monstrous truckling for the purpose of obtaining office, that the whole history of political tergiversation could furnish'. Canning, white with anger, rose and said, 'That is false!' There was, according to Hansard, 'complete silence during some seconds' before the Speaker invited him to withdraw the word 'false' as unparliamentary. Canning replied that 'He was sorry to have used a word which was a violation of the decorum of the House; but nothing—no consideration on earth—should induce him to retract the sentiment.' There was an anxious debate and a motion to commit both Canning and Brougham to the custody of the Sergeant-at-Arms had been proposed and seconded when Wilson rose and said that it was his belief that Brougham had referred to Canning 'in his official capacity either as Governor General of India or as Secretary of State for Foreign Affairs. Neither did he think that the interruption from the rt. hon. gentleman [Canning] arose from anything but the firm conviction of the moment that the expression was personal. With this view of the case, he thought the rt. hon. gentleman might, consistently with honour and feeling, say that it was under an impression that the language was meant to be personal that he applied the epithet which had called forth the present discussion.' This all but meaningless form of words satisfied all sides and the incident was closed.[29] Lord Holland, who had no high opinion of Wilson, wrote to his son, 'Sir Robert was of great use in preserving, or at any rate restoring, peace in the H. of Commons on Canning's late intemperate sally, and showed that, in a moment when real good heart and proper spirit are required, these qualities are so strong in him that they dispel his common want of judgment and discretion, and make him a useful man.'[30]

In 1827 Wilson had the opportunity to do more to bring Canning and Brougham together. In March of that year Lord Liverpool, who had suffered a paralytic stroke, resigned after thirteen years as prime minister. Canning was the obvious successor, the only alternative being the Duke of Wellington who then, and later, had no ambition for the post. Nevertheless, the ultra-Tories, wishing to see the Duke in office, refused to support Canning, and the Duke, who thought him 'a man of imagination, always in a delusion, who never saw things as they were', would not serve under him. If Canning was to succeed he had to have some support from the Whigs. Brougham, who was on circuit in Lancaster, favoured supporting Canning, believing him to be at least as liberal as some of the Whigs. He used Wilson, Canning's friend of long standing, as an intermediary, though Sir Robert needed more tact than he usually displayed to tone down Brougham's asperities on Canning's 'place-hunting'.

The result was that Canning was assured of some radical

support, including such unlikely adherents to a Tory ministry as Sir Francis Burdett. He ran into trouble over his approaches to the right-wing Whigs. Lord Lansdowne, who represented the Whig leadership in the negotiations, was prepared to allow the crucial question of Catholic Emancipation to be omitted from the government's immediate programme, but he insisted that the entire government of Ireland, including the Lord Lieutenant, should be appointed from those who supported emancipation. Canning, who had given his word to the King that this should not be the case, was forced to end the negotiations. That night, at 10 o'clock, Brougham and Wilson organized a protest meeting at Brooks's. William Lamb went to the club, 'where I found that among the people present, about thirty, perhaps forty, including Brougham, Burdett, Calcraft, &c, there prevailed a strong and almost general feeling of disapprobation of the decision to which Lansdowne had come. Some of them went to remonstrate with him, and I do not know whether some general representation upon the subject was not drawn up and sent to him.' The upshot was that Lansdowne was induced to change his mind and eventually four Whigs took their places in the Canning cabinet.

Acting as an intermediary was not the only service that Wilson had been able to do for Canning. The new Prime Minister's daughter had married Lord Clanricarde who, according to Mrs. Arbuthnot, had been made a Marquess for his trouble. Clanricarde was Under Secretary to his father-in-law and, in November 1826, accompanied by Lord Howth and two other worthies, took John Auldjo, a rich young minor, to dinner at Richmond. They filled him up with food and wine, the bill for dinner was £10 for the five of them, and induced him to play loo. In the course of the evening they fleeced him for £8,000 and when they parted Auldjo paid £100 to each of his creditors and asked for time to pay the rest of his debt. Next day, on the advice of his guardians, he told them that he would pay no more and, if he was pressed, that he would place the matter at the police office. Soon afterwards his solicitors wrote to one of the creditors threatening legal action if the money he had already paid was not refunded.

This was a crisis for Canning. With the succession to the Tory leadership in the balance, he could not afford to have his son-in-law involved in a card-playing scandal, the more so since his own reputation for probity was, probably unfairly, suspect. He turned to Robert Wilson, whose house in Chapel Street, Grosvenor Square, was adjacent to those of two of the creditors, and asked him to arrange the matter. Wilson was successful as far as Lords Clanricarde and Howth were concerned. Auldjo's solicitors wrote that they gave it as 'their unqualified opinion that there was nothing connected therewith in the slightest degree to impeach the honour of either Lords Howth or Clanricarde'. A charge of conspiracy was brought against the other two players but Clanricarde, and therefore Canning, was safe. Mrs. Arbuthnot commented, 'I suppose his lordship will be cut by his gentleman friends as he has long since been by blackguards and blacklegs who knew his conduct long since.'[31]

Wilson's services to Canning availed him little. The Prime Minister was unable to overcome the King's objections to reinstating him in the army and, on 8 August 1827, Canning died. For a few months Sir Robert had sat on the government benches, declaring that 'he had come to the ministerial side of the House, not by the circuitous path which gentlemen usually follow in moving from one side to the other, but boldly and unblushingly, because he had come with the colours of liberal principles flying.'[32] Canning's death left him politically isolated. The radicals distrusted him, the Tories believed him a dangerous radical, the old Whigs considered him a turncoat. Lord Grey, in particular, never forgave him. He had tried to pursuade Grey to join Canning but Grey loathed Canning, calling him 'the most detested of my enemies', and gave it as his opinion that, as the son of an actress, Canning was *de facto* disqualified from becoming premier.[33] Grey's hatred now turned against Sir Robert and, in July 1827, Lambton wrote, 'I am sorry to say that Lord and Lady Grey are very angry with him for the part he has played in the late arrangements.'[34] The breach soon became an open quarrel with hard words on both sides, and when Grey became prime minister in 1831 Wilson, who might have expected to receive some reward for years of loyalty and friendship, perhaps becoming Secretary at War, remained a backbencher.

If Wilson had lost Grey's support, he had gained some sympathy on the Tory benches. He became friendly with Robert Peel who was Home Secretary in Wellington's government of 1828. The reserved Peel seems an unlikely friend for the flamboyant Wilson but there was a link between them, since Peel's wife was the daughter of General Sir John Floyd, an old officer of the Fifteenth Light Dragoons. Not later than the middle of 1829 Peel was actively supporting the idea of Wilson's reinstatement and assuring him that the government would certainly not oppose such a proposal. He added, however, that the responsibility of bringing the matter forward lay with the Commander-in-Chief, Lord Hill.[35] No one could believe that Hill, the kindliest of men, would stand in Wilson's way, but the King still proved an insuperable obstacle. The Duke of Wellington was also opposed to the idea. Early in 1830 his confidante, Mrs. Arbuthnot, talked about Wilson to Henry Hardinge, the Secretary at War. 'He and the whole of the Horse Guards, Mr. Peel and indeed *every body* except the Duke, wish to see him restored to his rank. ... But I spoke to [Wellington] the other day and he is very violent against it.'

George IV died in June 1830, thus making reinstatement a practical proposition, and the combined pressure of Peel and Mrs. Arbuthnot persuaded the Duke to relent.[36] William IV raised no objection and Wilson's name was restored to the Army List with the rank of Lieutenant-General dating from 27 May 1825, the day on which he would have been promoted had he not been dismissed. Wilson went down to Brighton to thank the King but William, 'taking him by the hand said, "Don't thank me: I never tell an untruth. Your restoration was so strongly recommended to me by my ministers, that it was my duty to comply; for God forbid that I should ever stand in the way of the favours of the Crown towards a meritorious officer. I now have the satisfaction of congratulating you on your restoration because I know that, if ever your services are required, I shall find in you a brave officer and a loyal subject." '[37] 'This', wrote

Princess Lieven, no supporter of Wilson's, 'is generally approved, except for some friends of the late King, who think it an insult to his memory.'[38]

When Grey came to office in 1831, he not only declined to give Sir Robert office, he failed to recommend his name to the King for the knighthood which, in the past, he had frequently said that Wilson deserved. Instead he took the first opportunity to make his own brother a GCB. General the Hon. Sir George Grey had had a markedly dull army career. He had not seen a shot fired in anger since 1796 and had passed the years between 1806 and 1815 commanding the troops, successively, at the Cape of Good Hope and in Yorkshire. His pretensions to the honour were unquestionably lower than Wilson's and those of several other officers.

As early as 1820 Wilson had begun to lose his zest for politics and had said to Hobhouse that he was 'disgusted with the little figure he had made in the House and, said he, "You will be sick of it in half a year."'[39] As the years passed, his speeches became fewer as he learned the tedium of being a backbencher with little prospect of office or distinction. His passion for writing long memoranda was unabated and anyone of consequence was likely to receive a long screed, of dubious legibility, packed with unsolicited advice. In 1829 Greville noted in his diary that 'Wilson has written to the Sultan a letter full of advice, and says the Turk will be more powerful than ever. Wilson is always full of opinions and facts; the former are wild and extravagant, the latter generally false.'[40]

His swan-song came when the first Reform Bill was introduced in 1831. When he read it, he commented, 'I consider it as an initiatory measure of a republican form of government.'[41] Nevertheless, he voted for the second reading, believing that he had pledged himself to his constituents to support it. The government's majority in the division was one.

Four weeks later, on 18 April, General Gascoyne, MP for Liverpool, proposed a resolution 'that the total number of knights, citizens and burgesses returned for that part of the United Kingdom called England and Wales ought not to be reduced'.[42]

The underlying subtlety of the resolution was that the second reading had been carried by the votes of the Irish members. The MPs for England, Wales, and Scotland had produced a majority against the bill; the Irish had voted 54 to 38 in favour. While the government's proposals dealt largely with taking seats from rotten boroughs and giving them to the growing industrial towns, they had, in doing so, reduced the number of English seats. When challenged, they had given a number of conflicting explanations, none of which was plausible.

Isaac Gascoyne was a moderate Tory who had voted against the second reading but 'agreed with those who thought some reform was necessary'. He was one of Wilson's friends and the two of them had agitated in the House for various concessions for army officers and their widows.

On 19 April Wilson made his last speech to the Commons in support of Gascoyne's resolution. It ran to four columns in Hansard, shorter than many of his effusions, and was in his most high-flown style. 'The noble lord [Lord John Russell] who had introduced the reform bill had done honour to himself, and the administration with which he was connected, by the redeeming of their pledges to the nation, however objectionable in some of its details that bill must be considered. That he [Wilson] should be obliged to find some part of the bill objectionable was a most painful course for him, but he must openly avow that his objections to the reduction in the number of English representatives were insuperable. . . . The moment that he heard that proposition of his noble friend, he determined rather to relinquish his seat in the House, than to give his support to that part of the bill. . . . He was not the reformer who would change his opinion on the subject of reform every week. He was not a shifting reformer. He was not the reformer who put on and cast off his principles with as much readiness as his garments. He was not the reformer who by his indecision disparaged his own character, and threw doubt upon his own opinions. He was not one who could play the part of vacillation as it might meet the purpose of the passing moment; far less could he permit himself to be influenced to do so by the most base and sordid motives. . . . But the fluctuation of counsels on this point had been such that it seemed as if the government had set its fortunes upon a die which, in prudence, ought never to have been cast. He regretted that uncertainty of counsels as it endangered the measure upon which the peace and tranquillity of the country depended. He regretted it also on his own account, but he could not let mere personal considerations stand in the way of his zeal for the interests of his country, in whose service he had spent the best years of his life, and for which he had shed his blood. He felt himself placed by the fluctuating conduct of ministers in an embarrassing dilemma. . . . He was prepared to surrender to his constituents the trust which they had committed to him, if they disapproved of his conduct and withdrew their confidence. If that should be the consequence of the course which he pursued on that occasion, he should carry with him into retirement a grateful recollection of the courtesy which he had ever experienced in that House, and a perfect confidence that he bore with him into private life an unblemished character for political integrity.'[43]

The government speaker who followed him probably spoke for the whole House when he said that 'he had listened to the speech of the hon. and gallant member for Southwark with no ordinary amazement' and that was just what Sir Robert had intended the House to feel. He was tired of politics and was bidding them farewell with as much *éclat* as he could contrive.

He chose his moment well. Although he, in the end, abstained at the vote, the government was defeated by 299 to 291. Parliament was hastily prorogued and a general election called. Once more Wilson found himself the centre of a public storm but this time he was not on the side of the mob. All his windows in Chapel Street were broken that night. 'Poor Wilson,' wrote Croker, 'he has been assailed by his constituents, who call upon him to resign his seat, and call him rat, apostate, &c. He will hardly find his way back.'[44] Before the election he tried to call a public meeting in Southwark to explain the course he had adopted, but threats of violence forced him to postpone it until it was too late for him to stand. His seat was taken by Brougham's younger brother, William.

Retirement from politics left Wilson with time to nurse his resentment against Grey, especially after the preference given to the Prime Minister's brother. He was particularly anxious to be given the colonelcy of a cavalry regiment. When his old political ally, Sir Barnastre Tarleton, died he had hopes that he might succeed him as colonel of the Eighth Hussars. The Military Secretary wrote to apologize that this could not be arranged since the King had already promised it to Sir William Keir Grant, and Wilson wrote generously to admit that this was only just since Grant had been a lieutenant when he, Wilson, was only a newly joined cornet on the day when they had both charged with the Fifteenth Light Dragoons at Villers-en-Cauchies.[45] In fact the only three officers promoted to be colonels of cavalry during Grey's premiership were all senior to Wilson. Grey's successor made amends. In 1835 Lord Melbourne secured for Sir Robert the appoinment he would most have liked to have, the colonelcy of the Fifteenth Light Dragoons, recently re-mustered as Hussars, the regiment in which he had first made a name for himself. Among the many letters of congratulation was one from Robert Peel who wrote of 'a very honourable and most justly deserved reward for military service'.[46]

It was certainly not a political honour. Wilson had severed all but social ties with his Whig and radical colleagues. He had abandoned Brooks's Club for White's. Such political sympathies as he had now lay with the moderate Tories, but his friends ranged right across the political spectrum. He re-established friendly ties with the Duke of Wellington and was at a house-party at Stratfield Saye in January 1837, if not earlier. It is said that the Duke was once asked how he could have forgiven Wilson and replied that 'he himself had done many things which required forgiveness "and he hoped God, who was a God of Peace, would forgive him."'[47] The story may be true but a much likelier reason is that Wellington, however much he had disapproved of many of Wilson's acts, had always liked the man himself. Despite his severe façade, Wellington was fond of amusing company and nobody could deny that Sir Robert was charming and amusing even if his skill as a *raconteur* was marred for some by his anecdotes always centring on himself. Once he had given up parliament and his political views had moved to an acceptable middle ground there was no reason why Wellington, the least vindictive of men, should not share in the pleasure of his company.

In 1837 Wilson was sixty and had mellowed with age. He was also lonely. None of his private letters to his wife has survived but there is no doubt that he was devoted to her and her death had been a shattering blow to him. Of their thirteen children, nine had predeceased their mother, most dying as infants. Two sons and two daughters survived her, but one of the sons, Henry, who had been Queen Caroline's equerry, died in 1827 as a lieutenant in the Thirteenth Foot. The other son, Belford Wilson, went to South America and acted as aide-de-camp to Simon Bolivar. He made his career in that continent, becoming British consul at Lima and eventually gaining a knighthood after acting as *chargé d'affaires* in Caracas.

Wilson was still in demand at the dinner tables of London and at many of the great houses in the country, but he hankered for a post in the public service, preferably in a warm climate. He was short of money and longed for sunlight. He took a short holiday in the Isle of Wight, the furthest south that he could afford, and wrote, a little unconvincingly, to Peel that 'this is better than the Italian climate'.[48] He no longer longed for honours. The sovereigns of Austria, Portugal, Prussia and Russia restored his knighthoods to him in 1841 and he was satisfied that his colonelcy was a public recognition of his merits and services. He still longed for a well paid post where the weather was fine.

It was Peel, after he became prime minister in 1841, who gratified his wish. He appointed him Governor and Commander-in-Chief of Gibraltar, twenty-eight years after he had last held any but an honorary military appointment. Peel's letter must have added to the pleasure he felt.

Downing Street, 20th Aug 1842

My dear Wilson,

I wish you joy very sincerely on your appointment to an honourable and important trust.

I said less than I felt when you mentioned the subject of your desire for that active employment for which your habits, ability and experience qualify you, but you do me no more than justice in believing that I was very active to promote the object you had in view, on public grounds as well as feelings of personal regards for yourself.

Believe me,

Robert Peel[49]

Wilson's six years on the Rock were a quiet and dignified period, a fitting end to a long and turbulent life. With his taste for royalty he made friends with the nearest crowned head to Gibraltar, the King of Morocco, who sent him a fowling-piece of Moorish manufacture and a walking cane made of the horn of a unicorn, a fitting gift for a man whose own stories often verged on the fabulous. Almost the only excitement of his tour of duty was the negotiations to restore the Convent chapel which he found in 'a neglected, dark, unwholesome, abandoned state, and a sepulchral nuisance to the [Governor's] Residence'. There were five battalions of infantry in the garrison and Sir Robert conscientiously carried out their annual inspection. It is interesting that an officer who for more than fifty years had been complaining of the frequency of military punishments should think it worthwhile complimenting the Sixty-Seventh Foot because in less than four months they had had only nine courts-martial.

A year after he wrote that report he was back in London and died suddenly in Marshall Thompson's hotel in Oxford Street on 9 May 1849. They buried him in Westminster Abbey. Had he known, it might have been some compensation for the British knighthood which eluded him to the end.

BIBLIOGRAPHY

MANUSCRIPT SOURCES. In the British Museum are fifty volumes (Additional Manuscripts [ADMS] 30.095–30.144) of Robert Wilson's correspondence and journals. There is another considerable collection of Wilson papers scattered among the War Office papers (WO) in the Public Record Office.

PRINTED WORKS (giving the abbreviations used in the references; asterisks indicate works wholly or substantially by Robert Wilson)

Aberdeen	Frances Balfour, *Life of George, 4th Earl of Aberdeen* (2 vols.), 1923
Administration*	Robert Wilson, *Canning's Administration: Narrative of Formation, with Correspondence.* Ed. H. Randolph, 1872
Alison	Archibald Alison, *Lives of Lord Castlereagh and Sir Charles Stewart* (3 vols.), 1861
Almedigen	E. M. Almedigen, *The Emperor Alexander I*, 1964
Arbuthnot	*Journal of Mrs. Arbuthnot 1820–32.* Ed. Francis Bamford and Duke of Wellington (2 vols.), 1950
Aspinall	*Correspondence of George, Prince of Wales, 1770–1812.* Ed. A. Aspinall (8 vols.), 1963–71
Atkinson	R. H. M. B. Atkinson and G. A. Jackson, *Brougham and his Early Friends* (4 vols.), 1897
Avis	*Report of George Avis, Patrole belonging to the Public Office, Bow Street, 14th August 1821* (in the GLC (Middlesex) Record Office)
Bagot	*George Canning and his Friends.* Ed. Joscelyne Bagot (2 vols.), 1909
Barratt	Glynn R. Barratt, 'Sir Robert Wilson's Confidential Memoir on Turkey and Russia.' *Canadian-American Slavic Studies*, vii, 1973.
Bath	*The Bath Archives. A Further Selection from the diaries and letters of Sir George Jackson.* Ed. Lady Jackson (2 vols.), 1873
Berry	*Correspondence and Journal of Miss Berry.* Ed. Lady Theresa Lewis (3 vols.), 1865
Brett-James	Antony Brett-James, *1812. Eyewitness Accounts of Napoleon's Defeat in Russia*, 1966

Brougham   *Life and Times of Henry, Lord Brougham Written by himself* (3 vols.), 1871

Bruce   Ian Bruce, *Lavallette Bruce. His adventures before and after Waterloo*, 1953

Bunbury   Henry E. Bunbury, *Narrative of Some Passages in the Great War with France 1799–1810*, 1854

Burke   Peter Burke, *Celebrated Naval and Military Trials*, 1876

Burghersh   *Correspondence of Lord Burghersh.* Ed. Rachel Weigall, 1912

Bury   Lady Charlotte Bury, *Diary of a Lady in Waiting.* Ed. Frances Steuart (2 vols.), 1908

Calvert   *Journals and Correspondence of Gen. Sir Harry Calvert.* Ed. Sir Harry Verney, 1853

Cammisc.   'Some Letters of the Duke of Wellington to his brother, William Wellesley Pole.' Ed. Sir C. Webster. *Camden Miscellany*, xviii, 1948

Campaigns   *History of the Campaigns of the British Forces in Spain and Portugal* (5 vols.), 1812

Campbell   Neil Campbell, *Napoleon at Fontainbleau and Elba, 1814–15.* Ed. A. H. C. Maclachlan, 1869.

Canning's Ministry   Arthur Aspinall, 'The Formation of Canning's Ministry.' *Camden 3rd Series*, lix, 1937

Castlereagh   *Correspondence, Despatches and Other Papers of Viscount Castlereagh, 2nd Marquess Londonderry.* Ed. 3rd Marquess Londonderry (12 vols.), 1851

Cathcart   Hon. Geo. Cathcart, *Commentaries on the War in Russia and Germany in 1812 and 1813*, 1850

CCA   'The Correspondence of Charles Arbuthnot.' Ed. A. Aspinall. *Camden 3rd Series*, lxv, 1941

Colchester   *Diaries and Correspondence of Charles Abbot, 1st Lord Colchester.* Ed. 2nd Lord Colchester (3 vols.), 1861

Cornwallis   *Correspondence of Marquis Cornwallis.* Ed. C. Ross (3 vols.), 1859

Costigan   Giovanni Costigan, *Sir Robert Wilson: A Soldier of Fortune in the Napoleonic Wars*, 1932

Creevey   *The Creevey Papers.* Ed. Sir Herbert Maxwell (2 vols.), 1904

Croker   *The Croker Papers.* Ed. L. W. Jennings (3 vols.), 1884

Delavoye   Alex. M. Delavoye, *Life of Thomas Graham, Lord Lyndoch*, 1880

Diary*   Sir Robert Wilson, *Private Diary of the Travels, Personal Services and Public Events in the Campaigns* *of 1812, 1813 and 1814*. Ed. H. Randolph (2 vols.), 1861

Duffy   Christopher Duffy, *Borodino and the War of 1812*, 1972

D'Urban   *Peninsular Journal of Maj. Gen. Sir Benjamin D'Urban*. Ed. I. J. Rousseau, 1930

Egypt*   Robert Thomas Wilson, *History of the British Expedition to Egypt*, 1802

Farington   *The Farington Diary: Joseph Farington R.A.* Ed. James Grieg (8 vols.), 1922–8

Fortescue   Sir John Fortescue, *History of the British Army*. (vols. iv–x), 1915–20

Fox   *Journal of Henry Edward Fox, 1818–30*. Ed. Earl of Ilchester, 1923

George IV   *The Letters of King George IV, 1812–30*. Ed. A. Aspinall (3 vols.), 1938

Greville   *The Greville Memoirs*. Ed. L. Strachey and R. Fulford (7 vols.), 1938

HMC Bathurst   *Report on the Manuscripts of Earl Bathurst*. Historical Manuscripts Commission, 1923

HMC Fortescue   *Report on the Manuscripts of J. B. Fortescue at Dropmore* (vols. ix and x). Historical Manuscripts Commission, 1915 and 1927

Hobhouse   John Cam Hobhouse, Lord Broughton, *Recollections of a Long Life*. Ed. Lady Dorchester (2 vols.), 1909

Holland House   Earl of Ilchester, *The Home of the Hollands, 1605–1820* (vol. i); *Chronicles of Holland House, 1820–1900* (vol. ii), 1937

Jackson   *Diaries and Letters of Sir George Jackson*. Ed. Lady Jackson (2 vols.), 1872

JN   *Mémoires et Correspondance Politiques et Militaires du Roi Joseph*. Ed. A. Ducasse (10 vols.), 1854

Jones   L. T. Jones, *Historical Journal of the British Campaigns on the Continent in 1794*, 1797

Jourdan   *Mémoires Militaires du Maréchal Jourdan*. Ed. Viscomte de Grouchy, 1899

Lady Holland   *The Journal of Elizabeth, Lady Holland, 1791–1811*. Ed. Earl of Ilchester (2 vols.), 1908

Landsheit   *The Hussar, Sergeant Norbert Landsheit*. Ed. G. R. Gleig, 1837

Lavallette   Comte de Lavallette, *Mémoires et Souvenirs* (2 vols.), 1831

Leipzig	Antony Brett-James, *Europe against Napoleon. The Leipzig Campaign of 1812*, 1970
Letter*	*Letter from Sir Robert Wilson to his Constituents in refutation of a charge of dispatching a false report of a victory*, 2nd edn., 1818
Lieven	*Letters of Dorothea, Countess Lieven, 1812–34.* Ed. Lionel G. Robinson, 1902
Longford	Elizabeth Longford, *Wellington: Pillar of State*, 1972
Malmesbury Diaries	*Diaries and Correspondence of the Earl of Malmesbury.* Ed. 3rd Earl (4 vols.), 1844
Malmesbury Letters	*Letters of 1st Earl Malmesbury, his Family and Friends.* Ed. 3rd Earl, 1870
Mayne	William Mayne, *Narrative of the Campaigns of the Loyal Lusitanian Legion*, 1812
Military Force*	*An Enquiry into the Present State of the Military Force of the British Empire with a View to its Re-organisation, addressed to the Rt. Hon. William Pitt by Lt. Col. R. T. Wilson, KMT*, 1804
Napier	William Napier, *History of the War in the Peninsula and South of France.* Cabinet Edn. (6 vols.), 1852
Narrative*	Robert Wilson, *Narrative of Events during the Invasion of Russia.* Ed. H. Randolph, 1860
NC	*Correspondance de Napoléon 1er* (32 vols.), 1854–69
Nightingale	J. Nightingale, *Memoir of the Last Days of her late Most Gracious Majesty, Caroline, Queen of Great Britain*, 1822
Nollekens	John Thomas Smith, *Nollekens, his Life and Times* (2 vols.), 1816–33
Oldfield	T. H. B. Oldfield, *Representative History of Great Britain and Ireland*, 1816
Petrie	F. Lorraine Petrie, *Napoleon's Campaigns in Poland, 1806–07*, 1901
RMC	*The Royal Military Calendar or Army Service and Commission Book*, 3rd edn. (5 vols.), 1820
Russell	Spencer Walpole, *Life of Lord John Russell* (2 vols.), 1889
Russian Army*	Robert Wilson, *Brief Remarks on the Character and Composition of the Russian Army and a Sketch of the Campaigns in Poland in the years 1806 and 1807*, 1810
SD	*Supplementary Dispatches and Memoranda of FM the Duke of Wellington.* Ed. 2nd Duke of Wellington (14 vols.), 1852–72

Bibliography

Seton Watson   Hugh Seton Watson, *The Russian Empire 1801–1917*, 1967
Spanish Journal *The Spanish Journal of Elizabeth, Lady Holland*. Ed. Earl of Ilchester, 1910
Stanley   *Before and after Waterloo. Letters of Edward Stanley*. Ed. J. H. Adeane and M. Grenfell, 1907
Stewart   Charles Stewart (Vane), Marquess of Londonderry, *Narrative of the War in Germany and France in 1813 and 1814*, 1830
Tchitchagov   *Mémoires de l'Admiral Tchitchagoff, 1767–1849*, 1862
Temperley   H. W. V. Temperley, *Life of Canning*, 1905
Warre   William Warre, *Letters from the Peninsular 1808–12*. Ed. E. Warre, 1909
WCD   *Despatches, Correspondence and Memoranda of FM the Duke of Wellington, 1819–32* (vols. i–iii). Ed. 2nd Duke of Wellington, 1867
WD   *The Despatches of FM the Duke of Wellington*. Ed. J. Gurwood (12 vols.), 1834–9
Werry   *Personal Memoirs and Letters of Francis Peter Werry, Attaché to the British Embassies at St. Petersburg and Vienna, 1812–15*. Ed. Eliza F. Werry, 1861
Wellington and his Friends   *Wellington and his Friends. Letters of the 1st Duke of Wellington*. Ed. 7th Duke of Wellington, 1965
Wilson*   *Life of Sir Robert Wilson from autobiographical memoirs, journals, narratives, correspondence &c.* Ed. H. Randolph (2 vols.), 1862
Wright   G. N. Wright, *Life and Reign of William IV* (2 vols.), n.d.
Wylly   H. C. Wylly, *XVth (the King's) Hussars, 1759–1913*, 1914
Young   J. C. Young, *A Memoir of C. M. Young, Tragedian*, 2nd edn., 1871

References

CHAPTER 1   A Reputation in the Cannon's Mouth

1. Farington iii 29; Wilson i 1–10.
2. Wilson i 11.
3. Farington vii 183.
4. ib.
5. Wilson i 46.
6. ib. 55–6.
7. Fortescue iv 225
8. Wilson i 65.
9. ib. 75.
10. Wylly 107; Calvert 322.
11. Bunbury 28.
12. C. T. Atkinson, *Foreign Regiments in the British Army* iv 242.
13. Wilson i 112–14
14. ib. 118–32.
15. ib. 183.

CHAPTER 2   The Pen and the Sword

1. Egypt 72, 75.
2. Aspinall iv 511: RTW to McMahon, 23 Feb 04.
3. ib. v 112: —— n.d.
4. ib. 253, Moira to McMahon, 31 Aug 05; ADMS 30.116 f7.
5. Wilson i 241.
6. WCD vii 396.
7. Wilson i 249.
8. Castlereagh vi 133.
9. Landsheit 135.
10. ADMS 30.105 ff39, 43, 44; Wilson i 309.
11. Wilson i 319.
12. ib. 352; SD iv 507.
13. Fortescue vi 52.
14. Creevey ii 176; Bunbury 129; ADMS 30.125 f30; Aspinall iv 454
15. Bunbury 129; ADMS 30.125 f20; Jackson ii 108; Cornwallis iii 360.
16. Wilson ii 7–9.
17. ib. 32; Russian Army 83fn.

18. Wilson ii 33–9.
19. ib. 93; Almedigen 99; Jackson ii 101–2.
20. Wilson ii 184–9.
21. Campbell 236.
22. Jackson ii 108.
23. Wilson ii 195.
24. ib. 198.
25. ib. 282, 286; Almedigen 100.
26. Wilson ii 301.
27. ib. 354.
28. Malmesbury Diaries iv 393.
29. —— Letters ii 51: Ross to Malmesbury, 29 Sep 07.
30. Wilson ii 438: RTW to Canning, 29 Oct 07.

CHAPTER 3   Loyal Lusitanian Legion

1. Landsheit 267.
2. Junta of Oporto to Souza, 7 Jul 08.
3. ADMS 30.105 f144.
4. —— 30.099 ff29, 31, 69; WO i 230 f203.
5. WO i 230 ff207, 215, 220.
6. ADMS 30.099 f48.
7. —— 30.105 f106.
8. ———— ff38, 44.
9. ———— ff166–7.
10. ———— f169; WO i 417 f51; Castlereagh vii 200.
11. Castlereagh vii 194.
12. ib. 203.
13. ADMS 30.099 f79.
14. Castlereagh to Cradock, 24 Dec 08; ADMS 30.105 f241.
15. ADMS 30.099 ff88, 84.
16. ———— ff268, 270.
17. ———— f315.
18. MS dated 18 Jan 09 in possession of the author.
19. ADMS 30.105 f291: Guard to Mayne, 5 Jan 09.
20. ———— f294; HMC Bathurst 83.
21. Castlereagh to Cradock, 24 Dec 08; ADMS 30.105 f308.
22. ADMS 30.105 f302.
23. Spanish Journal 254, 19 Jan 09.
24. ADMS 30.105 ff333–5.
25. Napier ii 426: Morgan to Cradock, 19 Jan 09.
26. Cradock to Castlereagh, 6 Mar 09; ADMS 30.099, 25 Jan 09.
27. JN v 312, 365
28. D'Urban 24–5.

29. ADMS 30.106 ff10, 32–4.
30. —— 30.099 f105.
31. —— 30.106 f51.
32. —— 30.099 f133.

CHAPTER 4   A Separation by Detachments

1. ADMS 30.106 f40.
2. —— 30.099 f49.
3. Mayne 214; Spanish Journal 380.
4. Spanish Journal 381.
5. ib.
6. ADMS 30.099 f142.
7. —— ff148, 152.
8. —— 30.106 f84, 23 May 09.
9. —— f88, 25 May 09.
10. —— 30.099 f155; ADMS 30.106 f89, 29 May 09.
11. —— 30.106 f93, 1 Jun 09; ADMS 30.099 f159.
12. —— f95, 2 Jun 09; WO i 230 f245, 5 Jun 09.
13. —— 30.099 f159.
14. Spanish Journal 383; ADMS 30.099 f164.
15. SD xiii 330; WD iv 412, 526.
16. ADMS 30.099 f165–8.
17. —— 30.106 f109; QMG's orders, 18 Jul 09.
18. —— 30.099 f166.
19. —— 30.114 f5.
20. —— 30.099 f178.
21. —— f179.
22. —— 30.106 ff116–17; ADMS 30.099 f179.
23. SD vi 325.
24. —— xiii 348: Jourdan to Soult, 20 Jul 09.
25. ADMS 30.135 f9.
26. Mayne 86.
27. ADMS 30.135 f9.
28. —— 30.099 f190; ADMS 30.135 ff9–10: RTW to Wellesley, 13 Aug 09.
29. Letter 27–9.
30. ADMS 30.135 f10.
31. WD v 66: Wellesley to Castlereagh, 21 Aug 09.
32. Letter 25, RTW to Wellesley, 30 Aug 09; Cammisc. 33, Wellesley to W. W. Pole, 23 Apr 10.
33. WD v 111.
34. ADMS 30.099 ff197–8.
35. —— f213.

CHAPTER 5   Smolensk via Constantinople

1. HMC Fortescue ix 369.
2. ADMS 30.106 f185, 6 May 10.
3. ———— f224, 4 Dec 10.
4. *Quarterly Review*, Feb 1811; *Monthly Review*, Jul 1812.
5. Hansard, vol. xv, col. 461 & xvi 20 & 25, 16 Feb & 22 Mar 10.
6. Colchester ii 235.
7. Warre 122, 3 May 10.
8. ADMS 30.118 f10, 19 Jul 10; f14 29 Jul 10.
9. ————f22, 14 Aug 10; f40, 4 Oct 10; f44, 15 Oct 10; f54, 25 Oct 10.
10. ———— f63, 15 Dec 10; f80, 11 Mar 11.
11. ———— f108, 24 Jul 11.
12. Hansard xvii 543.
13. Lady Holland ii 271.
14. WO i 244 f243.
15. SD vi 519; WO vi 205 f366.
16. WO i 244 f243; WD vii 398.
17. WO i 244 f512; Beresford to Wellington, 14 Jun 10.
18. WD viii 451, 455.
19. WD viii 91, xi 294; ADMS 30.135 f12.
20. Bath i 222.
21. ib. 228.
22. Atkinson ii 99; Bath i 287.
23. ADMS 30.106 f248–9.
24. Bath i 348; ADMS 30.106 f256.
25. ADMS 30.119 ff6, 8.
26. Diary i 2–12.
27. ib. 14.
28. ib. 18.
29. ib. 60.
30. ADMS 30.106 f265.
31. HMC Bathurst 222.
32. Diary i 34, 63.
33. ib. 121.
34. ib. 125–32.
35. ib. 135–6.
36. ib. 136–7.
37. ADMS 30.132 f82.
38. ———— f87.
39. Diary i 139.
40. Tchitchagov 105, Czar to Tchitchagov, 18 Jul 12.
41. Diary i 140.
42. ib. 142.

CHAPTER 6 *Monsieur l'Ambassadeur des Rebelles*

1. Duffy 42.
2. Narrative 156.
3. Diary i 147.
4. ib. 149.
5. Narrative 384.
6. Diary i 149.
7. Narrative 109.
8. ib. 112.
9. ib. 386.
10. ib. 131.
11. ib. 388.
12. Werry 215; Castlereagh ix 28.
13. Cathcart 35, 41.
14. Narrative 382–4.
15. Diary i 157.
16. ib.
17. Narrative 114–17.
18. Diary i 156.
19. Narrative 117; Diary i 154.
20. Diary i 159–61.
21. Cathcart to RTW, 12 Sep 12; Castereagh to Cathcart, 20 Oct 12; RTW to Castlereagh, 12 Sep 12: quoted in Costigan 127–8; ADMS 30.106 f333, 10 Oct 12.
22. Diary i 162.
23. Narrative 157.
24. Duffy 133.
25. Diary i 164–5; Narrative 156.

CHAPTER 7 Advance from Moscow

1. Diary i 174.
2. Narrative 176.
3. ib. 183.
4. ib. 190.
5. Diary i 184.
6. Kurz, quoted in Brett-James 207.
7. Diary i 194.
8. Narrative 223–5.
9. Diary i 203.
10. Narrative 234.
11. ADMS 30.106 f300.
12. Werry 133.
13. Narrative 197.

14. Diary i 211.
15. Narrative 248.
16. ib. 245; Diary i 212.
17. Diary i 214–15.
18. Bath i 447.
19. Werry 133.
20. Diary i 222.
21. ib. 220, 223.
22. Narrative 353.
23. Diary i 243.
24. Werry 137.
25. Diary i 247.
26. Dumas, quoted in Brett-James 288.

CHAPTER 8   Disenchantment

1. Diary i 251, 263, 252.
2. Werry 163; Diary i 266.
3. Narrative 356.
4. Diary i 256.
5. ADMS 30.107 f11; ADMS 30.106 ff352, 370; Cathcart to Canning 4/16 Jan 13.
6. Diary i 307, 311.
7. ib. 282.
8. Werry 163.
9. Diary i 349, 357.
10. ib. 334.
11. ib. 354.
12. ib. 355.
13. ib. ii 17.
14. Stewart 52.
15. Delavoye 270; Croker i 347.
16. WD x 19.
17. Castlereagh viii 388.
18. NC 20070.
19. Diary ii 43, 63, 76.
20. Leipzig 80.
21. Arbuthnot ii 73; Fox 98.
22. ADMS 20.107 f183.
23. Diary ii 440, 443, 445, 449, 451.
24. Aberdeen i 145.
25. HMC Fortescue x 369.
26. Diary ii 179.
27. Aberdeen i 145.

28. Cathcart to Castlereagh, 4 Dec 13.
29. Alison ii 180.
30. Diary ii 296, 300.
31. ib. 297.
32. ib. 341, 490.
33. ib. 311.
34. ib. 343–5.
35. ib. 324, 327.
36. ib. 366.
37. ADMS 30.104 f104; ADMS 30.120 f25.
38. Diary ii 324.
39. ADMS 30.120 f29; Creevey i 195.
40. Diary ii 398; Bury i 255.
41. Burghersh 179.
42. ADMS 30.108 f9; Nightingale 422.
43. Greville i 41; Burghersh 184.
44. Creevey i 240.
45. Young 143.
46. ADMS 30.120 f194.

CHAPTER 9   Errant Knight

1. Hobhouse i 168; ADMS 30.120 f185; ADMS 30.125 f7.
2. Bruce 180; HMC Fortescue x 412.
3. ADMS 30.108 f70; Lavallette ii 317–29; RMC iii 323; Burke 384–93.
4. ADMS 30.108 f81; ADMS 30.127 f23.
5. ADMS 30.108 f80 & 89; ADMS 30.102 f23.
6. SD xi 276.
7. ib. 335–6, Bathurst to Wellington, 9 Mar 16.
8. Berry iii 92.
9. Stanley 294.
10. Berry iii 92.
11. HMC Bathurst 413.
12. Castlereagh xi 276; ADMS 30.108 f283.
13. HMC Fortescue x 412; ADMS 30.108 f117.
14. Hobhouse ii 133.
15. Oldfield iv 587.
16. *The Times*, 19–23 June 1818.
17. *Quarterly Review*, April 1818.
18. ADMS 30.108 f432.
19. Hansard xxxix 112; Fox 31; Greville i 71.
20. Bagot ii 91.
21. Russell i 135; Hansard xli 302, l 461.

22. *Quarterly Review*, April 1818, 131.
23. *The Courier*, 6 Sep 21.
24. HMC Bathurst 468.
25. ADMS 30.132 f120; ADMS 30.108 f206; Arbuthnot i 148.
26. Arbuthnot i 67.
27. Croker i 201; George IV ii 454.
28. Hansard NS vi 292, 329.
29. Nightingale 208–14.
30. Hansard NS vi 292.
31. Nightingale 221.
32. ib. 223.
33. Hansard NS vi 330, 957.
34. Brougham ii 426; Hansard NS vi 333.
35. Hansard NS vi 295–6.
36. Nightingale 408.
37. Hansard NS vi 307.
38. Nightingale 228.

CHAPTER 10   Transformation Scene

1. George IV ii 457.
2. Wellington & his Friends 14.
3. HMC Bathurst 514.
4. Colchester iii 236.
5. HMC Bathurst 511; Hansard NS vi 299.
6. Hansard NS vi 290, 302.
7. HMC Bathurst 515.
8. Hansard NS vi 300.
9. ADMS 30.110 f12.
10. Hansard NS vi 313–14.
11. ib. 325–6.
12. ADMS 30.110 f55.
13. ———— f57.
14. —— 30.125 f35.
15. Temperley 167; WCD ii 173.
16. Hansard NS viii 1040.
17. ib. xl 867.
18. ADMS 30.110 f163.
19. Arbuthnot i 247.
20. ADMS 30.110 f283.
21. ———— f342.
22. HMC Bathurst 543.
23. ADMS 30.111 f38, 52, 60, 95.
24. Holland House i 32.

25. ADMS 30.103 f184.
26. ———— f200.
27. Arbuthnot i 403, ii 25; WCD iii 316.
28. Hansard NS xii 932–63.
29. ib. viii 1091–8.
30. Holland House ii 33.
31. Arbuthnot ii 55, 56, 77; *The Times*, 4, 5, 19 Dec 1824.
32. Hansard NS xvii 1076.
33. Administration 17–18.
34. Canning's Ministry 245.
35. ADMS 40.299 f200–2.
36. Arbuthnot ii 340, 374.
37. Wright ii 624.
38. Lieven 229.
39. Hobhouse ii 118.
40. Greville i 338.
41. Administration vii (diary of 3 May 31).
42. Hansard (3rd Series) iii 1530.
43. ib. 1637–41.
44. Croker ii 116.
45. ADMS 30.112 f133.
46. ——— 30.115 f72.
47. Longford ii 406.
48. ADMS 40.428 f353.
49. ——— 40.514 f305.

Index

213

Index

Index

DATE DUE

21 June 78			

GAYLORD   PRINTED IN U.S.A